Colluding, Colliding, and Contending With Norms of Whiteness

A Volume in
Urban Education Studies Series

Series Editors
Thandeka K. Chapman
University of California, San Diego
Nicholas D. Hartlep
Metropolitan State University, St Paul, MN
Kenneth J. Fasching-Varner
Louisiana State University

Urban Education Studies Series

Thandeka K. Chapman, Nicholas D. Hartlep, and
Kenneth J. Fasching-Varner, Series Editors

Colluding, Colliding, and Contending With Norms of Whiteness (2017)
by Jennifer L. S. Chandler

Better Principals, Better Schools:
What Star Principals Know, Believe, and Do (2015)
edited by Delia Stafford and Valerie Hill-Jackson

Intersectionality and Urban Education:
Identities, Policies, Spaces & Power (2014)
edited by Carl A. Grant and Elisabeth Zwier

Colluding, Colliding, and Contending With Norms of Whiteness

by

Jennifer L. S. Chandler
Arizona State University,
Tempe, Arizona

INFORMATION AGE PUBLISHING, INC.
Charlotte, NC • www.infoagepub.com

Library of Congress Cataloging-in-Publication Data

CIP record for this book is available from the Library of Congress
http://www.loc.gov

ISBNs: 978-1-68123-691-9 (Paperback)

   978-1-68123-692-6 (Hardcover)

   978-1-68123-693-3 (ebook)

CONTENTS

SERIES EDITORS'S FOREWORD

The *Urban Education Studies* book series was created to give authors and editors the opportunity to share the lives and voices of educators, students, and parents connected to urban areas and the experiences of people of color in public schools. We seek to extend readers' understandings of events, perceptions, and practices that directly and indirectly relate to issues of race, gender, socioeconomic status, heteronormativity, and other issues of social subjugation that impact students and families. We are committed to increasing the visibility of urban issues from the perspectives and documented experiences of the people most affected by them, in order to converse about issues of equity and equality in complex urban contexts.

We hope to publish more complex analyses of people's lived experiences, implications for policies and practices in urban school settings, moments of joy, and slivers of hope for the future success of children of color and children disenfranchised by poverty and social oppression. It is not our intention to repeat well-worn conversations about educators and urban families in ways that re-instantiate dominant ideologies and hegemonic history. Rather, we wish to publish texts with new lenses, new quandaries, and that ask innovative questions, which reflect societal change *and* ongoing struggles for justice. In this series, we not only challenge stock stories and majoritarian tales, but traditional ways of thinking and constructing answers to the persistent questions plaguing urban stakeholders. We invite our audience to engage with us as we present radical methods, conceptual designs, and methodologies focused on emic and etic research

Colluding, Colliding, and Contending With Norms of Whiteness, pp. vii–viii
Copyright © 2017 by Information Age Publishing
All rights of reproduction in any form reserved.

designs of equity and equality, with the goal to enhance our knowledge of and compassion for the numerous realms of people thriving and surviving in rich urban settings.

In *Colluding, Colliding, Contending With Norms of Whiteness*, Jennifer Chandler takes on the difficult task of unpacking Whiteness within interracial family structures. Although it is more indirectly related to urban education, she translates her findings into a thoughtful argument about the ways in which White teachers embrace and resist race and racism. Chandler reaches past an analysis of identity tropes and personality dispositions to address the structural and societal factors that make it easier for White women to ignore race, and disobedient for White women to address issues of race. Chandler also problematizes White homogenous communities where race is never perceived as an "their" problem. Members of these communities do not welcome disruptions to the common sense rhetoric that keep these spaces disaffected by racism.

The balance, and often imbalances of how people relate to race become painfully apparent as Chandler carefully constructs her narratives about a diverse set of women. She is both empathetic and critical, generous and harsh, and insider and outsider in her task to portray the myriad experiences of White women who knowingly or ignorantly enter into hostile racial contexts in their families, neighborhoods, and schools. Chandler's book opens the door for further conversations about how educators can support White female teachers to address their complicity with racism as a step toward becoming better teachers and advocates for students of color in their classrooms.

Thandeka K. Chapman, PhD
Nicholas D. Hartlep, PhD
Kenneth J. Fasching-Varner, PhD

PREFACE

Moving away from the comfort of a complacent colour-blind world towards a colour conscious world [requires] an actual relinquishment of power.

(Smith & Lander, 2012, p. 346)

It is our job as social scientists to sift the silty soil for the petite grains of gold. It is also the responsibility of social scientists to critically analyze their own positionality and culpability in perpetuating Whiteness norms through their research. I attempt both. I identify as White and female. I am a biological mother of one son. My son identifies as Black. His father identifies as Black. My examinations of the meaning of race in my life as an adult are influenced by my enactment and my understanding of myself as a mother. My research and producing this book are part of my examination of the ways in which I continue to interact with Whiteness norms. I agree with Gordon's (2005) advice when she re-examined her research in which she concluded that "it is important for all of us to interrogate our own racism instead of deflecting attention to the racism of others" (p. 300). It is tempting to identify the more egregious acts of others and differentiate myself from them. However, "turning attention away from ourselves suggests that somehow we have "gotten it right," a stance which reinscribes the very racism we claim to want to overturn" (Gordon, 2005, p. 300). In all the interviews I conducted, rarely did we identify the race of the individuals we described. In all our conversations, we centered White people in the same way by only naming the race of people of color. Our conversations sounded

---

Colluding, Colliding, and Contending With Norms of Whiteness, pp. ix–xii
Copyright © 2017 by Information Age Publishing

as if the construct of race itself did not apply to White people; as if White people have no race. Colluding with the Whiteness norm that race does not apply to White people was one of the most prevalent norms of Whiteness I encountered. I also colluded with in the interviews.

In several of the interviews, it seemed that the mothers were operating on a belief that there is a safe, albeit narrow, passage to navigate safely through the maze of Whiteness norms without disturbing them. She creates a path of colluding, but not colluding too much and not annoying White people too much. Unfortunately, a strategy of safely colluding with the practices of Whiteness rests upon a belief that the practices of Whiteness norms remain stable and do not continually shift to always position non-Whiteness as deviant. It rests upon the notion that there is a safe passage through it for a few successful people willing to do the extra work necessary to navigate that narrow passage. The mothers were arguing at times that they simply wanted to mother their children of color and be accepted as normal in doing so. While I have often shared their desires, our very existence as White mothers of children of color disrupts a norm of White motherhood. So the paradox of trying to live with the Whiteness norms without attempting to disrupt them, but not being disrupted by them is an impossibility. Accepting this impossibility is a challenge itself.

Perhaps this paradox is also related to my struggles in writing much of this book. The debt I owe the mothers I interviewed is immeasurable. As I finalized my manuscript, I worried that the mothers I interviewed would not appreciate the book because it does not provide a rosy picture of our lives. I originally aimed to interview White mothers of daughters and sons of color across the country believing I would discover the ways that they were contending with Whiteness norms and that my resulting research would consolidate contention best practices. That is not what I discovered. I discovered pain, confusion, and frustration. I also discovered that, like me, many of these mothers were often unknowingly tripping over their own collusions every day as they strove for healthy and authentic relationships with their daughters and sons and their extended families as they also grew as women and mothers.

Our collusions are both in the present and in the past. Our collusions from our pasts can appear at any time. I recently uncovered one of mine when I recently moved from the Midwest to the Southwest. In the packing process I came across some calendars I owned as a teen. I read a notation written in my young hand on a Monday and the following Tuesday during the school year. The words were, "Buy Slaves" on Monday and "Slave Day" on Tuesday. Reading those words brought back the memories. During "Spirit Week" at the middle school I attended, one of the activities was "Slave Day." Students volunteered to be "auctioned off" on Monday and on Tuesday they followed the students who "paid for them" around to their classes and carried their books. Reading this calendar notation and recalling the experience, I saw the practice through my current mother-eyes and I felt a confluence of feelings that included fear, sadness, anger, resignation, and motivation. One of the mothers I interviewed described a similar reenactment of race-based oppression celebrated every year at the school her daughters attended. Every year, she debated whether to allow her daughters to participate. She weighed the consequences for her daughters of adhering to the norm and evaluated her capacity to ameliorate the harm inflicted. She also asked me to avoid providing the details of the school practice. All the mothers I interviewed faced comparable decisions in their lives.

Frankenberg's (1993) statement over two decades ago also applies to my research, "the ways in which the women I interviewed combined or linked discursive elements were neither random nor necessarily original, but for the most part repetitive and linked to larger social trends and movements" (p. 140). I argue that research focused on the social trends and movements can be illuminating. As the numbers of interracial families increases, research with them will likely increase as well. I caution future researchers who want to conduct research with interracial families because how researchers position their research impacts and shapes their results. Namely, I am referring to researchers who seek to identify differences <u>between</u> interracial families and monoracial families. Those who aim to find such differences, will undoubtedly do so, and in so doing, they will be colluding with a Whiteness norm when they assign those differences *to* the interracial families. That Whiteness norm declares that White people *are* the norm and everyone else is unusual and out of the ordinary.

I agree with Fine's (2015) assertion that "Our lives are filled with messy contradictions. Our debt to justice is to interrogate our privilege and our li(v)es" (p. 168). My research examined the experiences of White mothers of children whom they do not identify as White to uncover the ways in which they participate with norms of Whiteness. Research is also needed that examines the experiences of White mothers of White children. In what ways are they colluding, colliding, and contending with Whiteness norms?

I have many people who contributed in many ways to this book to thank and not all of them are listed. Andre Bennett, who serves the children in his community as a school principal, graciously set me on the path of discovery that led to this book. Thandeka Chapman relentlessly pushed me to improve my writing to reveal embedded meanings and the change that is possible. Janice Jones and Darnell Bradley taught me how to use the tools to excavate and build. The mothers I interviewed shared their pain, anxiety, and their humanity with me. My son, Adrian, shared this learning journey with me to Houston, Seattle, New York City, London, Indianapolis,

Los Angeles, Madison, Phoenix, and Philadelphia. The journey continues and we step up every day.

INTRODUCTION

Race matters for reasons that really are only skin deep, that cannot be discussed any other way, and that cannot be wished away. Race matters to a young man's view of society when he spends his teenage years watching others tense up as he passes, no matter the neighborhood where he grew up. Race matters to a young woman's sense of self when she states her hometown, and then is pressed, "No, where are you really from?" regardless of how many generations her family has been in the country. Race matters to a young person addressed by a stranger in a foreign language, which he does not understand because only English was spoken at home. Race matters because of the slights, the snickers, the silent judgments that reinforce that most crippling of thoughts: I do not belong here.

(SCHUETTE v. BAMN, 2014, pp. 45–46)

Through the same social mechanisms Justice Sotomayor referred to in her dissenting opinion quoted above, race matters to the White elementary school children whose White teachers read storybooks written by White authors filled with White characters in images by White illustrators. The social construct of race has real impact on lives. In 2013, the Pew Research Center released a report summarizing several indicators of "well-being and civic engagement" (p. 2) highlighting gaps between races in economic, educational, and health measures that have widened over the last 50 years and gaps that have narrowed. For example, the gaps between Black and White voter participation, life expectancy, and high school completion rates

Colluding, Colliding, and Contending With Norms of Whiteness, pp. xiii–xxii
Copyright © 2017 by Information Age Publishing
All rights of reproduction in any form reserved.

have decreased while the gaps in median household income and wealth have increased (Pew Research Center, 2013). The report also included survey results exploring the public's views on the amount of progress made toward eliminating race-based inequities in U.S. society revealing that 49% of all Americans agreed that "a lot more needs to be done to achieve racial equality" (Pew Research Center, p. 1). Yes, race certainly does matter. It inescapably matters in college applications, job interviews, workplaces, board rooms, family rooms, coffee shops, city streets; and it gravely matters in schools.

About half the current population of U.S. elementary and secondary public school students are students of color and while the majority of their teachers are White women (Goldring, Gray, Bitterman, & Broughman, 2013; Kena et al., 2015; Snyder & Dillow, 2015). The number of students of color is projected to continue growing while the number of White students is projected to shrink in the coming decades (Kena et al., 2015). Some researchers point to this racial demographic shift as one of the triggers challenging the entire education system because the system is built upon and exists to inscribe behaviors that benefit White people (for example, see Leonardo, 2009). Those behaviors are norms of Whiteness and previous research (Case & Hemmings, 2005; DiAngelo, 2010; Fasching-Varner, 2012; Gordon, 2005; Lensmire, 2012; Parks, 2006; Pennington, Brock, & Ndura, 2012; Picower, 2009; Sleeter, 2005; Yoon, 2012) describes ways that teachers and preservice teachers perpetuate Whiteness norms which impede their teaching effectiveness.

Many university teacher preparation programs and individual school districts are grappling with how to address this teacher competency gap. To investigate options for addressing that gap, instead of focusing on White female teachers, I examined another group of White women who regularly interact with children of color. The White women I interviewed are mothers of children of color. Asking what can be learned from White mothers of children of color that can assist White female teachers, my study focused on mothers' interactions with their children's caregivers, family members, colleagues, doctors, strangers, and teachers. By focusing on mothers, my study acknowledged the position that Dancy (2012) argues mothers hold with their children—they are their children's first teachers. While mothers are not teachers paid through taxes and tuitions, they perform many teaching functions with their children. Thus, mothers' experiences are a valid location for exploring possibilities that could assist paid teachers. Furthermore, exploring mothers' and fathers' experiences is a common approach in researching educational processes (for examples, see Hill & Tyson, 2009; Hughes, et al., 2006; Noel, Stark, Redford, & Zukerberg, 2013). So examining mothers' experiences is not a novel approach for exploring innovative approaches for addressing educational system challenges.

In my study, I discovered that the 30 mothers I interviewed colluded with some of the same Whiteness norms that were revealed in previous research conducted by Case and Hemmings (2005), DiAngelo (2010), Fasching-Varner (2012), Gordon (2005), Lensmire (2012), Parks (2006), Pennington, Brock, and Ndura (2012), Picower (2009), Sleeter (2005), and Yoon (2012). However, in my research I discovered that the mothers' interactions with norms of Whiteness varied revealing three different social processes. Those three processes were: collusion, collision, and contention. I created a model that depicts these social processes. The mothers did always collude with the norms of Whiteness. At times, some mothers balked and refused to collude with Whiteness norms. In other words, they collided with Whiteness norms. Their collisions were often fraught with anger, frustration, and confusion. For some of the mothers it was their repeated collisions with Whiteness norms that propelled them to take action to increase their racial literacy and after increasing their racial literacy, many of those mothers adjusted their responses to Whiteness norms. Rather than colliding repeatedly with the same Whiteness norms, those mothers developed ways to actively and productively contend with those norms. The model I created illuminates the path of learning and growth that many of the mothers in my study journeyed. Their learning journeys addressed their competency gaps. The model and its constructs can be applied in school districts and by White female teachers across the nation to create their own learning journeys.

The 30 White women across the nation I interviewed were all mothers of sons or daughters whom they did not identify as White. Appendix A lists some information about the mothers interviewed and also provides details about my study. The information provided about the mothers is brief to not only respect their privacy, but it also keeps the focus on them as a group of mothers. Certainly, the mothers' unique intersecting identities matter in their lives. For example, their educations, their families of origin, their economic situations, their professions, their ages, their locations, and many other aspects of their lives matter. But for my analysis, the focus was on motherhood and race. In the announcements for my study, it was clear that the scope included mothers who identify as White who identify any of their children as not White and that included any racial classification. While my study was broad and open, the mothers who volunteered to participate in this study did not have sons and daughters representing all possible race categories. The majority of the mothers in my study identified their sons and daughters as Black (again, for a full list of information about the mothers, the fathers, and the sons and daughters, see Appendix A). This is telling. I argue that these mothers were responding to my study in part because of their feelings regarding the danger that their sons and daughters face in the United States.

The national stories receiving attention while I was recruiting and interviewing mothers for my study included President Barack Obama's reelection and the recurring battles between the federal government executive and legislative branches. Additionally, that winter, the nation grieved over the loss of many young lives in Newtown, Connecticut. The following spring, George Zimmerman murdered Trayvon Martin and the national conversation turned to race along with gun control and associated laws like "stand your ground." Thus, my study was conducted before the #BlackLivesMatter movement began and before Justice Sotomayor wrote her words above. Yet, many of the mothers I interviewed were not oblivious to the constant threat of harm against Black bodies that exists in the United States. However, because the mainstream media had not yet begun focusing on the number of Black people killed by police and the status of indictments or trials, our interview conversations encompassed the ordinariness of how Whiteness norms operated in these mothers' lives. In part, it is the norm's ordinariness that keeps them in place.

Grappling with how to dismantle those norms in schools requires addressing their ordinariness. So this book includes interactions that mothers had with employees at the schools that their sons and daughters attended and it also explores interactions in the mothers' lives that led up to those experiences. The social experiences that led up to interactions with school employees include interactions between the mothers and their own mothers, their pediatricians, daycare providers, and women that they did not know who asked them questions in public. I argue that those early interactions were the locations where mothers began to establish patterns of behavior that later shaped their interactions with education system employees.

CONCEIVING THE SELF AS A MOTHER

This book is about a variety of mothers' experiences with family members, care givers, service providers, teachers, principals, other school employees, and strangers. To provide a basis of understanding motherhood, I direct readers to Miller's (2005) *Making Sense of Motherhood* because it positions motherhood as an ongoing process which "provide[s] opportunities to explore the ways in which selves are constituted and maintained" (p. 10). Unfortunately, Miller (2005) does not explore interracial mother-child relationships. Furthermore, she addresses race as an immutable characteristic as if every White mother has the same experiences or every Latina mother has the same experiences. However, her focus on the process of constituting oneself as a mother through evolving narratives does apply to my work because Miller (2005) argues that mothers create their narratives by borrowing from or parroting available dominant narratives in order to make themselves understood to others and to themselves. In other words, mothers' stories about themselves are not always unique constructions based on detailed personal reflections and revelations, rather they are fabrications or performances created in order to present the self in ways that can be understood. The goal of understanding is situational. Thus, borrowing from dominant narratives is like using a shortcut because tapping into a common story allows one to skip past certain well-understood details in order to get to the crux of the story. There is a vulnerability that arises when repeating a dominant narrative that helps explain one's life to others because doing so also has the capacity to harm the self. hooks (2014) cautioned her audience "to look at the language that we use for ourselves and the language that people use against us because a lot of the times we are vulnerable to pushing that language" in her recent public dialogue at The New School in New York City. In this same way, the mothers I interviewed picked up and used the same language that ensnared them in norms of Whiteness while they were also colliding with those norms.

All mothers operate within a culture that provides a multitude of messages about what mothers do and what they do not do and Whiteness norms are embedded in that culture. Those messages impact the understanding that each mother fashions for herself in her own motherhood. Mothers assess their own mothering actions, choices, and beliefs against those messages. This entire process for every mother is one that is constantly in flux. Mothers talk about other mothers and compare themselves to other mothers. Some of the mothers I interviewed compared themselves to White mothers of White children and argued that they are no different. Some of the mothers I interviewed argued that they are different in that they have more work than White mothers of White children. The idea that mothering children of color is more work for a White mother has appeared in previous research (Cabellero & Edwards, 2010; Twine, 1999). Another narrative comparing White mothers of children of color to White mothers of White children that I heard was that White mothers of White children do not address race in their lives at all. I argue that neither of these are accurate conceptions, rather they both reflect Whiteness norms. For example, the idea that White mothers of White children do not address race in their lives at all belies their actions that enforce Whiteness norms in their families by avoiding references to race explicitly. "The key to producing whiteness, of course, is not to refer to it explicitly, but to make it an all-encompassing field of communication to have it so visible that it is not noticed" argued McLaren, Leonardo, and Allen (2000, p. 110). Therefore, not talking directly about race is one of the norms of Whiteness that many White mothers comply with. Whiteness norms also contain images and meanings conveying what it means to be a good White mother. Though the word "White" is rarely included in that phrase, it is embedded in the meaning of a good mother for White women. What is a positioned as a good White mother is almost always constructed by contrasting it with what is a bad White mother. Woodward (2003) explains:

> Who is allowed to be a mother is strongly contested.... Motherhood is up for public debate in all manner of different places and the key issue is often to pinpoint the "bad" mother and by implication the good mother. (p. 23)

Furthermore, the definitions and boundaries of good motherhood are also racialized. Behavior that is considered being a good mother is judged according to the race of the mother and the race of her children. The mothers who participated in this study experienced many social sanctions and the people imparting those sanctions were colluding with Whiteness norms that dictate such sanctions can and must be applied.

The way in which Whiteness norms function in the lives of White mothers with daughters and sons of color is complex so this book advances along two avenues. One avenue is through identifying the Whiteness norms themselves. These norms, like all norms, are often left unspoken. The second avenue is through an explication of the ways in which the mothers interacted with the norms. My model depicts the ways of interacting and it is a social process model. While the model can apply to any set of social norms, the focus here is on Whiteness norms. The model and its underlying constructs are presented in chapter one. The three ways of interacting with Whiteness norms it presents are by colluding with them, colliding with them, and contending with them.

ORGANIZATION OF THE CHAPTERS

Collusions, collisions, and contentions in action are messy and complex. To further complicate an examination of these processes, retelling events as stories in interviews is also fluid and organic. Therefore, the excerpts from my interviews are sometimes long and they include the actual language from the conversations. This is intentional for two reasons. One is to emphasize that these stories are just that, stories. This does not mean that these stories are fictional. The emphasis here is on these stories the mothers are telling others of themselves as mothers. They are stories that the mothers tell to present and portray themselves (i.e., perform) as mothers who identify as White. The way the stories are framed and told by the mothers is as important as the events described in the stories. The other reason that there are long excerpts is to present and expose some examples of collusions, collisions, and contentions that occurred in the interviews. The mothers interviewed were frequently not aware of their own collusions, collisions, and contentions. These mothers are not alone. Existing research (Bonilla-Silva, 2010; Case & Hemmings, 2005; Frankenberg, 1993; Low, 2009; Parks, 2006; Pennington, Brock, & Ndura, 2012; Picower, 2009; Sleeter, 2005; Smith & Lander, 2012; Yoon, 2012) reveals that it is common for White people to be unaware of their participation with Whiteness norms. Increasing awareness of the ways in which collusions, collisions, and contentions with Whiteness norms occur is one aim of this book. Because the specifics of each collusion, collision, and contention differ, many individual conversations were examined in detail. Including the details of the conversations rather than limiting them to skeletons allows the reader to recognize the mundane ways that these processes occurred. At the detail level, many of the collusions appear blandly innocuous. Seeing through their blandness to distinguish the collusive nature of the interaction is key in being able to critically analyze Whiteness norms and the social processes that maintain them. Motherhood research and theory that continues to frame race by colluding with the Whiteness norm that *White women mother White Children* (Glenn, Chang, & Forcey, 1994; Miller, 2005; Rich, 1986) are operating within and perpetuating this norm rather than critically examining it and its function within motherhood.

The structure of chapters two through four roughly follow a trajectory of mothering to keep the focus on these White women as mothers. The mothers' stories are organized generally based either on the age of their child or children when the events occurred or on the type of experience. Many of the mothers with more than one child were grappling with a range of experiences and several of the mothers interviewed told stories from years past. So do not look for a strict timeline. Also, not every story that every mother provided in the interviews is included in this book. Additionally, there are stories from some mothers in multiple sections of the book because they told me stories from when their sons or daughters were very young and other stories when they were older. The chapter and section titles refer to the mothering activities with which the mothers engaged. Therefore, the chapter titles do not highlight the causes nor the impacts of the experiences in the mothers' stories. In other words, the chapter titles are not themes from the interviews.

Using a general chronological order through the lives of the mothers helps keeps the focus on mothering and mothering activities change over time as daughters and sons develop. Similarly, mothers' interactions with people outside family expand and shift as their sons and daughters grow and participate in activities with people outside the immediate family. The evolution of mothering activities and the widening span of people with whom mothers interact as their children grow are not the only threads woven together forming the fabric of a mother's life, but they are the two that I draw the reader's attention to here because they were largely responsible for creating the locations where these mothers collided, colluded, and contended with Whiteness norms. At the end of each chapter is a table that presents a summary of the Whiteness norms addressed in the chapter and the mothers' various participations with those norms.

I ask the reader to avoid the temptation to label the mothers or categorize them while reading their stories. It can be tempting to label any of these mothers as a colluder or a collider. In my study, there was no evidence to support the notion of classifying mothers as generally colluders, or colliders, or contenders. On the contrary, all these mothers have colluded and collided many times. Contention was somewhat less prevalent for these mothers, but that is not surprising. Contending with any social norm is a process of actively engaging with people in ways to disrupt and modify it. Doing so, itself, is not a social norm. Additionally, Leonardo (2009) asserts that White mothers of mixed-race children "may not know the extent of their participation in racism, but they are not dupes of it either" (p. 39). This statement may appear to support a binary configuration, but I urge readers to steer away from binary thinking and use critical thinking instead.

While it might be tempting to identify unique circumstances or characteristics of each mother to explain her experiences, doing so can draw the reader's attention away from motherhood and away from race. For that reason, I minimized the descriptions of the mothers as much as possible while providing their stories. I also urge readers to steer away from comparing these mothers to each other. Furthermore, I ask readers to refrain from comparing these mothers to White mothers who have only White children. Lastly, I urge readers to avoid comparing them to mothers of color of children of color. The mothers I interviewed, like all mothers, participate in many complex social interactions in the pursuit of their goals. In living their lives, they are colluding with dominant norms much of the time, colliding with those same norms at times, and sometimes contending with those norms. The mothers I interviewed are not villains nor are they heroines. Please do not pity them, nor vilify them. I also recommend readers focus on the Whiteness norms uncovered in this study and consider using the model in analyzing the ways all people interact with Whiteness norms. The Whiteness norms that the reader experiences are worth exploring; as are the ways in which the reader interacts with those norms.

REFERENCES

Bonilla-Silva, E. (2010). *Racism without racists* (3rd ed.). Lanham, MD: Rowman & Littlefield.

Cabellero, C., & Edwards, R. (2010). *Lone mothers of mixed racial and ethnic children: Then and now.* London: Runneymeade.

Case, K. A., & Hemmings, A. (2005). Distancing strategies: White women preservice teachers and antiracist curriculum. *Urban Education, 40*(6), 606–626.

Dancy, R. B. (2012). *You are your child's first teacher* (3rd ed.). New York, NY: Ten Speed Press.

DiAngelo, R. J. (2010). Why can't we all just be individuals?: Countering the discourse of individualism in anti-racist education. *InterActions: UCLA Journal of Education and Information Studies, 6*(1), Article Number 4.

Fasching-Varner, K. J. (2012). *Working through Whiteness: Examining White racial identity and profession with pre-service teachers.* Lanham, MD: Lexington Books.

Frankenberg, R. (1993). *White women, race matters: The social construction of whiteness.* Minneapolis, MN: University of Minnesota Press.

Glenn, E. N., Chang, G., & Forcey, L. R. (Eds.). (1994). *Mothering: Ideology, experience, and agency.* New York, NY: Routledge.

Goldring, R., Gray, L., Bitterman, A., & Broughman, S. (2013). *Characteristics of Public and Private Elementary and Secondary School Teachers in the United States: Results From the 2011–12 Schools and Staffing Survey.* Washington, DC: U.S. Department of Education.

Gordon, J. (2005). White on White: Researcher reflexivity and the logics of privilege in White schools undertaking reform. *The Urban Review, 37*(4), 279–302.

Hill, N. E., & Tyson, D. F. (2009). Parental involvement in middle school: A meta-analytic assessment of the strategies that promote achievement. *Developmental Psychology, 45*(3), 740–763.

hooks, b. (2014). Are You Still a Slave? New York: The New School. Retrieved from http://events.newschool.edu/event/bell_hooks_scholar-in-residence_-_are_ you_still_a_slave_liberating_the_black_female_body#.Vgas1t9VhBc

Hughes, D., Smith, E. P., Stevenson, H. C., Rodriguez, J., Johnson, D. J., & Spicer, P. (2006). Parents' ethnic-racial socialization practices: A review of research and directions for future study. Developmental Psychology, 42(5), 747-770.

Kena, G., Musu-Gillette, L., Robinson, J., Wang, X., Rathbun, A., Zhang, J., … Dunlop Velez, E. (2015). *The Condition of Education 2015.* Washington, DC: U.S. Department of Education.

Lensmire, A. (2012). *White urban teachers: Stories of fear, violence, and desire.* Lanham, MD: Rowman & Littlefield Education.

Leonardo, Z. (2009). *Race, Whiteness, and education.* New York, NY: Routledge.

Low, S. (2009). Maintaining Whiteness: The fear of others and niceness. *Transforming Anthropology, 17*(2), 79–92.

McLaren, P., Leonardo, Z., & Allen, R. L. (2000). Epistemologies of Whiteness: Trangressing and transforming pedagogical knowledge. In R. Mahalingam, & C. McCarthy (Eds.), *Multicultural curriculum: New directions for social theory, practice, and policy* (pp. 108–123). New York, NY: Routledge.

Miller, T. (2005). *Making sense of motherhood: A narrative approach.* Cambridge, England: Cambridge University Press.

Noel, A., Stark, P., Redford, J., & Zukerberg, A. (2013). *Parent and Family Involvement in Education, From the National Household Education Surveys Program of 2012.*

National Center for Education Statistics, U.S. Department of Education, Washington, DC.

Parks, M. W. (2006). I am from a very small town: Social reconstructionism and multicultural education. *Multicultural Perspectives, 8*(2), 46–50.

Pennington, J. L., Brock, C. H., & Ndura, E. (2012). Unraveling the threads of White teachers' conceptions of caring: Repositioning White privilege. *Urban Education, 47*(4), 743–775.

Pew Research Center. (2013). *King's dream remains an elusive goal: Many Americans see racial disparities.* Washington, DC: Pew Research Center. Retrieved August 23, 2013, from http://www.pewsocialtrends.org/2013/08/22/kings-dream-remains-an-elusive-goal-many-americans-see-racial-disparities/

Picower, B. (2009). The unexamined Whiteness of teaching: How White teachers maintain and enact dominant racial ideologies. *Race Ethnicity and Education, 12*(2), 197–215.

Rich, A. (1986). *Of woman born: Motherhood as experience and institution.* New York, NY: W. W. Norton & Company.

SCHUETTE v. BAMN, 12–682 (Supreme Court of the United States April 22, 2014).

Sleeter, C. E. (2005). How White teachers construct race. In C. McCarthy, W. Crichlow, G. Dimitriadis , & N. Dolby (Eds.), *Race, identity, and representation In education (critical social thought)* (2nd ed., pp. 157–171). New York, NY: Routledge.

Smith, H. J., & Lander, V. (2012). Collusion or collision: Effects of teacher ethnicity in the teaching of critical Whiteness. *Race Ethnicity and Education, 15*(3), 331–351.

Snyder, T. D., & Dillow, S. A. (2015). *Digest of Education Statistics: 2013.* Washington, DC: U.S. Department of Education. Retrieved from National Center for Education Statistics.

Twine, F. W. (1999). Bearing Blackness in Britain: The meaning of racial difference for White birth mothers of African-descent children. *Social Identities, 5*(2), 185–210.

Woodward, K. (2003). Representations of Motherhood. In S. Earle, & G. Letherby (Eds.), *Gender, identity and reproduction: Social perspectives* (pp. 18–32). Houndmills, Basingstoke, Hampshire, England: Palgrave Macmillan.

Yoon, I. H. (2012). The paradoxical nature of whiteness-at-work in the daily life of schools and teacher communities. *Race Ethnicity and Education, 15*(5), 587–613.

CHAPTER 1

MODEL AND
SUPPORTING THEORIES

These are things that happened [in the past] and this is how far we've come ... to make him [my son] understand that it is not like that anymore and that we, you know, we're a better society, in many ways.

Wendy, one of the mothers interviewed.

Wendy's words above reflect the color-blind, post-racial fantasy that life in the United States has been steadily getting better for people of color. That fantasy is part of a dominant narrative that asserts that some aspects of life in the past were not as good as they are now. The dominant narrative asserts that the present is better than the past and the future will be even better. Such narratives are examples of presentism, which is a logical fallacy (Stocking, 1965). That fantasy suggests that there is nothing in particular that needs to happen for life to get better for people of color and that the simple passage of time will bring about change. That fantasy is a part of the grand narrative that suggests that no work is required to effect social change. This is an appealing fantasy. For example, a White woman whose grown son and daughters are White and whose grandchildren are White recently told me that she likes to think about how much better life will be in 50 or 100 years. I asked her how the passage of time alone, as more and more families in the United States are interracial, will bring about social change. She didn't have an answer. While I don't disagree with her that things could be better, I also acknowledge that a great deal of work is needed to effect change. Another example of this fantastical kind of thinking appears in the logic that some college students use. They refer to the natural process of generations passing away as the mechanism through which the U.S. society will become more racially equitable. They believe that as the elderly die, all racist social practices will die with them. These narratives lack a critical analysis of the systems that perpetuate social inequities.

CRITICAL WHITENESS THEORY

Frankenberg (1993) argued over two decades ago that one of the three linked dimensions of Whiteness is that it refers to "a set of cultural practices that are usually unmarked and unnamed" (p. 1). Critical Whiteness studies have expanded in the intervening years, and yet framing Whiteness as a set of norms remains central to understanding Whiteness. For example, Garner (2007) described in his overview of Whiteness that one of the four common conceptions of it is as a set of social norms. Explicating specific norms of Whiteness is one way of interrogating Whiteness not with the goal of listing every normative behavior, but rather as a way of making the familiar unfamiliar. Leonardo (2009) explains that Whiteness takes different forms in different societies in different times, but its purpose and function has always been oppression. Leonardo (2009) distinguishes the concept of Whiteness from the behaviors and practices of individual people who identify as White and that Whiteness is not the collective action of such individuals. How this is accomplished, Leonardo (2009) argues, "is quite simple: set up a system that benefits the group, mystify the system, remove the agents of actions from discourse, and when interrogated about it, stifle the discussion with inane comments about the 'reality' of the charges" (p. 88). As is addressed later in this chapter, Leonardo's (2009) explanation aligns with Goffman's (1959) description of collusion.

Whiteness as an epistemology is enacted and supported not just by individuals who identify as White. Colluding with Whiteness norms benefits all who collude. People need not identify as White to reap some benefit from colluding. Whiteness, according to Leonardo (2009, p. 104), "exists to prey upon its racialized counterparts and *it has always existed in this manner*" [emphasis in original]. Whiteness is a system of oppression to be sure, but its current formations and results in the United States impact everyone. That reality makes Whiteness difficult to understand for some people. Whiteness is not <u>just</u> what White people do and it is not everything that <u>only</u> White people do.

Using critical Whiteness theory to ground my study, I examined White mothers' narratives about their experiences in order to identify specific Whiteness behaviors or practices. I analyzed the behaviors and practices by applying Sherif's (1965) theory of social norms. Thus, I refer to norms of Whiteness or Whiteness norms. I compared the norms I discovered to the practices discovered in research done with White female teachers and preservice teachers (Case & Hemmings, 2005; DiAngelo, 2010; Fasching-Varner, 2012; Gordon, 2005; Lensmire, 2012; Parks, 2006; Pennington, Brock, & Ndura, 2012; Picower, 2009; Sleeter, 2005; Yoon, 2012) and found several similarities. I also discovered there were three interrelated processes occurring. All the mothers were not interacting with the Whiteness norms in the same manner in every situation. I identified the social process involved and the next section briefly describes the theoretical origins of the three social processes I identified and it presents the model I developed.

COLLUSION, COLLISION, AND CONTENTION: THEORETICAL ORIGINS

This section summarizes the theoretical origins of the constructs of collusions, collision, and contention included in my model in Figure 1.1. My specific application of the constructs of collusion and collision with Whiteness norms is not unique. These two constructs have been explored by Smith and Lander (2012) in their examination of the varied ways in which their university students studying to become teachers enacted Whiteness norms with them as teachers. Both Smith and Lander are education professors in England teaching critical Whiteness study courses with predominantly White students. They examined their students' experiences with Whiteness norms during their classes as collisions and collusions (Smith & Lander, 2012).

Additionally, my discussion of collisions with norms aligns with Sullivan's (2014) discussion of what she refers to as etiquette ruptures. Sullivan (2014) argues that a "critical philosophy of race needs to examine the personal side of whiteness and white privilege, that is, how whiteness and white privilege are experienced by the lives of flesh and blood people" (p. 19). Her analysis addresses the ways in which White children are socialized to abide by social norms regarding race and those practices constitute the White etiquette rules. Thus, when someone does not comply with those rules, they are creating an etiquette rupture. Complying with the norms on the other hand is collusion and doing so supports the etiquette rules.

Collusion is a social process. Goffman (1959) discussed the concept of collusion within his construct of teams. Goffman (1959) defined a team as "a set of individuals whose intimate co-operation is required if a given projected definition of the situation is to be maintained" (1959, p. 104). Collusion is cooperation among team members to maintain a performance. Goffman's (1959) concept of collusion is "any collusive communication which is carefully conveyed in such a way as to cause no threat to the illusion that is being fostered for the audience" (p. 177). These definitions of Goffman's (1959) frame all social interaction as performance, so references to an audience are not of auditoriums full of seated viewers. The audience includes everyone; we are all audience members and we are also performers. Social performance in the United States includes many Whiteness norms and those norms provide the unwritten scripts for the performers. When performers go off script, they are colliding with the norms and disrupting the performance.

My use of the construct collision combines Garfinkel's (1967) concept of a breach in social expectations with Goffman's (1959) concept of collusion within team performances. Garfinkel (1967) conducted experiments to explore what he referred to as breaches with social expectations. In his (1967) experiments, he manipulated the situations for the participants in a way to completely upend their perceptions of reality. The participants struggled to grapple with falsified descriptions and data to make sense of the false reality they were given. There was a range of responses from the participants. Some drastically and quickly revised their meaning structures to fit the falsified data. Some did that but then quickly returned to their previous perceptions, waffling between the two in confusion. A few refused to continue participating in the experiment, and some were convinced it was a trick. All the participants reported a disturbance in their sense of reality and described their emotional reactions. The participants were experiencing collisions with social norms. Thus, a breach is when a person behaves in an unexpected way that does not support the performance illusion. Breaches in the social expectations are collisions. A collision is when a team member commits a breach that disrupts or threatens the performance. In other words, collisions are when an individual stops performing in accordance with the social norms.

The concept of contention used here does not mean only disagreements, debates, arguments, and battles revealing opposition. The concept of contention in my model relies on the work by McAdam, Tarrow, and Tilly (2001) who addressed contention as a necessary and healthy process. They "treat social interaction, social ties, communication, and conversation not merely as expressions of structure, rationality, consciousness, or culture but as active sites of creation and change" (McAdam, Tarrow, & Tilly, 2001, p. 22). Thus, the coexisting sets of processes in my model work together in societies. Participating in the norms within social groups is part of performing and negotiating identities. Norms are embedded in identities. We enact our identities when we interact with social norms.

MODEL

My model of collusion, collision, and contention with social norms adds to existing related models, namely:

Helms's (2008) White identity development model,

Trepagnier's (2010) racism continuum, and

Stevenson's (2014) "recast theory (Racial Encounter Coping Appraisal and Socialization Theory)" (p. 113) and model.

My model is a process model rather than a classification model. Because people do not perform the same behaviors in all contexts, it is challenging to classify individuals using only a few examples of their behavior. They may behave one way in a particular context and behave another way in another similar situation in a different context and my model accounts for this complexity and changeability of human behavior. My model provides a lens for analyzing social interactions rather than a model for locating individuals relative to their level of racial understanding like the Helms (2008) and the Trepagnier (2010) models. Consequently, my model can be used to examine the entire expanse of variability of behaviors and practices, and it can also be used to examine the behaviors and practices of individuals in organizations.

Two of the existing classification models mentioned above (i.e., the Helms's (2008) White identity development model and Trepagnier's (2010) racism continuum) each consist of a linear scale with opposite ends. These scales portray the concept under examination as a substance that individuals can possess. The type and amount of the substance that individuals possess varies. Using those models requires one to assess the degree to which a person possesses the specified substance. If the person possesses a great deal of the substance, they are positioned near one end of the continuum and another person possessing very little of it is positioned near the other end of the continuum. The substance could be "awareness," "friendliness," or "intelligence." Intelligence is one psychological concept that has been portrayed this way for over a century. However, more recent conceptions of intelligence have moved away from it being considered as a substance. Recent understandings of intelligence position it as a complex set of malleable abilities that fluctuate over time rather than a static amount of something from birth (Dweck, 2007).

Researchers using the continuum type models mentioned above depict their findings by positioning their study participants on a spot along their continuums (Helms, 2008; Trepagnier, 2010). Classifications that place individuals along a continuum imply a static position that obscures the variability and contradictory explanations, beliefs, and understandings that are operating for each person. In contrast, my model depicts how the processes of collusion, collision, and contention function to maintain social norms. Thus, using my model allows for comprehending complex and seemingly contradictory behaviors.

Another reason I am advancing a process model rather than a continuum type model is that a process model shifts the focus from classifying or labeling individuals as possessing more or less of something to understanding how individuals are participating in systemic processes. Research demonstrates that White people resist being labeled racist (Bonilla-Silva, 2010). Therefore, a model that does not result in a score for individuals that can be interpreted as a "good" score or a "bad" score may be more palatable. That is not to say that using my model will not result in disagreements over whether an interaction was a collision or a collusion, or who was colluding and who was colliding, and what norms were operating. Indeed, such disagreements are to be expected. In fact, through authentic and meaningful engagements that include disagreements people can explore perspectives other than their own. Through exploring these perspectives, it becomes possible for people to do what Delpit (2006) refers to as allowing "the realities of others to edge themselves into our consciousness" (p. 47). Delpit (2006) argues that such explorations are a necessary learning step for White adults to become effective teachers of students of color. In my study, the collisions the mothers experienced allowed many of them to grasp those realities and the ways in which their own behaviors have contributed to those realities.

As mentioned above, my model draws from the theoretical work on social norms by Sherif (1965). Harro's "Cycle of Socialization" (2013, p. 46) is also anchored in Sherif's (1965) concepts and addresses some of the same processes included in my model. Thus, my model is consistent with her discussion of the ways in which social norms work to sustain racial oppression. The constructs of collusion, collision, and contention briefly outlined above are further discussed in the next section and my model is presented in Figure 1.1.

The model includes the processes of introducing and instilling social norms with newcomers. This process is depicted on the left side of the figure in a clockwise direction. Newcomers are children born in a society and individuals of any age who move into a society other than the one they were born into. Everyone in the society has opportunities to introduce and instill norms with newcomers in direct and indirect ways. Teaching

newcomers the norms is positioned as benefitting the newcor
comers will benefit by understanding the social rules because a
the rules identifies that they belong to the social group. Belonging to the
group bestows protections from others in the group. Much of the time,
people are oblivious to their participation in the social processes included
in the model; even those teaching and reinforcing the norms are doing so
without awareness (Sherif, 1965). Adherence to norms is collusion in my
model. Individuals who comply with norms benefit in two ways. Tangible
rewards are dispensed after compliance. The other benefit is avoiding the
consequences for non-compliance. Part of the process that teaches newcomers the norms is when they observe the consequences meted out to
non-compliers. Once newcomers have become accustomed to the norms,
they are enlisted in teaching other newcomers and they are no longer considered newcomers. For example, older siblings are enlisted to help teach
younger siblings and older students or experienced employees mentor and
guide less experienced ones.

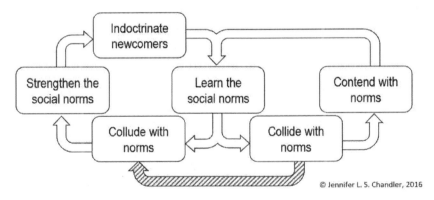

Figure 1.1 Model of colluding, colliding, and contending with norms.

Not everyone abides by the all the norms all the time. Instead of complying, some individuals balk, disagree, complain, or refuse at times. So
the divided arrow exiting the "Learn the social norms" box represents that
movement can go either way. Refusing to comply with norms is not only
out of ignorance. A person may fully comprehend that they are expected to
conform to the norm. Whatever the reasons are for resisting, the resistance
itself is represented by the arrow pointing to the "Collide with norms"
box. Refusing to collude is moving away from the processes that sustain
the norm.

Refusing to conform, balking, recoiling, resisting, or arguing could all be part of a noticeable response or it could be unobserved. In any case, the person has moved away from the processes that maintains the norm by refusing to comply with the norm. The refusal could pertain to one norm or it could include several related norms. A person could comply with the norm sometimes and refuse at other times. The refusal could be short-lived. After initially refusing to comply with the norm, a person may rejoin the processes that maintain that norm. Rejoining the processes that sustain the norm is represented by the shaded arrow that points from the "Collide with norms" box to the "Collude with norms" box.

The amount of time a person is outside the processes that sustain the norm and what they do while they are there differs with every collision. Additionally, the decision to return to collusion after a collision may be preceded by a variety of behaviors by those who are also colluding and are inviting the person who collided to rejoin them. Those invitations may be expressed repeatedly and more fervently the longer a person remains outside. Thus, they function to highlight the benefits of compliance. Compliance, at least, will end the incessant pressure to collude.

Not everyone returns to the processes of perpetuating the norm after every collision. Sometimes a person decides to not return to complying with the norm and they remain in the collision process, repeatedly colliding with the norm. They may voice indignation and outrage about the norm in an attempt to bring attention to what they feel is unjust, unfair, or unhealthy. Being stuck repeatedly colliding with the norm is a location that several of the mothers I interviewed found themselves in at times.

Moving beyond a collision process to begin exploring ways to re-engage with the norm in a way that pushes for changes to the norm itself is the process of contending in my model. Moving from colliding to contending involves a decision to move away from continual collisions and is represented in the model by the arrow pointing to the "Contend with norms" box. That movement includes a learning process. The learning could be of any kind. It could be experiential and result from trial and error; it could include advice from community or family members; or it could involve classes, workshops, videos, online resources, and books. The learning referred to in this model is purposeful in that it helps the person focus on working for change because the function of the learning is to re-engage with the norming processes further upstream. Reengagement is purposeful and it is primed with learning about the norms themselves and their outcomes.

My model of collusion, collision, and contention applies to any norms, not just norms of Whiteness. Norms are not static, they evolve. Their evolution is brought about, in part, through accommodating pressures for change. There is a set of processes that perpetuates existing norms. It is represented by the processes operating in a clockwise direction in the left half of my model. There is another set of processes operating in a counterclockwise direction in the right side of my model. Both sets of processes are ongoing and are impacting each other. Individuals are participating in multiple places in the model at all times because they are interacting with many social norms at once. Locating specific actions within these processes can be a revelatory step that can lead to change. This applies for individuals and for organizations. At the organizational level, the model could be used to analyze the norms operating within the organization and the ways in which individuals collude, collide, and contend with those norms. The norms that function within organizations could be examined without ascribing labels to specific individuals. Once the existing norms are understood, then choices regarding those norms can be undertaken. Are the norms assisting the organization in reaching its goals? Would replacing some of the norms better support the actions for reaching the goals? Recommendations for using the model in such a change effort in school settings are contained in chapter six.

The next three chapters present details from my interviews. The organization of the chapters was explained above in the Introduction. The interviews reveal many collusions, collisions, and some contentions with Whiteness norms. In these chapters, I define the Whiteness norms encountered and explain how the mothers interacted with them.

REFERENCES

Bonilla-Silva, E. (2010). *Racism without racists* (3rd ed.). Lanham, MD: Rowman & Littlefield.

Case, K. A., & Hemmings, A. (2005). Distancing strategies: White women preservice teachers and antiracist curriculum. *Urban Education, 40*(6), 606–626.

Delpit, L. (2006). *Other people's children: Cultural conflict in the classroom.* New York, NY: The New Press.

DiAngelo, R. J. (2010). Why can't we all just be individuals?: Countering the discourse of individualism in anti-racist education. *InterActions: UCLA Journal of Education and Information Studies, 6*(1), Article Number 4.

Dweck, C. S. (2007). *Mindset: The new psychology of success.* New York, NY: Ballantine Books.

Fasching-Varner, K. J. (2012). *Working through Whiteness: Examining White racial identity and profession with pre-service teachers.* Lanham, MD: Lexington Books.

Frankenberg, R. (1993). *White women, race matters: The social construction of whiteness.* Minneapolis, MN: University of Minnesota Press.

Garfinkel, H. (1967). *Studies in ethnomethodology.* Englewood Cliffs, NJ: Prentice Hall.

Garner, S. (2007). *Whiteness: An introduction.* New York, NY: Routledge.

Goffman, E. (1959). *The presentation of everyday self.* New York, NY: Anchor Books.

Gordon, J. (2005). White on White: Researcher reflexivity and the logics of privilege in White schools undertaking reform. *The Urban Review, 37*(4), 279–301.

Harro, B. (2013). The cycle of socialization. In M. Adams, W. J. Blumenfeld, C. Castaneda, H. W. Hackman, M. L. Peters, & X. Zuniga (Eds.), *Readings for diversity and social justice* (pp. 45–52). New York, NY: Routledge.

Helms, J. E. (2008). *A race is a nice thing to have: A guide to being a White person or understanding White persons in your life* (2nd ed.). Hanover, MA: Microtraining Associates.

Lensmire, A. (2012). *White urban teachers: Stories of fear, violence, and desire.* Lanham, MD: Rowman & Littlefield Education.

Leonardo, Z. (2009). *Race, whiteness, and education.* New York, NY: Routledge.

McAdam, D., Tarrow, S., & Tilly, C. (2001). *Dynamics of contention.* Cambridge, England: Cambridge University Press.

Parks, M. W. (2006). I am from a very small town: Social reconstructionism and multicultural education. *Multicultural Perspectives, 8*(2), 46–50.

Pennington, J. L., Brock, C. H., & Ndura, E. (2012). Unraveling the threads of White teachers' conceptions of caring: Repositioning White privilege. *Urban Education, 47*(4), 743–775.

Picower, B. (2009). The unexamined Whiteness of teaching: How White teachers maintain and enact dominant racial ideologies. *Race Ethnicity and Education, 12*(2), 197–215.

Sherif, M. (1965). *The psychology of social norms.* New York, NY: Octagon Books.

Sleeter, C. E. (2005). How White teachers construct race. In C. McCarthy, W. Crichlow, G. Dimitriadis, & N. Dolby (Eds.), *Race, identity, and representation In education (critical social thought)* (2nd ed., pp. 157–171). New York, NY: Routledge.

Smith, H. J., & Lander, V. (2012). Collusion or collision: Effects of teacher ethnicity in the teaching of critical whiteness. *Race Ethnicity and Education, 15*(3), 331–351.

Stevenson, H. C. (2014). *Promoting racial literacy in schools: Differences that make a difference.* New York, NY: Teachers College Press.

Stocking, G. W. (1965). On the limits of 'presentism' and "historicism" in the historiography of the behavioral sciences. *Journal of the History of the Behavioral Sciences, 1*(3), 211–218.

Sullivan, S. (2014). *Good White people: The problem with middle-class White antiracism.* Albany, NY: State University of New York Press.

Trepagnier, B. (2010). *Silent racism: How well-meaning White people perpetuate the racial divide* (2nd ed.). Boulder, CO: Paradigm.

Yoon, I. H. (2012). The paradoxical nature of Whiteness-at-work in the daily life of schools and teacher communities. *Race Ethnicity and Education, 15*(5), 587–613.

CHAPTER 2

BECOMING A MOTHER

Some of the mothers interviewed became mothers through giving birth and some through adoption. Some of the mothers were single, some were partnered with a man, and some were partnered with a woman. Of the mothers who were partnered, some were partnered with a person of color and some were partnered with a White person. While some of the mothers referred to their partners and some of those references are included in the vignettes I discuss, an examination of the choices of partners these mothers made is not included in this book so that the focus stays on these women as mothers. This way, we are looking back on the process of partnering or the process of making parenting choices regarding adoption from the standpoint of their motherhood that was already in place. This allows the mothers' stories to unfold here for the reader similarly to how their stories unfolded in the interviews. Once these mothers became mothers, they never returned to being non-mothers. Consequently, their descriptions and explanations and recollections at the time of the interviews were always through their current experiences and identities as mothers.

Before beginning with details of the interviews, it is necessary to become familiar with the history in the United States that casts its long shadow on the mothers interviewed. It has been the norm in the United States for White females to partner with White men and to give birth to White children. Social sanctions to create this norm were enacted into law before the United States was formed, starting in 1662 in Virginia (Hening, 1823). ACT XII specified that the status of all children born in the territory to match that of the mother. "All children borne in this country shalbe held bond or free only according to the condition of the mother...." (Hening, 1823, p. 170).

Another Act of note was passed in 1691 in Virginia and is included in its entirety in Appendix B. The law was "ACT XVI—An act for suppressing outlying Slaves" (Hening, 1823, p. 86). Act XVI is frequently referred to as the first anti-miscegenation law in the United States. It is also frequently noted that the Act did not prohibit marriage among people of color. It only stipulated a punishment for White men or women marrying "a negroe, mulatto, or Indian man or woman bond or free" (Hening, 1823, p. 86). There was no punishment for a man of color and a woman of color who married. Battalora (2013) argued that the 1691 Act was an initial step in a concerted effort on the part of the British elite men who "made a connection with European laborers, in part through a claim of shared authority over 'white' women" (p. 28) and her analysis examined the laws that followed to restrict the partnering options for White women. Since there were few White women in the colonies at that time, they had the upper hand, so to speak, in selecting partners. The laws enacted restricted their selection options (Battalora, 2013).

However, because the 1691 Act did not distinguish between White men and women, another interpretation is possible. The restriction in the 1691 Act on the partnering choices of "whatsoever English or other white man or woman" (Hening, 1823, p. 86) to reduce the number of "mulattoes" must be read in conjunction with the other restrictions of the Act. The goal of the Act was to address the problem that "negroes, mulattoes, and other slaves unlawfully absent themselves from their masters and mistresses service, and lie hid and lurk in obscure places killing hoggs and committing other injuries to the inhabitants of this dominion" (Hening, 1823, p. 86). The Act contained three stipulations to address the problem: (1) empowering of justices of the peace to issue warrants for the apprehension of "negroes, mulattoes, and other slaves" (Hening, 1823, p. 86) and allowing the killing of those individuals if they resisted; (2) reducing the number of "mulattoes;" and (3) removing free "negroes and mulattoes" (Hening, 1823, p. 86). The goal of reducing the number of "mulattoes" (Hening, 1823, p. 86) in general coupled with the removal of free "negroes and mulattoes" (Hening, 1823, p. 86) can be interpreted as a strategy for reducing the number of individuals whose status was not discernable from their physical appearance. Reducing the number of individuals who could not have been easily classified as either White or "negro" (Hening, 1823, p. 86) would ease the burden on the sheriffs given the charge to capture enslaved people.

In any case, however one interprets the 1691 Act, since both White men and White women were to be punished if they were to "intermarry with a negroe, mulatto, or Indian man or woman bond or free" (Hening,

1823, p. 86), there was a critical difference for a "mulatto" (Hening, 1823, p. 86) whose mother was White because having a White mother most likely meant freedom whereas a White father did not. Thus, alongside the legacy of social sanctions against White women for partnering with men who are not White, is the legacy of the benefit for individuals who were not White whose mothers were White.

Some might argue that since the *Loving v. Virginia* (1967) decision by the Supreme Court declared anti-miscegenation laws unconstitutional, we are long past those days and that interracial couples are currently supported and embraced by society. The stories from my study as well as results from other previous studies (Cabellero & Edwards, 2010; Harman, 2010; O'Donoghue, 2005; Twine, 1999) do not support that notion. Maillard (2009) argues that while U.S. law no longer prohibits a White person from marrying a person of any race, it does not promote such relations either; in fact it continues to treat such relationships as uncharacteristic.

> *Loving* and similar laws that preceded it assume that interracial marriage begins from a clean slate. But as long as this legacy of separation persists, current deviations from the norm of racial purity will remain just that— deviant. (Maillard, 2009, p. 15)

None of the mothers I interviewed referred to the *Loving v. Virginia* case nor the earlier Virginia Acts before the United States was formed. Nevertheless, the long shadows cast by those and many other cases, laws, incidents, and family circumstances from history continue to impact the daily lives of the women I interviewed.

ANNOUNCEMENTS

My parents to this day have never met my husband.

Fran, one of the mothers interviewed.

Wedding announcements and baby announcements are generally portrayed as happy times. But, some of the mothers interviewed did not have happy memories of their announcements. Some of the mothers talked about their own parents who expressed feelings about them violating the norm of White women partnering with White men and having White children. Onwuachi-Willig (2013) addressed the impact of interracial partnering, explaining that "multiracial families destabilize rigid categories of race in our society, a society, which ... continues to promote the monoracial family as the normal ideal" (2013, p. 278). Some of the mothers' descriptions of their parents' reactions exemplified the idea of familial destabilization and some of those parents eventually developed close and supportive relationships with their grandchildren such as Riley Stevenson's parents.

Riley, her husband, their daughter in elementary school, and their three year old son lived with her parents when I interviewed her. Her husband's work required that he travel during the week and Riley worked full time. At the time of the interview, Riley's parents looked after her son while she worked and they took care of her daughter after school. In Riley's description of her children's relationships with her parents, her reference to the intimacy between her parents and her children was telling.

> **Riley:** Because I'm not there—They have their own little relationship that is just them and even I've noticed my son whose three, is starting to get his own little things—where I'm like "Don't do that" and [one of her parents responds] "Oh no, this is what we do." And I'm like, "Ok." So—you take it one way and it's something special I guess between them interacting—so. I mean [my son] walks by now and if my dad has a glass of water—he'll take the water and "Can I have a sip?" and then drink half of it and then give it back to him. Or "What are you eating?" and sit down. It's cute. I like it. That it's like that. So—when—he—with my mom—he'll come in and say "I want to go lay in Grandma and Grandpop's bed—because she'll go in there with them— she reads. So she'll read and then he'll either have a book next to her like he's looking at his book or watch something on tv and stuff so that's—pretty neat. Then there's my poor husband <chuckle, shakes head>. But no, everybody gets along—and my parents really like my husband and stuff so.

The intimacy between her parents and her children that Riley emphasized above contrasts with her description of her announcement to her parents that she was pregnant. Riley underscored the distance her parents moved from their original reaction to her announcement in detailing the intimacy they share with her children. It also provided a sharp contrast with her words about her husband's relationship with her parents.

> **Riley:** We've been through <pause> When I was pregnant with my daughter it was not good. My parents were—upset because I wasn't married—I was 20 almost 21—so number 1 I'm not married and I'm pregnant and number 2—I'm not married and it's biracial—child—it was not good. They were mad and my dad didn't talk to me. But I found out they were more worried about what everybody else was going to think and react versus how they really felt. And it took, actually the ladies at the church that

I grew up with that knew me—threw me a baby shower—and then even the church just didn't point a finger or shake their head—just embraced me and [my daughter]. And my whole family—and I mean I couldn't—especially my dad kind of go, "Oh, It's not so bad." That was the hard—that was probably the only prejudice—I guess if that's what you want to say—was from my parents. And I've learned that—that most people that feel that way it's because they're worried about what everybody else is going to think about it or perceive it and thinks it's bad versus how they really feel about it—it doesn't really bother them. So—it's—been through a lot—but the day she was born—you know my dad was like "I don't care, the first person that makes a comment will have to answer to me! This is my grandchild." So and she is very special—she—when I think of her—I think of her in the middle and she just has a circle <makes a circle with her hands> of people that have just surrounded her with love. And even my mom has said "There's a purpose for everyone in this world" and she was like, "Look what [your daughter] taught us." You know, cuz we went from couldn't talk about it—and—I mean they never said not to have her or to give her up, but they really did have to get over the fact of the—interracial. They had friends and stuff of all races but, I guess—I mean obviously they didn't have to deal with that, but they were worried about how everybody else was going to think or not accept it. My dad even asked, "Don't you realize, that there's people probably in our family that disagree—doesn't that bother you?" <Shaking head> I said, "No not really. Cuz that's them, not me and I don't really see those people often enough for it to matter." And stuff—so I think they really—I mean it was kind of a blunt harsh way to bring it on them, but to think of where we started—and I thought I was just going to be miserable and something I couldn't get through—just completely turned around—opposite.

Riley expected that her parents were going to be displeased when she originally announced to them that their grandchild was going to be biracial. Riley expected her parents to be displeased and braced herself for her parents' displeasure. Riley's father did not speak to her for a while and both he and Riley were colluding with the norm of Whiteness, *Good White parents do not approve of their White daughters partnering with Black men.* By extension, Riley was also colluding the norm, *Good White women mother White Children.* They were both enacting their roles within those norms. Riley's father was disapproving and Riley was acquiescently accepting her father's disapproval. She explained that "it" doesn't really bother her parents now, over a decade later, and that her parents came to realize, "it's not so bad."

Because Riley accepted that her parents could have disowned her, she positioned them as being the "opposite" of their initial position when they learned she was pregnant. She also described how 13 years later, her parents are still not comfortable talking about race. Talking about race is more work than they were comfortable doing; they had done enough. Furthermore, Riley's reference to her "poor husband" suggested a relationship between him and her parents that was less intimate than the one her children enjoyed. By presenting her parents as having done a great deal by embracing her children, Riley colluded with the norm of Whiteness that positions White people who simply refrain from behaving abominably as good. The norm is to behave atrociously and any other behavior is considered laudatory. Thus, Riley was colluding with the Whiteness norm that, *White grandparents who accept and love their grandchildren who are not White are doing more work than White grandparents of White grandchildren.* The extension of this Whiteness norm is that *it is more work for a White woman to mother a child who is not White than for a White woman to mother a White child.*

Riley explained how her parents closed ranks around her while she also acknowledged that "others" were not going to be accepting. This positioned her parents in opposition to unnamed others. This is another indication of the "more work" she saw her parents doing. However, examining her parents' positions in terms of the degree to which they learned about and were addressing systemic racism that impacted their grandchildren's lives could lead one to conclude that they have done very little. By positioning her parents in opposition to "others" Riley can view them as not like those "other" people. Because her parents' initial position was so oppositional, the distance they moved is what Riley focused on, rather than the fact that they continued to collude with Whiteness norms and were still incapable of discussing race. In this way, Riley colluded with the Whiteness norm that *racism is only a problem because there are some overtly racist people. Good White people do not behave in overtly racist ways.*

In Riley's story, becoming a mother and marriage occurred abruptly from her parents' point of view. Amy Kaster explained that she and her husband had been together for a long time before they had their daughter who was five years old at the time of the interview. Amy talked about the time before she and her husband married as a time when she "worked through things." One of the things that she worked through was other people's perceptions of her and her assumptions about their perceptions.

> **Amy:** We had waited 10 years to get married—I think until we were totally sure that—uhm—you know until we had kind of worked through everything ourselves and—uhm—and partly in terms

of the racial issue—in terms of just feeling like it was going
to be ok with family and there was a lot that we both had to
resolve—and—and then there at the end everybody wanted
to come to the wedding, you know even people I would have
thought would have been hostile to it. I was wrong. They wanted to come and show that they were people who were not racists. I had just assumed from my own upbringing and—and—
you know—I didn't hear people saying terribly racist things,
but it's in the culture. I knew—I thought I knew what people
were thinking. Uhm. You know—just from absorbing the culture <laughs> and I think that is what they were thinking.
And there's also part of people that really want to be open and
reach out—they don't want to be the—you know racist asshole
in the—uhm—you know who is yelling things at people. They
want to be the nice guy.

Amy recognized that people position themselves as the "not racist" by
aligning their outward actions in contrast to the "racist asshole yelling
things at people." Again, this positioning was similar to Riley's description
of her parents with respect to the Whiteness norm, *racism is only a problem
because there are some overtly racist people. Good White people do not behave in
overtly racist ways.* Amy colluded with this norm. Anyone who doesn't do
something overtly racist is behaving "well." In Amy's story, she seemed to
be implying that attending her wedding was all that the attendees felt was
necessary to earn a non-racist stamp of approval. Amy's story also acknowledged that racism is not simply yelling obnoxious things.

Amy was looking back on her life before she had her daughter through
her five years of motherhood when she talked about her extended family
and their reactions to her planned marriage. She said, "I knew—I thought
I knew what people were thinking. Uhm. You know—just from absorbing
the culture <laughter> and I think that is what they were thinking." She
started off her statement referring to her ability to know without anyone
saying anything what they were thinking about her, then she caught herself
and corrected herself when she said "I thought I knew...." Then after her
stressed laughter, she came back to her original assertion that she did know
what they were thinking about her. On face value, it may seem like Amy
could not make up her mind. On the contrary, she was attempting to deal
with the slippery nature of Whiteness norms. Amy's first assertion that
she knew what "they" were thinking was referring to years ago when she
and her husband first became involved. Then when she stopped, she was
imposing an idea that she talked about later in the interview and I address
in her stories presented in the next chapter about giving people the benefit
of doubt. In her conversation with me, she was trying to give people from

her past the benefit of doubt. Then she laughed and resignedly admitted, that she really did know what they were thinking. Her references to "what they were thinking" all stem from the same dominant narrative that White women who partner with men who are not White are deviant. This is one example of Amy's collision with the Whiteness norm, *Good White women mother White Children*.

The word "deviant" is used here as Erikson (2003) defines it. Deviance is defined by communities. Identifying behaviors and individuals who are not considered members of the community is one way communities define themselves as communities; that is, it is one of the ways that communities establish their boundaries.

> The interactions which do the most effective job of locating and publicizing the group's outer edges would seem to be those which take place between deviant persons on the one side and official agents of the community on the other. (Erikson, 2003, p. 86)

The official agents that Erikson (2003) referred to are official organizations for enforcing rules and laws, like police. The same process of boundary policing to identify who is a good White woman continues, though it is no longer official agents of the state performing the policing as was described earlier in this chapter. Individuals in society act as boundary enforcers by identifying deviants.

Amy grappled with the dominant narratives of White motherhood as a White mother of a daughter who is not White. No one actually said those dominant storylines to her and yet she collided with the ubiquitous nature of those narratives. No one has to shout the overtly racist things—they simply exist. And just because no one is shouting them, does not diminish their power. That is the slippery nature of Whiteness norms that Amy, and all the mothers in this book, grappled with. Amy wanted to give people the benefit of doubt, and yet, she understood the ways in which they were colluding with Whiteness norms. Amy was also colluding, at times, with norms of Whiteness. I include these vignettes not to draw your attention to the fact that these mothers' first step toward motherhood was labeled deviant because they chose partners who are not White. I include them to emphasize the pervasiveness and magnitude of the impact of such positioning on these mothers which began long before they became mothers. Whiteness norms operate like an overarching invisible shell that encompasses the lives of all these mothers. Some of the mothers did not realize it nor analyze it until after they became mothers. Amy was one who described her awareness of this shell before she had children. Fran's Johnson's awareness also began before she had her daughters and it evolved as her daughters grew.

Fran's parents made their position clear to her before she married and they had not substantially moved from that position in over 27 years. Thus, they did not play a central role when Fran announced the births of her three daughters. Fran's parents have not participated in her daughters' birthday parties, school performances, holidays, nor graduations. While her parents did not participate, their absence impacted Fran and thus through their absence they were still a part of her announcement experience. Their absence drew attention to her motherhood as deviant. Normal White mothers' parents are happy and they joyfully participate in their daughter's news and preparations. Not for Fran. Fran's parents had never met her husband and had only seen their granddaughters a handful of times.

> **Fran:** My parents to this day have never met my husband. And we met when I was 18 and I'm 45. Yeah. They've seen my kids a handful of times and—I mean—that's just a whole nother—another can of worms <laughing> for a different conversation. It's sad. It's sad. Uhm—yeah—yeah—they probably would say—and I know at this point <heavy sigh> they would say today that they've changed and you know, blah blah blah. But I think as long as—if you change, then I think it would be really simple to get on an airplane and come down and meet my husband and say, "You know what, I am so sorry." They just behaved—you know—that—that—just—we—"We reacted terrible and from this day forward would love a relationship with you and understand if that's not possible. I just want to say, I'm sorry." But it hasn't happened.

By essentially staying away from their daughter for almost three decades, Fran's parents had been enacting the norm, *Good White parents do not approve of their White daughters partnering with Black men.* Thus, Fran has repeatedly collided with that norm and by extension, the corollary norm that *Good White women mother White Children.* Her collisions were no longer fresh, stinging with anger, frustration, and pain. Fran had long ago resigned herself to the fact that her parents were not a part of her daughters' lives. While she did not sound bitter or angry with her parents, she said that life is short and that grandkids are wonderful. Thus, she positioned her parents as the ones who lost the opportunity to experience loving relationships with her amazing daughters. Later she spoke about her parents again.

> **Fran:** I think that things that happen to me that are used for good— you don't even know—<heavy sigh> in high school, I liked a Black guy and my parents like beat me to death. Beat the crap

out of me and took me out of that school and put me into another school for writing notes back and forth with a Black kid. And so <pause> ultimately I've had to get to a place of feeling and think—you know what—maybe with me—things had to be so extreme for me to be a doer. Otherwise, I could be just like everybody else and be passive and not do anything and then you know—you know what they are only [refers to the diversity work she does]—but they send a diversity message to everybody who [interacts with them]. And the next time [they do that] they might remember that message and—you know— react a little different in the next situation. So, I don't know, I just kind of have to look at my experience as this is part of my plan and maybe it had to be <sigh> that bad, that extreme for me to go do what I'm supposed to do. So. I just get confused on what I'm supposed to do sometimes.

Fran collided violently with the Whiteness norm to which her parents adhered early in her life, *Good White parents do not approve of their White daughters partnering with Black men.* Fran was in high school when her parents attempted to prevent her from having an emotional relationship with a Black boy. Even though Fran referred to that experience as being pivotal, she was still trying to make sense of it in her life at the time of the interview. She wove that early experience into her references to her recent actions advocating for diversity, but she sounded tentative and unsure. When she referred to her early experience with her parents as extreme, she drew on the metaphor of distance similar to Riley's description of her parents' original reaction to her news that she was pregnant. These distances are positioned as gulfs that are significant because of their size. The gulfs are referred to as if they were actual long distances traveled. The size of those distances convey value. The further someone traveled, the more valuable their journey. Fran's parents were literally not willing to make the journey.

Fran referred to her experience in high school with her parents as pivotal and yet in the passage below she revealed that it was not until she was a mother that she collided with the Whiteness norm, *White people are the norm. There is no need to depict or display people of any race but White. A White person can be displayed and it will be understood that it represents a raceless human in books and advertising.*

> **Fran:** When I had my first daughter and I realized, wait a minute, you know, probably one of the first things was, I pass this billboard and it had these group of people on there, and I'm thinking oh well, I don't see her in that billboard, and then it became I went to the bookstore and I started just leafing through

books and I am thinking I don't see her there either and that, that was my Aha moment of oh wait a minute she's gonna have more challenges than the average White kid being born in this world.

After Fran became a mother, she began noticing all the images around her that did not include her daughter. She could not see the reality of her daughter reflected in any of the advertisements or children's books she saw. However, even in Fran's description of her "Aha" moment, she referred to "the average White kid" as the norm against which she compared her daughter and she declared that her daughter would have more challenges. While framing her daughter's life as more challenging, Fran remained silent about her own challenges. By positioning her daughter's life as more challenging, she also positioned her mothering as being more work than if she had a White daughter. It is more work because it is her responsibility to assist her daughter through the challenges she projected that her daughter will face. Thus, Fran is colluding with the Whiteness norm, *it is more work for a White woman to mother a child of color than for a White woman to mother a White child*.

Not all the mothers experienced rejection from their parents like Fran did. Betsy Caruthers experienced overt rejection not from her parents, but from two extended family members before she and her husband married. Before their marriage, Betsy and Greg attended a holiday gathering with her extended family, some of whom were meeting Greg for the first time. Focusing on the holiday celebrations and her joy in introducing her partner to her family, Betsy was stunned and embarrassed when two of her uncles refused to speak with her or Greg during the holiday gathering. Betsy struggled to overcome her feelings of confusion and disgust stemming from the fact that no one rebuked nor scolded the uncles for their disrespectful behavior. Betsy's family shushed, whispered, and generally acted as if the uncles' behavior was best ignored and gotten over, rather than challenged. This was a public collision for Betsy with two Whiteness norms. One was that *it is best to avoid overtly racist people because they cannot change. If one cannot avoid overtly racist people, tolerate their behavior and do not participate in it. Not participating in it signifies that one is not a racist.* The second Whiteness norm was that *adults who become parents make sure their races match. People whose race matches go together. People whose races do not match, do not belong together.*

After the event, in Betsy's conversations with her now husband, she realized that his experience of the event was but one experience in his life that has included overt or covert racist behavior from people. She recalled coming to "recognize the privilege that I had that I had been able to ignore a lot of things in our society up until that moment." Because she and Greg did not live near her extended family, she began to think of the event as the type of thing she would avoid in the future and she "kind of let it all ride and be under the rug." In this way, Betsy was colluding with the same Whiteness norm she had collided with, *it is best to avoid overtly racist people because they cannot change. If one cannot avoid overtly racist people, tolerate their behavior and do not participate in it. Not participating in it signifies that one is not a racist.*

Years later, after Betsy and Greg married and Betsy was pregnant with their daughter, in thinking about her daughter's life inside her, Betsy reflected back on that family gathering and thought, "I can't have my daughter around this—I can't let her see those people treat us like that—I can't let them treat <u>her</u> like that." It was not only her uncles' behavior that she was remembering, it was that everyone accepted their behavior, including her immediate family, herself, and her husband. Betsy recognized her own collusion. I asked Betsy to review the way I summarized her story above and she agreed that it reflected what had occurred and expanded on it as follows.

> **Betsy:** I think part of what made me so reluctant to stand up against my family was my age. My now-husband and I were young (20, I think) at the time of this incident, and I was a very "good" kid who respected elders and authority. Growing up in that rural, conservative, Christian-ethos filled environment, my assumption that my family members were good, kind, fair people was such a naïve, blanket force. When I looked around and saw everyone reacting with hushed whispers like this was just a little embarrassment to look away from until it disappeared left me dumb-founded. I was used to trusting these people to do the right thing, and I knew their reaction was wrong, but I didn't know how to articulate that in the moment. Also, I want to make sure that I don't give the impression that I kept taking my husband to these events and forcing him to sit idly by while these people treated him this way. After that initial Christmas dinner, we didn't go to many more family functions. We've maybe been to three eventsin the 10+ years we've been together that included these relatives, often weddings where we wanted to support the bride and groom and couldn't avoid being around them. While my concern for my husband was not as deep or as protection-focused as my concern for my daughter, I never expected him to silently accept their treatment to keep the peace, either.

Betsy collided with the norms of Whiteness enacted by her family members and her response was to reduce the number of interactions with those family members. Disengagement from her White relatives was Betsy's strategy to protect her husband and her daughter. After those collisions, not only did she disengage from her extended family, she also sought to further her learning about the social processes she experienced. She increased her understanding of how systemic racial oppression works and began using that learning to contend with the norms of Whiteness. Examples of Betsy's contentions with Whiteness norms are included in the next sections.

In this section, I presented some Whiteness norms with which mothers collided and colluded before or as they became mothers and as they began to envision their lives as mothers. The norms from this section are listed at the end of the chapter and all the norms are summarized in chapter five. I included these early experiences from the mothers because the mothers themselves referred to these experiences as meaningful. By continuing to draw on their early experiences in ongoing sense-making of their motherhood, the mothers had opportunities to re-tell their stories and incorporate their experiences in their ongoing formation of their selves as mothers. In the next section, their children have arrived and the physical care of children takes center stage. Meanwhile, as the mothers moved about in society, their visibility as White mothers of children of color often played a prominent role in some of their experiences.

MOTHERING BABIES AND TODDLERS

We know that we're not racist, because we gave birth to them.

Emma, one of the mothers interviewed.

While pregnancy is only one route to motherhood, it is a time that can create opportunities for women to conceptualize themselves differently as mothers (Miller, 2007). Planning for children often serves as a catalyst for new mothers to analyze themselves as women and as prospective mothers. For any mother, the conceptualization process might include speculations and reflections on race. A White woman pregnant with a child whose father is not White who is in the process of comparing and contrasting her identity before and after the child's birth cannot escape the Whiteness norm that *good White women mother White Children.* Likewise, a White woman adopting a child of color is reminded in many ways that her relationship with her child will not be the norm.

The dominant narratives that make use of that norm include those that position the lives of White mothers of children who are not White as deviant from the lives they would have had if they had mothered White children. This means there is an ever-present comparison of their lives with a normal White mother's life. This constant comparison not only continuously marks these mothers' lives as deviant, it also raises race to a superordinate position impacting these mothers lives. What this means is that race becomes the first consideration for interpreting and understanding her experiences. This type of thinking was evident in the comments made by strangers and family members. But for the mothers in my study, race was not at all separable from all other aspects of their lived experiences and this finding mirrors Frankenberg's research (1993). The White people with whom the mothers interacted seemed to be using an overly simplified framework which explained everything as a consequence of the race of the mothers' children as not White. The result was that these mother's lives were often reflected to them by others in ways that were gross oversimplifications. Thus the images of themselves given to them by others did not contain their own meanings and understandings. Because these experiences were so frequent, it can be likened to moving through a funhouse full of mirrors providing one distorted view of oneself after another.

Some of the mothers incorporated aspects from the dominant narratives in their stories. For example, a dominant narrative can be heard in Betsy's description of a series of experiences that included her story below. She realized her perspective was shaped by her experiences as a White woman who was married to a Black man and as the mother of their two year old biological daughter. Betsy brought up the incident about the following tweet by *The Onion* "Everyone else seems afraid to say it, but that Quvenzhané Wallis is kind of a cunt, right? #Oscars2013—The Onion (@ TheOnion) February 25, 2013" (2013).

> **Betsy:** I think a good example is with the Quvenzhané Wallis—when *The Onion* tweeted that—uhm—that she was a cunt. I—I ah—I have some friends—who I know are great people who were like, "Oh you're being too sensitive to this. It has nothing to do with race." Well, but it does have something to do with race because Black women are sexualized more often and younger and in more violent ways than White women are, so *The Onion* ignored that part of her identity like they were calling her out because she was a young girl so they thought it would be funnythat it would be incongruous. But it wasn't incongruous because people actually do say these things about young Black girls. Like the humor doesn't work because of this racism that's underneath of it.

In her conversations with her friends who are "great people" Betsy collided with the Whiteness norm that *many people of color and some White people are "too sensitive" about race. They think every situation has something to do with race when most situations have no racialized meaning whatsoever.* She was also colluding with a Whiteness norm in describing her White friends as great, *racism is only a problem because there are some overtly racist people. Good White people do not behave in overtly racist ways.* Betsy's discussion of the tweet continued.

> **Betsy:** And—uhm—but I realized was that I could never figure out if I would have thought that way if my own daughter hadn't just two weeks earlier pointed to a picture of Quvenzhané Wallis and said her own name. Cuz, she, you know, she has the big curly hair and brown skin and huge bright eyes and she saw the little girl on the screen and rec- literally—recognized herself in her. And so it really put it into perspective for me. It's like, well, maybe if I didn't have this personal connection, I wouldn't see it either, and that's a problem that I would be blind to it if I didn't have that touchstone. And I don't—I guess I'll never know how I would have reacted to it if I were living in a different situation.

Betsy explains that her own realization stemmed from observing her daughter connect herself to the image of Quvenzhané Wallis on the screen. That connection opened a door and Betsy saw the social meanings applied to her daughter that she had not seen previously.

Betsy also acknowledged that she was aware that her experiences were outside the dominant narrative of White motherhood. Betsy's statement "I'll never know how I would have reacted to it if I were living in a different situation" encompassed a broad range of differences that could include having partnering with someone other than her husband. Yet, Betsy was not referring to a wide array of different situations she could be living. She was comparing her actual motherhood to the norm of White motherhood. In so doing she shifted between colluding and colliding with norm of Whiteness, *Good White women mother White Children.* This is but one example of how powerful the pull to compare one's experiences to some unspecified yet omnipresent idea of what one's life would have been if one had had White children.

Many of my study's participants mentioned that their families do not look like most of the families where they live. That positioning was just one of the ways in which the mothers recognized that they are not participating in the dominant narrative of White motherhood. Some of them also pointed out that they are not alone in their position and yet the mothers also told stories that revealed their genuine surprise. So while each mother acknowledged her position as outside the norm, paradoxically, several also described experiences in which that understanding escaped them.

Beth Danforth, like Amy and Fran in the previous section, was aware that in some ways her choices were not consistent with the dominant narrative about White mothers. In the vignette below, Beth's actions colluded with the Whiteness norm that *if a person can identify as White, do it, it will be beneficial to identify that way*. At the time of the interview, Beth's husband had not yet been allowed to enter the United States and she had not seen him in person for over a year. The two married in Italy and Beth moved back to the United States in preparation for having their son. The immigration process took longer than they had expected so Beth's experiences as a mother for a year and a half were as if she were a single mother, even though she was not. Beth's son was 18 months old when we spoke and he was in the room with us toddling around during the interview. In the beginning of the conversation, Beth referred to the U.S. Census race options.

> **Beth:** Yeah, so when I was pregnant—I remembered back to when I was pregnant and when you go to the doctor for the first time and they ask you all these questions about the mother and the father and so it asks the race of the father and I sat there and I looked at it and I thought "What race is he?" Cuz I—I—he's—he's Muslim, he's from Morocco, he's brown—I had no idea so I just left it blank and so then after talking to my sister-in-law saying I was going to do this interview she said, "Well is he [Beth's son] biracial?" So I had to Google it. And Google says that the U.S. government says that Arabic people are—uhm—White race—racially but Arabic ethnically.

Beth's discussion of the U.S. Census race and ethnicity options and whether or not her husband can claim White identity according to the 2010 Census categories is in stark contrast to the more flexible understanding of race put forward in Root's (2004) "Ecological Framework for Understanding Identity Development" (p. 116). Root's (2004) flexible framework describes biracial and multiracial identity development, arguing that multiracial racial identity is fluid. According to Root (2004) a person may identify as several different race categories during one period in their life depending on their social circumstances. Additionally, that same person may use only one racial identity for all occasions during various periods of their life. The variations are many and there is no one linear progression of identity development. Nor is there one correct racial identity choice for any person at any given time. Beth was not applying flexible racial identity framework to her son. Beth acknowledged that when people see her and her husband together, people do not see him as as White. However, she focused on explaining that her husband was White according to the 2000 U.S. Census racial categories and therefore, her son was White as well. Beth seemed to be using the official census categories to prove that her husband and her son were White.

Soon our conversation turned to discussing how we as mothers are viewed by others, and regardless of the U.S. Census race categories chosen by the fathers of our children, we are compared to White mothers of White children. In this part of the conversation, the focus was on how we look in comparison with our children. In the quote above, Beth referred to her husband's country of origin, his religion, and the color of his skin. In talking about her son, she focused on his physically observable self. It is not unusual for mothers to focus on their babies' bodies. Much of motherwork is focused on the physical care of bodies. In that work, mothers learn to be alert to all facets of their sons' and daughters' lives through attentive observation. It is common for a first time mother to be observing her infant's physical self a great deal. When others ask questions about a child's physical self, the mother is the person who knows the most about her child's body. Beth and I had wrapped up the interview and I was packing up my camera and we were still chatting when she described a conversation about her son's physical appearance with a close friend whom she visited after her son was born. I asked Beth if I could turn the camera back on and if she would repeat what she had said. She agreed and I did. Beth described an experience with her friend in which she collided with the Whiteness norm that *asking or commenting to White mothers about the physical features of their children who are not White is excusable as curiosity. It is an acceptable way to draw attention to deviant mothers and their children and still claim to be a good person. It is acceptable to ask questions in ways that position the children as objects. It is also acceptable to touch the children as if they were objects.*

> **Beth:** So one of my closest friends—after he was born, she probably said it at least three times—I think—well, I think when she first saw pictures of him and then when we went to visit she made the comment of "I can't believe how White he is!" And I was surprised that she was saying and I was like "Well, you know, cuz nobody's met my husband in person in the United States. Uhm, but they've seen pictures of him and he's tan and I'm like, well, you know he's been to the beach so he's pretty tan and you know whatever, and I was surprised when she said "I can't believe how White he is—I just thought he'd be tanner"
>
> **Jennifer:** And how did you respond?
>
> **Beth:** I said, "Well, I don't know, I guess you know his family's pretty light too, I don't know. I don't know how he got it."
>
> **Jennifer:** It's—it's—did it catch you off guard?

Beth: It did. It definitely did. Especially coming from her. I didn't really expect anything like that coming from her, I guess. It was strange.

Jennifer: Are you satisfied with how you responded?

Beth: Probably not. Because I was caught off guard so much that I probably would have—I don't know if I would have corrected her more—maybe. Cuz I was just so surprised that she said it that my only thought was "Well I guess some of his family is Whiter" You know?

Jennifer: Do you feel like it—Did you have the sense of "How dare you?"

Beth: Almost. Yeah—almost. Like where's that coming from? That's weird. I think part of that was surprising to her because I don't know if there's a perception that darker skin, darker hair, darker features in general are more dominant than those of us with lighter features so maybe that was part of the expectation—uhm—but. Yeah. And I think maybe because—she surprised me so much because she's my friend I talked about earlier that's Korean and she's adopted. She was born in Korea—in South Korea—and adopted by a Puerto Rican family in New York—so you would think—<held out her hand like an offering and raised her eyebrows and her tone in question> That of all people that's the last person that would make a comment like that.

The behavior of Beth's friend has been described as simply being curious. Beth did not experience it as harmless curiosity, nor did many of the mothers interviewed when they encountered similar behaviors with family, friends, and strangers. The mothers who described these types of incidents collided with the Whiteness norm that positions their children as objects. Some of the mothers also colluded with this norm and is discussed in the next section.

While I mentioned above that several mothers focused on their awareness that their motherhood is outside the norm of White motherhood, not all the mothers positioned themselves in that way. Darlene Eckard used a narrative of universality to connect herself to all mothers. Thus, she provided an argument that she is not any different than any other mother. All mothers are the same, we all love our children and want what is best for them was the narrative that Darlene parroted.

Darlene: You don't see color, especially with a newborn. I mean I can't imagine—I mean my experience wasn't anything like "Oh, she going to experience this or that because of this or that." I just saw her as my baby and that's my responsibility and I have to do the best I can to take care of her. I'm pretty sure that's what every mom feels like—you know—except if you're—ahh—you know—a bad mom—a deadbeat mom then you might focus something else, but I would imagine that every mom's experience is very similar. Especially a first time mom. I was like 27 when I had [my daughter], I wasn't any—I mean I wasn't new—uhm—I wasn't young compared to some other mothers, but I felt like it was a good time and I felt like I was finally mature enough to handle it. Well then, I mean—you almost change instantly <does a flipping motion with her hands> when you know that suddenly you're responsible for this life growing and you change your bad habits and hopefully you step up and do the things you need to do. And so—I know all moms don't so that—but I would imagine that the same no matter what your child's—you know—background is. Uhm. I can't imagine that being pretty much different for any mom.

Darlene relied on normative statements to explain her recollections. She said "you don't see color" which is the claim of colorblindness. Darlene also argued that she was no different than a White mother of White children. She compared her actual life to the imagined one in which she had White children. That imagined life is ever-present and provides constant comparisons. By arguing that she was no different than that imagined life, Darlene positioned herself as just as good as that mother. That narrative presents White mothers of White children as the normative ideal. All mothers can be compared to the normative ideal. They are the standard to which all other mother-child relations are compared. Therefore, by referring to that positioning, Darlene colluded with the Whiteness norm, that *there is a hierarchy of races involved and types of relationships in which White women mother children of color. The circumstances will be valued differently. It is best to be recognized as belonging to the highest level group possible. The ideal to strive toward is that of a White mother of White children. Be like White mothers of White children as much as possible.*

While Darlene argued how she is like every other mother, there were several mothers who told stories similar to Beth's interaction with her friend described above. In those kinds of interactions, the mother is not given the message that she is like every other mother. She is repeatedly told that she is deviant. Laura Moritz told me about her experiences of this. People repeatedly have asked her where she "got" her daughter. All of the mothers who brought up this kind of interaction with strangers interpreted the questioner as operating on a premise that their children were adopted.

> **Laura:** I was walking up to see a client, and she was with her client and I had my daughter with me—she was sick that day or something I don't remember why I had her with me, but I needed to bring her with me for a short meeting, and this old—it was an older woman—much, much—probably like a seventies or eighties and this is [Southern state where she lives] so—so she looks at me and she just went "Where did you get that child—she's beautiful?!" And my client froze cuz you know she knows that [my daughter] is mine—was—you know—my biological child—and she's—and she laughed nervously and I said, "I gave birth to her." <laughs> And then she like—hurried her off. <laughs> I wasn't really offended, but it was so like—blatant—you know. And I—I—I wasn't—I mean I was like whatever—I can take it, but what bothered—I didn't—I wonder like—how - - even—how—that was about—that was a while back because [my daughter] was probably three—three and a half maybe when that happened so I'm like—she's taking all of that stuff in and I wonder what she's doing with it. She's never—she's never said anything—I—I wait—I figure—I either wait until she raises things up like that or if I feel like it's gonna happen like if —

Sharing these stories is part of what occurred in many of the interviews I conducted. Laura said she can "take" it. What that means is she was planning on enduring being positioned as the deviant mother without contesting those norming actions. Her objection was because her daughter was with her and heard the interaction. Laura differentiates what she can "take" and what experiences she wanted for her daughter. Thus she collided and also colluded with the Whiteness norm that *asking or commenting to White mothers about the physical features of their children who are not White is excusable as curiosity. It is an acceptable way to draw attention to deviant mothers and their children and still claim to be a good person. It is acceptable to ask questions in ways that position the children as objects. It is also acceptable to touch the children as if they were objects.* Through Laura's claim that she can "take it," she also positioned herself as a mother who has more work because "taking it" is a way of referring to a burden. Thus, Laura also colluded with the Whiteness norm that *is more work for a White woman to mother a child of color than for a White woman to mother a White child.* These experiences were not isolated nor were they infrequent. They were, however, easy to classify as "more work" by employing the ever-present narrative of what their lives would be like if only they had had White children instead.

Some of the mothers had not developed effective responses and strategies for handling their repeated collisions. However, some mothers were resigned about them and seemed to smoothly move back to colluding, helping the person with whom they were interacting pretend that it hadn't happened. But many of the mothers expressed frustration and anger in describing their experiences similar to how Laura framed hers. Yvette Zanders' feelings of dread related to her experiences was evident in her description of her ongoing conversations with her mother about her children.

Yvette and I had been discussing "nosy" questions that strangers ask mothers in public. Yvette mentioned that her mother "always does that" and expressed her frustration with her mother when her mother did that. Then Yvette described another source of frustration with her mother.

> **Yvette:** She just says what she sees, and you know it's not malicious and she's not trying to be unkind, but she just wants to say <u>something</u>. Every time she comes over to my house we always have to discuss—my children's—the fact they're multiracial. The last time I was there—the last two times I was there—she discussed with me how she likes their squinty eyes. And I was like Mom! You can't say—you—you can't say—you can't talk about the kids that way. She's like, "But I'm <u>complimenting</u> their eyes." "Yeah, but you're saying they are squinty—that's not—you know what......" <sigh—pause> She's not doing it to be malicious. And it just—it drives me bananas. And you know, I'm like "Mom, it's just….."
>
> **Jennifer:** You are SO tolerant. You've—She's been doing this for <u>three</u> years?
>
> **Yvette:** She—it's just—well the squinty comments are new. So that's the last few times I've seen her. And, I—you know, my husband has got a real good attitude about it too you know I came home and I was like "You won't <u>believe</u> what my mother said!" And he goes, "You know, she could have said a lot worse." And I was like "Yes, I know, but it's just, it's—it's putting my kids in this box again that I don't like and so how would be a good way to handle it because I—you know I just couldn't come up with the words. I said "Mom, I just—it's not a nice thing to say." And she said, "Why, I'm complimenting them." And I said "I—ah—I know

you—you're pointing out that feature on them..." But it is not a compliment. And she says "but it's a good comment, they have beautiful eyes." So how do you explain that? I mean, I know it's not an ok thing to say, but I can't put it into words. Like how do I explain that to her?

I conveyed to Yvette that I did not have answers for her dilemma, and I encouraged her to continue discussing the issue with her mother and try a variety of strategies for talking about race until she became comfortable making herself clear. I encouraged her to keep using her voice to find her voice.

New mothers may look to and rely on their own mothers for advice, assistance, and a sympathetic ear. Through that relationship, the new mother can try out and develop her nascent repertoire of motherhood practices and behaviors. The relationships with the women in her family is one of the locations where a mother develops her patterns of behaviors. In other words, it is one of the locations where norms are shared, taught, learned, and reinforced. Thus, it is one of the locations where the norms of Whiteness are passed on—mother to mother. It is in those relationships that collusion with Whiteness norms is expected. It is also the location where mothers begins to develop, use, and practice behaviors that may serve as the basis for their later interactions with daycare providers, pre-school teachers, teachers, principals, and other school staff.

One way to examine Yvette's ongoing struggle with her mother is to focus on the way she talked about it enduring. Yvette said the squinty eyes comment was new, but she said "we always have to" as if she was resigned to it. Yvette was frustrated with her mother and she was hurt by her mother's comments. Her strategy to get her mother to stop was simply to tell her mother that "it's not nice." Yvette was referring to the norm of niceness and what "nice" people do and what they do not do. Yvette described cringing when she saw her mother make similar "not nice" comments to people in public. Her mother's comments about her children place Yvette with the group of people to whom Yvette saw her mother say "not nice" things. Yvette's mother's comments about the children are a continual signifier that Yvette has deviated from a norm of Whiteness. Reminding people of the norms is part of the process of perpetuating them. Subtle reinforcements are made when people comply with the norms and when people do not comply with them. Yvette's mother is complying with the norms of Whiteness by her continual references to her grandchildren lack of belonging. Yvette collided with the Whiteness norm that *asking or commenting to White mothers about the physical features of their children who are not White is excusable as curiosity. It is an acceptable way to draw attention to deviant mothers and their children and still claim to be a good person. It is acceptable to ask questions in ways that position the children as objects. It is also acceptable to touch the children as if they were objects.* Yvette wanted it to stop. Yvette framed having to endure the conversations as more work and that was one way in which she colluded with the Whiteness norm that *it is more work for a White woman to mother a child of color than for a White woman to mother a White child*. Yvette's husband's acceptance of her mother's behavior further complicated Yvette's quandary. It felt wrong to Yvette. She believed it would be better if her mother no longer said those comments. Yvette provided a follow-up to our interview in an email.

> **Yvette:** My husband and I had a long conversation about this last night. He is actually on the other side of things, he thinks there is nothing wrong with people asking immediately about the ethnicity of our children. His thoughts were that people always point out what is different, that is just how humans are. I think I have a unique view on this situation because all my life I have been White, no one has ever come up to me and immediately asked about my Irish or German roots, or commented on my blonde hair. Then suddenly, I have these children and now ethnicity is always a part of the conversation when I first meet someone. So I have kind of seen both sides of it.

When Yvette relayed that her husband said that people "always point out what is different," the statement was arguing that such questions are inevitable. They are expected. They are normal. However, the practice of using the word different as a label or descriptor only carries meaning in a relational sense. Two things or two people must be compared to discover differences between them. One apple is red and small, the other apple is green and large. Comparing them reveals a difference in sizes and a difference in colors. But which one is different? Neither <u>is</u> different. There are differences <u>between</u> them. Declaring one of them as different requires an understanding of a norm for apples. The word "different" is often used as a label for the person who is not like the dominant group in some way. Using the word "different" in this way signals social meaning that has little to do with actual differences. The word "different" is a signifier of not belonging to the dominant group.

Also, in Yvette's story, she emphasized that through having her children she came to recognize changes in how she was treated in public. She did not link those realizations to getting married to her husband. It is also interesting to note her use of the word "suddenly." Her biological children did not appear suddenly. However, she may be revealing that while she was pregnant she did not consider, examine, nor speculate on the ways in which she herself would be racialized differently once her children were born. The important aspect here is that the public encounters that these mothers experienced and the strategies they developed for grappling with them began with their reactions and responses within their more intimate sphere of contacts, which frequently included their own mothers.

Jane Kopfeldt described her challenges with her mother and other family members regarding her daughter. Jane described her discomfort with her family's use of the word "special" to refer to her daughter. Jane believed that her daughter was no more special than any other person. Thus, Jane's understanding of the word "special" used to describe her daughter carries the same meaning as "different" discussed above.

> **Jane:** It's tough though because she is the biracial child in a White family, people immediately wanna go to 'special,' like we need to couch her and wrap her in bubble wrap, 'you're special, you're special, you're special' <u>because</u>—in their heads they are thinking she's different—you're different, you're different, your different so let me make up verbally like let me make up for that lacking or something. I don't think that they mean it. I don't think it's a conscious thing, but every time I hear it I just have this whole physical and emotional and mental, just, UGH! Shudder and cringing. It's like, don't teach her that. Don't!

Jane is full of frustration describing her collisions when she hears her daughter described as "special" by her family. Based on the readings on race that Jane has completed, her understanding of the word "special" as her family used it, is that it was a way of continually marking her daughter as not White and positioning her as an object. The Whiteness norm Jane collided with was *asking or commenting to White mothers about the physical features of their children who are not White is excusable as curiosity. It is an acceptable way to draw attention to deviant mothers and their children and still claim to be a good person. It is acceptable to ask questions in ways that position the children as objects. It is also acceptable to touch the children as if they were objects.* Jane was visibly upset in the interview and she seemed to be arguing that her position as the only single White mom in her family of origin who has a biological biracial child legitimizes her authority to demand that her family stop using the word "special" to refer to her daughter.

Cathleen Dillard also had a very strong emotional reaction to an experience. Cathleen was traveling alone with her two year old son in a public space. Her son was not happy sitting in her lap and he was fussy and she anticipated that people around her were not going to have favorable feelings toward him.

> **Cathleen:** Uhm. Ah. <nervous laugh> Well, you know, just in general, we—going in [to the public space where it occurred] with

your child at that age, when you know that they don't want to sit still is—probably the most suffocating feeling ever—because you know what's going to happen—you know at some point they're going to freak out and cry and people around you are going to hate them and whatever. Uhm. But, to actually have it—like have somebody do that—and—show anger and hatred toward your child is awful.

Cathleen's description of her emotional state revealed that she was nervous and concerned about how people around her were perceiving her son and her mothering capabilities. Was she able to soothe and calm her son? In other words, was she a good mother? Her description of the experience as "suffocating" was as if she felt she did not have any resources or options for coping with the situation. The entire incident was so traumatizing for her that she planned to never put herself in a position where something similar could happen.

Cathleen: It's—I feel like I never want to [be in that kind of public space] alone with him ever again. In fact, I'm not going to.

When Cathleen said, "In fact, I'm not going to" she was referring to her plans to modify her life so that she is not in similar public spaces with her son without her White husband. To protect herself and her son, she wants her husband with her; however, reliance on people complying with Whiteness norms will not ensure protection for her son, nor for her.

As Cathleen continued her story, she referred to what people told her that they would have done in her situation and she argued that their speculations were flawed. Startled as she was, she was unable to fully comprehend what happened, much less react the way her friends suggested when the White man sitting next to Cathleen leaned toward her and said in her ear, "Shut that little n----- up!" and slapped her son.

Cathleen: It sucks, but he—uhm—like every time I'd have to tell my story it was like it was coming back to life and honestly like when it was happening—uhm—it happened so fast that I couldn't really react the way that I wanted to like you know people would be like, "Oh if I was there, I would have hit him back" or whatever. You can't—you can't—it happens in like point two seconds and I have a 22 pound kid on my lap and in—within a split second that it happened I moved—I removed from the situation. And not that I have that in me anyways, but still—it was like I was still not able to react and—and—I was in such shock from that whole experience that I literally got moved and I sat there and I went blank. Wait—did this just happen? What just happened? And until I looked at [my son] closely again and saw his eye, I was like yup—he hit my kid. And he—he called him the N word. I just could not believe it—it was like—just—I—when he said it—it was like everything slowed down because I have never heard that word outside of a movie or a rap song. And then it was being directed towards—my child. It was—it was the most insane feeling I have ever had in my life. <shakes head side to side> It just really never—I didn't think people said that ever. I'm still in shock. I truly thought there was no more of that! I really did! And I don't know why I would think that. But, I just never—I don't hear people talking like that. And it kind of opened my eyes because even just hearing that word towards my baby who I—because he is a baby—and I think he's adorable and he's doing new things every day and I was like wait—you just called him a derogatory Black name! He's not doing anything.

Cathleen was in disbelief. Then she was shocked, angry, and frightened. The people near her who overheard the exchange were as well. Some people immediately began attending to Cathleen and her son, but only so much could be done because of the larger circumstances of the situation, and soon everyone dispersed. Cathleen collided with the Whiteness norm that *White people can and do harm Black people who are innocent*. Cathleen argued that her son was innocent because he was "not doing anything" to deserve such treatment. Furthermore, she explained that she believed nobody behaved like that anymore because she does not observe that behavior. She caught herself and asked "I don't know why I would think that?" revealing that she realized she had blinders on. In many respects, Cathleen's experience was similar to Betsy's with her husband at the family gathering that was discussed in the previous section. Both mothers were unable to completely process the experience at the time, and it prompted a great deal of reflection. While Cathleen's situation was drastically different in that she was surrounded by strangers and Betsy was surrounded by family, their descriptions both contained the same sense of surrealism. Their experiences triggered a period of self-reflection and then prompted a search for learning for both mothers.

Cathleen's shock, anger, and disbelief about the incident were not solely focused on her son. She was also concerned about what people were thinking about her.

Cathleen: I was like—I was just shocked. And I was like well who is thinking that but not saying it. You know and especially happen

> like—"White blonde mom" now what are you thinking about <u>that</u>?! Because they didn't see me with the dad. Often times as a mom you are alone with your kid everywhere—so. What are people thinking?

Her son looks like he could be her biological son, and Cathleen seemed uncomfortable with the thought that people could position her as a White woman who partnered with a Black man resulting in the birth of a biracial baby. Was she only comfortable as her son's adoptive mother? A complete discussion of transracial adoption is beyond the scope of this book; see Appendix C for some notes about transracial adoption. Cathleen was not alone with her discomfort on this topic during the interview. I was acutely aware of her discomfort because as she told her story, she seemed to suddenly remember that I am a White mother of a biological son whose father is Black. She let the topic drop. I did not press her on her statements, because I was trying to stay within the boundaries of nice White woman discourse. Thus, we were both colluding with the Whiteness norm that *there is a hierarchy of races involved and types of relationships in which White women mother children of color. The circumstances will be valued differently. It is best to be recognized as belonging to the highest level group possible. The ideal to strive toward is that of a White mother of White children. Be like White mothers of White children as much as possible.*

The incident with the stranger was not the only story Cathleen told me. She also described her discomfort when people wanted to touch her son's hair. Note how she referred to her son in telling her story.

Cathleen: It's almost like—ah—people never saw one. And it was a lot of people, "Ohhh I just want to touch his hair" <she touched her hair> After a while it was really frustrating—just ok! God, like haven't you seen one of these before. I mean really? But they really haven't. There's just not a lot of diversity in this area. But other—that would be the only experiences that I feel was negative. Like I said, when we first introduced him to family and friends it was very positive, however, it was like overkill with the "Oh my gosh his hair!" <she rubbed her hair> You know, it's like are we going to have to go through that when he is school all the time I mean it's like the first person they've ever seen like that. And that's strange to me. To obsess about it. You know—I mean—I don't know—it—I mean—that bothers me—it's just—there's—I don't know— like our neighborhood—there's not one other Black family—I'm like—so—nobody's treating him differently, but he is different and I don't want that at all. Not for his future.

Cathleen referred to her son's hair before as an afro, so it is possible that when she used the word "one" in the above she was referring to an afro. Even if that is the case, she was referring to either her son or his hair as an object. So the same time she was colliding, Cathleen was also colluding with the Whiteness norm that *asking or commenting to White mothers about the physical features of their children who are not White is excusable as curiosity. It is an acceptable way to draw attention to deviant mothers and their children and still claim to be a good person. It is acceptable to ask questions in ways that position the children as objects. It is also acceptable to touch the children as if they were objects.* Furthermore, Cathleen's explanation that the people who touched her son's hair did so because they had never been face to face with a Black child before supports the Whiteness norm that *it is collectively the responsibility of people of color to teach White people how to behave because there is no other way for White people to learn to behave in respectful ways with people of color.* That dominant narrative also defends their behavior that they are not trying to be offensive, it is because they don't know any better. The narrative continues that since they don't know any better, they could learn to behave differently if people of color taught them how to behave.

Cathleen referred to her faith in people diminishing. She was starting to recognize that the Whiteness norms are not something she can rely on to benefit her and her family. She speculated about future incidents that could happen.

Cathleen: Hm-hmm. Because of what I'm not hearing or what I'm not seeing. That's what bothers me. Specially now. My eyes are way more open to it because I just thought like "This is really cool. This is great." But do they really because I don't know now. You know this guy was really vocal to us. What about people who aren't vocal about it? You know, and—yeah—it bothers me. Like what—I don't know what experiences I'm going to run into with parents, I never imagined I'd have to deal with the situation that I did deal with so who knows you know maybe [my son] will make a friend and his parents won't want him to be friends with him. I don't know. I'm sure that can happen anywhere but in particular here. He's the only him around, you know it would lead me to believe that was why. <pause> I had more faith in people before this happened. I never thought that way—ever—until now.

Cathleen positioned the White man who slapped her son as a racist. As she began to wonder what other people were thinking but not saying she also collided with the Whiteness norm that *racism is only a problem because there are some overtly racist people. Good White people do not behave in overtly racist ways*. This norm implies that harm only comes from the overt racist actions like what happened with Cathleen and her son. Cathleen started wondering about the harm that can come from "good White people." She started to wonder about what Trepagnier (2010) labels "silent racism" and what Bonilla-Silva refers to as "racism without racists" (2010).

Cathleen's traumatic collisions with Whiteness norms added to the smaller collisions she experienced and endured earlier when strangers and friends insisted on touching her son's hair. Together, they contributed to her decision to begin seeking information online related to her experiences as a White mother of a Black son. Her search was one step in her process of learning that could lead to her moving to contending with Whiteness norms similar to other mothers I interviewed. Cathleen's steps to learn more about how racism actually operates was also a tacit acknowledgement of her previous collusion with the Whiteness norm that *there is no reason to acknowledge nor examine structural or systemic racism. It is not the responsibility of White people to educate themselves or their children about race-based oppression. It is acceptable to be recognized as an educated person and claim ignorance about race-based oppression.* Cathleen was not the only mother who experienced a traumatic public experience that included overt racist behavior directed at her and her child. The mothers who described such stories referred to those experiences as "opening their eyes" about racism.

This section explored several collisions and collusions with Whiteness norms that the mothers experienced when their children were very small. The ways in which each mother handled her collisions were unique in many ways to her family circumstances. The extent to which these mothers were aware of their collusions varied. The next section addresses experiences mothers had with care providers or in relation to their preschoolers. The mothers brought their own expectations for the kind of care their child would receive and their expectations for how they as mothers would be treated into their relationships with care providers. They also had expectations for their interactions involving their preschoolers. In part, these expectations were created based on these earlier experiences they had with family, friends, and strangers.

CARE PROVIDERS AND PRESCHOOL SITUATIONS

In our playgroups, my son was not the only mixed kid and mixed doesn't only mean Black and White, mixed meant anything. And now he is the only mixed kid. People stop me and say, [laughs] all the time people stop me and say, "Awhhhhh, he looks just like my niece's—daughter." You know, like every mixed kid looks alike. And that just really irks me. I don't know. It bothers me when people say that. I don't go up to every single White kid and go, "Ohhhhh, he looks like my niece who is like two."

Hannah, one of the mothers interviewed.

Some of the mothers I spoke with stayed home with their children until preschool or kindergarten and some found daycare in order to return to work, so I didn't discuss preschool and daycare with every mother. The mothers I spoke with about childcare all had some flexibility when it came to selecting who would care for their children. None of the mothers referred to financial challenges as a factor in their childcare decision making. As middle-class White women they had the privilege of assessing the factors they considered to be their own personal priorities. Research shows that parents use a variety of factors and their priorities differ among communities based on the childcare options available (Fram & Kim, 2008; Weber, 2011). Additionally, parents modify their criteria over time. In considering what she wanted from caregivers and what she was looking for in the care environment, each mother had another opportunity triggered by that decision-making process to examine her own beliefs, attitudes, and actions regarding race.

Some of Jane's stories appeared in the previous section. Jane made arrangements with her younger sister to live in her home and care for her daughter during her daughter's first year. After that, Jane shopped around for a daycare provider. This notion of shopping for childcare and preschool is key because it positions mothers as customers. As customers, mothers are not only seeking certain features, they are positioning themselves as purchasers of a service. That role differs from the role mothers occupy when interacting with public school employees. Public school employees do not always follow a customer service model like private childcare or preschools are likely to do. So the approach in choosing a childcare service provider involves some aspects that are missing when selecting a school. I mention that here so readers keep this in mind while reading these stories and the stories in the next chapter. Jane described how she selected the childcare provider that she chose.

Jennifer: So does your daughter go to uhm, daycare or anything like that?

Jane: She does, uhm, I actually got really lucky in that from her first year she was at home the whole time. Uhm I went back to work after 10 weeks, wasn't able to take any more time than that off but my sister … stayed [as] a nanny for me—uhm—through—until [my daughter's] first birthday. But then I wanted to get her you know a little bit more socialized around other kids a little more structure and so she started daycare after—just before her first birthday. Uhm, so she's been there for a year at the same daycare the whole time. Uhm she goes to [name of the organization] which is like national chain. Uhm and it's a really great daycare and I think one of the things that I really—that I liked the most about it was that there was a lot of structure. Uhm and also when I did the tour that it was very multicultural. Like with teachers and students. Uhm and when you look at her especially when she started—now she's getting older she's starting to look—uhm—I guess more African American, but she's still pretty racially ambiguous. I think that's probably the best way I can put it. People look at her and everywhere we go people look at her and kind of give her a double take and the first question is you know, some variant of "What is she?" Uhm, and you know, I've gotten Greek and Middle Eastern and Persian and Brazilian and Latin and Hispanic and I think I even I got Asian and Filipino and you know it's like she's just half Black. Um, but she's very light skinned, very, very light skinned. Uhm—and she—her hair is just curly—it's just thick curls and so I think that a lot of people look at her and you know—and no one knows what she is. Uhm and I think that's what I wanted for her was to be around a lot of other kids that weren't just White. Especially being that her family and the people that she's around the most are all White. Her father and his family are not in-volved at all and so she's not—uhm just by nature of my family alone she's not going to have a sort of —a—mm—diverse—uhm—experience and interaction. So like I said, that was one thing that I was specifically looking for in her school—I wanted to make sure that it wasn't going to be her being the odd man out.

In entering the space of organized for-profit childcare, Jane came into contact with a wider set of people with her daughter. In discussing those experiences, Jane, at the same time, drew attention to the people who challenged her daughter's identity and Jane excused their actions. Thus, Jane was colliding and colluding simultaneously with the Whiteness norm *asking or commenting to White mothers about the physical features of their children who are not White is excusable as curiosity. It is an acceptable way to draw atten-tion to deviant mothers and their children and still claim to be a good person. It is acceptable to ask questions in ways that position the children as objects. It is also acceptable to touch the children as if they were objects.* From the way Jane said, "What is she?" it was clear that Jane knew this was not a question of inno-cent curiosity and yet she excused and tolerated the behavior. Jane stated, "Everywhere we go people look at her and kind of give her a double take and the first question is you know, some variant of 'What is she?'" Jane was indicating how common the occurrence was for her. It was so common that she expected it. Expecting it, she seemed to treat it as not worth reacting to any longer; and yet, from the way Jane talked about the questions it seemed that she would prefer to not experience them. That type of collusion appeared in several of the mothers' stories.

At one point, Jane mentioned that she found herself beginning to buy into "the stereotypes of the single White mother of a biracial child whose father is Black." She realized that about herself and decided she wanted to change that. Jane collided with the Whiteness norm, *there is a hierarchy of races involved and types of relationships in which White women mother children of color. The circumstances will be valued differently. It is best to be recognized as belonging to the highest level group possible. The ideal to strive toward is that of a White mother of White children. Be like White mothers of White children as much as possible.* The stereotype she referred to includes many images and meanings that warn White girls and women that partnering with men who are not White will garner them serious adverse repercussions. While Jane did not describe details about the stereotype she referred to, White women who partner with Black men are portrayed and perceived as promiscuous and incapable of partnering with a White man. Single White mothers of biracial babies whose fathers are Black are positioned as the lowest level of these White mothers. Such stereotypes serve to instruct all White women of the consequences they will endure if they choose a path that could include mothering children whose fathers are not White. Their status among other White mothers will be dramatically lowered. Thus, in order to keep instructing White girls with this message, public questions directed at single White mothers of biracial children must be continued. That is how norms are enacted. Norms are enforced through sanctions that are imposed on those who violate the norms. Sanctions are imposed through several mechanisms in order to teach those who have not violated the norms but who are observing the interaction (Posner & Rasmusen, 1999). Thus, the purpose of the mothers' public interactions in which they were repeatedly marked as deviant in public, was not solely to punish them, but more importantly those interactions were repeated as warnings for all young White girls and women.

When family members and strangers asked the mothers about the physical appearances of their children, their questioning identified those mothers as having transgressed the norms of Whiteness. Witnesses to those questioning interactions are therefore instructed on the Whiteness norms. Thus, young people who overhear such interactions are instructed as to how things are done, whether their parents are immediately involved or not. Parents in public with their children who are bystanders of such interactions who say and do nothing are colluding with the Whiteness norms as well. They are socializing their children to collude with those same Whiteness norms.

Hannah Isling's collisions and collusions can be seen in the following vignette. Hannah's stories that dealt with childcare were with her son and her brother's children. Hannah cared for her two sons together with her brother's children frequently. Hannah and her husband and her two young sons had recently moved in with her parents. The difference between the social norms where she lived (Central region) and where she moved from (West region) still surprised her several months after the move. Hannah described some interactions among her children and the other children she was taking care of one day.

Hannah: My sister has three kids, 10, 8, and 5. Daniel [her son, not his real name] will be three and [my younger son] will be one. And my brother has a two year old who is a boy as well. So my brother's son and my son and my other son, they are—they pretty much are the three Musketeers—they're always stick together. Because I keep my brother's son a lot, not that he ever keeps mine, but that's—<laughs> There's another— my sister's friend has a mixed child—it's not hers—it's her sister's child and she has custody of her. And it's funny, like whenever—Frances—her name is Frances [not her real name] whenever she comes around, my sister's kids always say, "Oh, Daniel and Frances are going to get married!" You know? And—and—I'm like yeah, I guess that makes sense— like. They are the same age—and they're the same—you know—race—so they look kind of—so they would think that.

When Hannah said, "I'm like yeah, I guess that makes sense.... They are the same age—and they're the same—you know—race" she was colluding with the Whiteness norm that the children were enacting that *adults who become parents make sure their races match. People whose race matches go together. People whose races do not match, do not belong together.*

Hannah: And our neighbors—I live at my mom's house and the neighbors there—they have—uhm—they're grandparents to a girl who's mixed, her dad's not in the picture. Uhm—that's what I find here in [city where she lives] more too is a lot of times I find White moms with mixed children, but the dad isn't often present. In [where she used to live] I feel like there's more—just mixed couples. You know, course you're going to have like your single mom, with—you know—Black—you know half Black baby, but you find, out here—predominantly what I find mixed kids to be. The two I can think of that are Daniel's age—neither of their fathers are in the picture.

> Which makes me sad. And also makes me not want to—not not want to be here—because I do think it is important for those mixed kids to see that my boys' dad is around and a presence—I don't know—it's interesting.

Jennifer: So—ah—are—is what you're saying—like—you—cuz you don't want people to think that that's your situation?

Hannah: You know that's interesting. I think—I wonder if it's the [place I learned about your study where I heard about a concern] of being concerned about a stereotype about her husband and always being sure to let people know she was married. Even before I lived here, when I came back to visit, I noticed that whenever I went to the grocery store or wherever, I would be sure to make sure people saw my wedding ring with me and my mixed kids. And I thought that was interesting.

Here, Hannah collided with the Whiteness norm as she described her collusion with it, *there is a hierarchy of races involved and types of relationships in which White women mother children of color. The circumstances will be valued differently. It is best to be recognized as belonging to the highest level group possible. The ideal that to strive toward is that of a White mother of White children. Be like White mothers of White children as much as possible.* Hannah explained that she not only made sure she wore her wedding ring, she explained that she made "sure people saw my wedding ring" when she was in public with her children. She did not provide details about what that behavior entailed. Hannah came to her own awareness of her collusion with this Whiteness norm (i.e., she collided with it) when she read online about another White mother of children of color who described her own realization of her collusion with this same Whiteness norm.

Hannah also described being "blown away" by "how White it was" when she and her husband moved in with her parents recently. "It" referred to the experience of living in the area where her parents lived. What follows is one of her descriptions that revealed her discomfort living where it is "so White" because she collided with the norms of Whiteness more frequently than she did before they moved. In this way, Hannah colluded with the Whiteness norm that *locations with low percentages of people of color are not good places for people of color to live. It is better for people of color to live in areas with higher percentages of people of color.* I asked her to expand on what she mean by being "blown away" and she revealed another collision of hers with the Whiteness norm *asking or commenting to White mothers about the physical features of their children who are not White is excusable as curiosity. It is an acceptable way to draw attention to deviant mothers and their children and still claim to be a good person. It is acceptable to ask questions in ways that position the children as objects. It is also acceptable to touch the children as if they were objects.*

> **Hannah:** I don't know, it's just interesting, like in [name of large metropolitan area she and her family lived in before in the West region of the U.S.] in our playgroups my son was <u>not</u> the only mixed kid and mixed didn't just mean Black and White mixed mean anything and now it's like he's the only mixed kid and people stop me and say—all the time people stop me and "Ohhhh, he looks just like my—niece's—daughter" you know like every mixed kid looks alike and it just really irks me. I don't know. Uhm, it bothers me when people say that, like I don't go up to every single White kid and say "Oh she looks like my niece who is 2." That's just kind of, you know, bothers me.

Hannah stated that she does not go up to White kids and say they look like someone she knows. Some people do that, of course. White adults tell White parents of White children that their child looks just like some child they know. But the comment does not carry the same meaning when it is said by a White person to a White mother of children of color. The "they all look alike" trope carries a meaning stemming from the dominant discourse regarding race in the United States. White people looking at White faces "see" more and distinguish more details regarding a White person's features than when they look at faces of people of color (Levin, 2000). Thus, the comment serves to mark people of color as not being unique individuals; they are positioned as only one of a group. The individual is marked as indistinguishable from all others in the same group. So it is within that context and reality, that the commonly heard comment, "Oh your child looks just like my cousin's neighbor's child" was received by the mothers interviewed.

Similar to Jane's experiences discussed earlier, Ursula Vale described an interaction that she and her husband have had with strangers that happened frequently. She explained how acclimated to it they were. While she explained that she was acclimated to the experience, she also seemed to prefer to not experience that kind of interaction. But both Jane and Ursula described these incidents as so commonplace, that they rarely got upset about them any longer. Ursula described her and her husband's interactions with the staff at the preschool facility they visited.

> **Ursula:** One thing that we've run across—ok—so my older son— we're just starting to look at possibly preschools for him for next year and we went to look at one just last week, really

like it—very friendly, everybody is very nice, my husband went with me and one thing that happened there that we notice that happens a lot is that when both of us is there even if we're both asking questions people always talk to me. Instead of to him. And I don't know if it's just they feel more comfortable with me like this is another White woman so maybe she felt more comfortable talking to me or if it's—ah—I don't know. Because I mean, he's—he's—actually he's from Costa Rica and so he has a little bit of an accent so I don't know if sometimes people are worried like maybe he won't understand them—even though he speaks English so well, I don't know if why it is, but that's something we've noticed in many different situations. And I used to try and say it's just your imagination and it's not. It's pretty—and it's pretty across the board—happens to us all the time.

Thus, Ursula repeatedly collided with the Whiteness norm that *when inter-acting with interracial couples, focus on the White person. Direct your questions to that person and look at that person.* Repeated collisions take their toll and one response is to become hardened to them. Ursula collided, and it was a collision that she was used to so she quickly and smoothly moved back to colluding. Ursula referred to the frequency of experiencing interactions with people that she and her husband met as the reason why she did not address the behavior of those people. On the face of it that sounds plausible. However, she did not refer to nor describe trying to encourage people to stop interacting with them in that way. Did her collision impact her view of the preschool?

Jennifer: And then—how did—did that have an impact on your assessment of that—uhm preschool, then?

Ursula: Ah—I guess, no because it happens so often. It's more—it probably would have made a really positive impression if that <u>hadn't</u> happened. And she wasn't—she talked to him some—it wasn't that she wasn't friendly so we didn't really have a negative impression overall. But it's more that it would have been really nice if she had maybe felt as comfortable talking to him, but uhm. No I mean, like I said, I think it happens so often that we didn't really—it didn't change our minds—it didn't really sway our decision about whether we were going to choose that preschool or not. At least not in this case. I mean there are sometimes when people are—I don't know—it kind of depends on how they do it—their attitude—and she was very friendly—just maybe not talking to him directly—so—so it was ok. If she had maybe had a less friendly attitude it would have made a difference. And I don't know—actually—we didn't even talk about it afterwards. I noticed it, but when we were talking about the preschool, he didn't mention it and I don't think I even thought to bring it up either. Although I definitely noticed it at the time.

Ursula described their assessment of the preschool facility by focusing on how much she valued the friendliness of the woman who gave the tour. That White woman's friendliness carried more weight than the fact that she did not speak directly to her husband. Ursula also excused the behavior by suggesting reasons why the nice White woman at the facility was behaving as she did.

Jennifer: And when you say it happens so often, you mean in like other—other social environments?

Ursula: Yes. So it can be if we're—say we're at some kind of social gathering and we meet somebody new—and you know, now that I say it—I don't know if it's just—I'm trying to think if it's just White women or if it's just people in general. But say we're at a party or dinner at a friend's house and we meet somebody new, they almost always talk to me even if I don't directly ask them a questions, they start to answer him, <shifting her body one way and then the other to imitate what occurs> and then they turn to answer to me, and uhm—it happened one time when we were—that I remember very clearly when we were at the doctor's and this was—ah—actually when we had a miscarriage—and so both of us were there and both of us were very emotional and he was, you know, talking to the doctor about the situation and about our options and about—you know—and she didn't look at him the entire time. And we switched doctors after that. That was one of many reasons we switched doctors, but that was the main one that she wouldn't even address him.

Ursula and her husband did not tolerate the behavior from the doctor. They switched doctors. So maybe there was also an evaluation of the severity of the situation they were assessing and deciding how they to respond. It seemed that Ursula's range of responses were to tolerate (i.e., collude) or end the encounter or relationship. Did Ursula and her husband feel uncomfortable the first few times it happened and did they never develop strategies for requesting the people interact with them differently? Did they just tolerate it and explain why they don't do anything about it as if it would be too much work? Perhaps Ursula's years of learning how to be a White woman when she was a younger taught her to accept the treatment that she and her husband received.

Some of Betsy's experiences were discussed already above. In her experience described below with a pediatrician, Betsy collided and then attempted to contend with two Whiteness norms that the pediatrician was enacting at the same time. In her attempts to contend with them, she also colluded with them. One was *there is no reason to acknowledge nor examine structural or systemic racism. It is not the responsibility of White people to educate themselves or their children about race-based oppression. It is acceptable to be recognized as an educated person and claim ignorance about race-based oppression.* The second Whiteness norm was, *asking or commenting to White mothers about the physical features of their children who are not White is excusable as curiosity. It is an acceptable way to draw attention to deviant mothers and their children and still claim to be a good person. It is acceptable to ask questions in ways that position the children as objects. It is also acceptable to touch the children as if they were objects.*

Betsy: Well, uhm—so she was—I go to—I went to—her pediatrician is in a teaching hospital and so that doctor asked me one time if I would be okay with allowing her—one of her students to do her physical examination. And I said sure. You know, I'm a teacher—that's fine. And so—he comes in, he's a nice guy—uhm young, White guy, and he's going through the list of questions and I was already kind of getting irritated with him because I didn't feel like he was really listening to me like—he was like—I—like at one point he asked me what she was eating and I listed off a bunch of—this is when she was really little—she was like maybe 8—or 9 months old and he asked me what she was eating—what kind of solid foods she was eating and I was like, "Oh, you know we give her green beans, and apples, and nectarines." And he was like, "We really like for them to stay away from those things—like—like candy and cake and nectarines." And I'm like, "Candy, cake, nectarines? One of these things is not like the others." <laughs> So I already felt like he was kind of like not really—like he kind of had a script that he had in mind and he wasn't really paying attention to me. Uhm—so then in the midst of all of these questions—he's asking me about her physical—like milestones—like is she pulling up on things—and he's like, "So is she adopted or—what's up with that?" And uhm—I think he caught himself—and said, "So is she crawling?" And I'm like, "No, she's not adopted." And he's like, "Oh. Okay." And you could kind of tell that he realized that he had said something inappropriate. On top of all this—I was breastfeeding [and I had already] I <u>told</u> him I was breastfeeding—and I guess it's technically possible for people to breastfeed an adopted child, but—probably he should have been able to—you know—even if he was trying to figure it out in his own mind there were enough clues that—it was just really weird. Uhm—it was so weird that I like didn't know how to handle it in the moment but I went and thought about it later and I'm like, "I need to say something." Like it was really—really—the "what's up with that?" is what really kind of got to me.

In Betsy's story about the pediatrician in training, her first descriptive word about him was that he was "nice," the second is that was "young" and the third was that he was "White." It would have been helpful to investigate what about him she saw that led her to categorize him as nice because in her next words, she described how irritated she was with him because he was not really listening to her. At the same time that Betsy was clearly upset and annoyed that this young pediatrician failed to accept, acknowledge, and honor her legitimate biological motherhood, she also clearly felt awkward about the incident.

Betsy: Right—I mean even if he's—even if he had been like "So is she adopted?" I think I—it still would have been—sort of taken aback—but I would been "Oh, okay. You know he's just trying to figure it out." The "What's up with that?" I'm like what is that? Her brown hair? Her brown skin—I mean what's the "that" that you're seeing here. And so—uhm—I thought about it for a little while and I decided to send an email to my—uhm—my pediatrician—and she was very, very, very like, "I'm so sorry about that. I will talk to him immediately—uhm—the next time you come in just—if they ask you if you're willing to have one of my students come in, just say no. You can deal directly with me. She was very—you could tell—like very embarrassed that it had happened and very apologetic. And I wasn't even mad—so much as just kind of like—this is weird. Right? Like how do you go through med school and not understand that—you know—a White woman can have a brown baby—it can physically happen right. And so—he called me. And when I saw the number on the phone I knew that that's what—I knew she was making him call, right, to—to—apologize or—to—and I thought about just not answering—cuz I'm like I really don't want to deal with this—but I'm like—well I started—you know—like I—I—I emailed so I should follow through—you know—and so we had actually had a pretty good conversation. He was—he was very apologetic, but he was also—like I think as soon as he heard my voice he could tell that I wasn't going to like yell at him or anything—I could kind of feel him feel relieved and he just kind of started babbling. He was like, "and I didn't grow up around here and where I grew up there wasn't a lot of racial diversity and it's just not something that I'm used to seeing but I realize that I may need to work on and da – da – da." And so like, I felt like that incident – it made him reflect on kind of some assumptions that he was making so – in the end I felt like I was glad that I sent her the email – but it was definitely it was a weird moment when it happened.

Later in her phone conversation with the doctor, Betsy was contending with the Whiteness norm that *there is no reason to acknowledge nor examine structural or systemic racism. It is not the responsibility of White people to educate themselves or their children about race-based oppression. It is acceptable to be recognized as an educated person and claim ignorance about race-based oppression.* However, when the doctor used a dominant narrative of "I didn't grow up with a lot of diversity" to excuse his actions, he was enacting another Whiteness norm and Betsy accepted it. She also provided him the absolution he was seeking. His excuse is the same dominant narrative that Parks (2006) and Fasching-Varner (2012) have found with their teacher students. Both Parks (2006) and Fasching-Varner (2012) found White college students studying to become K–12 teachers explained that their lack of cultural competence and racial literacy stemmed from their growing up in cities and towns that were predominantly White. There are many paths through which people (including professionals such as pediatricians and teachers) can use to acquire the racial literacy skills necessary to competently perform their jobs. When White people claim that they cannot be expected to possess racial literacy skills because they were not exposed to people of color, they are relying on the Whiteness norm that places the responsibility for educating White people about race onto people of color.

In the next vignette, Amy described an incident in which her daughter's teacher met with her daughter, another female student, and that girl's mother at the school to discuss something that happened between the girls at school and Amy was not invited to the meeting, nor did the teacher inform her of the meeting. The teacher classified Amy's daughter's actions toward the other girl as unkind. Amy learned about the meeting after it happened from another person.

Amy: When she was three in her Montessori school, right at the be- ginning of the year—there was an incident where one of the other girls had been going—I think my daughter was saying—I can't remember now—but it was just normal basic kid stuff, but maybe [my daughter] was saying, "No, I don't want to do that." Or maybe even, "No, you can't play with us." But really in the realm of normal—like—it hadn't even—it was in the realm of normal, but this one girl who's real sensitive told her mother and so the mom had come—and the mom is kind of—a person who is a difficult person is always up there complaining—like a real helicopter parent and so I think the teacher in the interest of just—later she told me, in the interest of just nipping it in the bud, sat down with that mother, the other girl, [my daughter] and the teacher to talk about—you know—to me it seemed like to talk about was about [my daughter] being unkind to the other girl. And when I heard that—I just—even now—I just totally flipped my lid that because somebody told me that it had happened. That they didn't think that was right.

In this incident, Amy collided forcefully with the Whiteness norm that *White female teachers and school administrators can be trusted to take care of the students in the school. They work for the best interests of all children by following a color-blind approach.* Amy also colluded with that norm by absolving the teacher by shifting the focus onto the mother of the other girl. Amy continued to describe how upset she was and she continued to excuse the teacher's position in the situation.

> **Amy:** My daughter was traumatized—you know because her teacher is actually very good, and she was trying to—I think—because the other—because when they had the girls talk neither of them knew what the mother was talking about. It was not an actual issue. I felt like that mom was—like—you know—projecting that [my daughter] somehow—and she's not even like a ringleader bully—but that somehow she got it into her mind that [my daughter] was being mean. And so, I was really angry—yeah—that I wasn't included in the conversation. Yeah, and I think it was just spur of the moment and the teacher really apologized for that and uhm—because I brought it up—I was so pissed. I—you know—Yeah, I was really mad. I mean <heavy sigh> it—because of this mother—I mean, I can see why the teacher—later I could say, "Yeah, she was just trying to deal with this mom, and" The teacher was never going to allow [my daughter] to be hurt—uhm—<u>and</u> it still was not appropriate for this—and—but—this can happen!

Amy's disbelief that the teacher acted the way she did is as strong as her support for the teacher. This conflict and tension of colliding while also colluding with the same Whiteness norm was a common occurrence for other mothers in my study. I can empathize with those experiences as I have had many of them myself and they provided fodder for my own reflections. The complex entwined experience of collusion and collision happening at the same time is also evocative of the experiences that Garfinkel's (1967) experiment participants endured that were discussed in chapter one. The difference between his experimental participants and the mothers in my study is that while the disruption to their sense of reality was just as great, the mothers were not part of an experiment. This was their lives. Their confusion and disorientation stunned them and many of them were still grappling with making sense of their experiences years later.

SUMMARY

Before moving onto the next chapter which explores mothers' experiences when their daughters and sons were school-aged, it is helpful to consolidate the Whiteness norms discussed in this chapter. Whether the mothers realized it or not at the time, their early experiences provided them places for trying out responses and reactions to their collusions and collisions. Thus, these early experiences provided the mothers experiences in which they had opportunities to increase and practice their racial literacy. Table 2.1 summarizes the Whiteness norms and the ways in which the mothers interacted with them during the motherhood stages addressed in this chapter. Many of these Whiteness norms also appear in the following chapters because collision, collusion, and contentions with them were not restricted to this time period in the mothers' lives. Chapter five presents all the Whiteness norms.

Table 2.1. Mothers' Collusions, Collisions, and Contentions With Whiteness Norms Identified During the Becoming a Mother Stage

Whiteness Norms: *Social Processes and Discursive Practices*	*Mother*	*Type of Interaction*
White people are the norm. There is no need to depict or display people of any race but White. A White person can be displayed and it will be understood that it represents a raceless human in books and advertising.	Fran	Collision
If a person can identify as White, do it, it will be beneficial to identify that way.	Beth	Collusion
Asking or commenting to White mothers about the physical features of their children who are not White is excusable as curiosity. It is an acceptable way to draw attention to deviant mothers and their children and still claim to be a good person. It is acceptable to ask questions in ways that position the children as objects. It is also acceptable to touch the children as if they were objects.	Beth	Collision
	Laura	Collusion and Collision
	Yvette	Collision
	Jane	Collusion and Collision
	Cathleen	Collision
	Hannah	Collusion and Collision
	Betsy	Collision
Adults who become parents make sure their races match. People whose race matches go together. People whose races do not match, do not belong together.	Hannah	Collusion
	Betsy	Collusion
Good White women mother White Children.	Amy	Collision
	Riley	Collusion
	Fran	Collision
	Betsy	Collusion and Collision
Good White parents do not approve of their White daughters partnering with Black men.	Riley	Collusion
	Fran	Collusion
White grandparents who accept and love their grandchildren of color are doing more work than White grandparents of White grandchildren.	Riley	Collusion
Racism is only a problem because there are some overtly racist people. Good White people do not behave in overtly racist ways.	Amy	Collusion
	Riley	Collusion
	Cathleen	Collusion and Collision

(Table continues on next page)

Table 2.1.   (Continued)

Whiteness Norms: Social Processes and Discursive Practices	Mother	Type of Interaction
It is best to avoid overtly racist people because they cannot change. If one cannot avoid overtly racist people, tolerate their behavior and do not participate in it. Not participating in it signifies that one is not a racist.	Betsy	Collusion and Collision
There is no reason to acknowledge nor examine structural or systemic racism. It is not the responsibility of White people to educate themselves or their children about race-based oppression. It is acceptable to be recognized as an educated person and claim ignorance about race-based oppression.	Cathleen Betsy	Collusion Collusion, Collision, and Contention
It is collectively the responsibility of people of color to teach White people how to behave because there is no other way for White people to learn to behave in respectful ways with people of color.	Cathleen	Collusion
It is more work for a White woman to mother a child of color than for a White woman to mother a White child.	Riley Fran Yvette Laura	Collusion
There is a hierarchy of races involved and types of relationships in which White women mother children of color. The circumstances will be valued differently. It is best to be recognized as belonging to the highest level group possible. The ideal to strive toward is that of a White mother of White children. Be like White mothers of White children as much as possible.	Darlene Cathleen Jane Hannah	Collusion Collusion Collision Collusion and Collision
When interacting with interracial couples, focus on the White person. Direct your questions to that person and look at that person.	Ursula	Collusion and Collision
Locations with low percentages of people of color are not good places for people of color to live. It is better for people of color to live in areas with higher percentages of people of color.	Hannah	Collusion

(Table continues on next page)

Table 2.1.   (Continued)

Whiteness Norms: Social Processes and Discursive Practices	Mother	Type of Interaction
White female teachers and school administrators can be trusted to take care of the students in the school. They work for the best interests of all children by following a color-blind approach.	Amy	Collision
White people can and do harm Black people who are innocent.	Cathleen	Collision
Many people of color and some White people are "too sensitive" about race. They think every situation has something to do with race when most situations have no racialized meaning whatsoever.	Betsy	Collision

REFERENCES

Battalora, J. (2013). *Birth of a White nation: The invention of White people and its relevance today.* Houston, TX: Strategic Book Publishing.

Bonilla-Silva, E. (2010). *Racism without racists* (3rd ed.). Lanham, MD: Rowman & Littlefield.

Erikson, K. T. (2003). On the sociology of deviance. In D. H. Kelly, & E. J. Clarke (Eds.), *Deviant behavior: A text reader in the sociology of deviance* (6 ed., pp. 85–92). New York, NY: Worth.

Fasching-Varner, K. J. (2012). *Working through whiteness: Examining white racial identity and profession with pre-service teachers.* Lanham, MD: Lexington Books.

Fram, M. S., & Kim, J. (2008). Race/ethnicity and the start of child care: A multi-level analysis of factors influencing first child care experiences. *Early Childhood Research Quarterly, 23*(4), 575–590.

Frankenberg, R. (1993). *White women, race matters: The social construction of Whiteness.* Minneapolis, MN: University of Minnesota Press.

Garfinkel, H. (1967). *Studies in ethnomethodology.* Englewood Cliffs, NJ: Prentice Hall.

Harman, V. (2010). Experiences of racism and the changing nature of White privilege among lone White mothers of mixed-parentage children in the UK. *Ethnic and Racial Studies, 33*(2), 176–194.

Hening, W. W. (Ed.). (1823). *The statutes at large; Being a collection of all the laws of Virginia from the first session of the legislature, in the year 1619* (Vol. II). New York, NY. Retrieved from http://vagenweb.org/hening/vol02-09.htm

Levin, D. T. (2000). Race as a visual feature: Using visual search and perceptual discrimination tasks to understand face categories and the cross-race recognition deficit. *Journal of Experimental Psychology, 129*(4), 559–574.

LOVING V. VIRGINIA, 395 (Supreme Court of the United States 1967).

Maillard, K. N. (2009). Miscegenation: An American leviathan. *Human Rights, 36*(3), 15.

Miller, T. (2007). "Is This What Motherhood is All About?": Weaving experiences and discourse through transition to first-time motherhood. *Gender & Society, 21*(3), 337–358.

O'Donoghue, M. (2005). White mothers negotiating race and ethnicity in the mothering of biracial, Black-White adolescents. *Journal of Ethnic & Cultural Diversity in Social Work, 14*(3/4), 125–156.

Onwuachi-Willig, A. (2013). *According to our hearts: Rhinelander v. Rhinelander and the law of the multiracial family.* New Haven, CT: Yale University Press.

Oscars: The Onion Under Fire for Calling Quvenzhane Wallis the C-Word. (2013, February 24). Retrieved from The Hollywood Reporter: http://www.hollywoodreporter.com/news/onion-calls-quvenzhane-wallis-c-424113

Parks, M. W. (2006). I am from a very small town: Social reconstructionism and multicultural education. *Multicultural Perspectives, 8*(2), 46–50.

Posner, R. A., & Rasmusen, E. B. (1999). Creating and enforcing norms, with special reference to sanctions. *International Review of Law and Economics, 19*(3), 369–382.

Root, M. P. (2004). Multiracial families and children: Implications for educational research and practice. In J. A. Banks & C. A. Mcgee Banks (Eds.), *Handbook of research on multicultural education* (2nd ed.). San Francisco, CA: Jossey-Bass.

Trepagnier, B. (2010). *Silent racism: How well-meaning White people perpetuate the racial divide* (2nd ed.). Boulder, CO: Paradigm.

Twine, F. W. (1999). Bearing Blackness in Britain: The meaning of racial difference for White birth mothers of African-descent children. *Social Identities, 5*(2), 185–210.

Weber, R. (2011). *Understanding parents' child care decision-making: A foundation for child care policy making.* Washington, DC: Office of Planning, Research and Evaluation, Administration for Children and Families, U.S. Department of Health and Human Services.

CHAPTER 3

MOTHERS AND SCHOOLS

People in the United States typically attend school while developing from children to young adults. The school class "may be regarded as the focal socializing agency" (Parsons, 1959, p. 298) because there is more than reading, writing, and math that is taught and learned in U.S. schools. Social norms are taught and reinforced in schools and those social norms teach young people what it is to be an American. This chapter describes mothers' experiences within the context of their daughters and sons attending schools. Schooling brings families into contact with a wider set of individuals than the network of interactions they experienced before starting school. Schools provide a place for mothers and children to interact with more people. Those interactions were locations where the mothers I interviewed colluded, collided, and contended with Whiteness norms.

Watching my son climb the school bus steps on his first day of kindergarten was an experience I share with many mothers across the country. I am not the only mother to wonder how big everything must have seemed to my son and to wonder how I could possibly let my precious little boy go. Relinquishing our children to a school system with confidence that the school employees will care for our children with the same degree of care that we have as mothers for our children demands a great deal of trust. Not every parent relinquishes their child to a school, but most do. The majority of children in the United States are attending and are projected to attend public school. Homeschooled students represented only 3% of students in the 2011–12 school year according to surveys conducted by the

---

Colluding, Colliding, and Contending With Norms of Whiteness, pp. 57–111
Copyright © 2017 by Information Age Publishing
All rights of reproduction in any form reserved.

Department of Education (Noel, Stark, Redford, & Zukerberg, 2013) and private school enrollments decreased by 11% from 1997 to 2011 and are projected to decline another 5% by 2022 (Hussar & Bailey, 2014). Believing that children will be well cared for by the employees at public schools requires trust. Trust in schools is:

> the willingness to be vulnerable to another party based on the confidence that the other party is benevolent, honest, open, reliable, and competent.... In schools, principals, teachers, students, and parents all have expectations that the other parties will behave in ways that are deemed to be right and good. (Tschannen-Moran, 2014, p. 57)

Parents have ideas about what is right and good. There is no perfect alignment between what every parent believes is right and good and what is enacted in the school as right and good. A parent who believes that there is enough overlap between what they believe to be right and good (i.e., their norms) and what the school employees deem to be good and right have a basis for trusting that their children will be cared for while they are at school. However, this trust does not exist for all parents. Some parents experience what many of the mothers I interviewed did. Those mothers discovered that the overlap between their ideas of what is right and good for their children and what was deemed good and right by school employees was smaller than they expected. What the mothers believed was good and right for their children was not deemed as good and right by some school employees. Additionally, those mothers discovered behaviors approved by school employees that were, in reality, harmful to their children. Those discoveries often destroyed their trust.

For some mothers, their loss of trust in school employees was similar to what occurred with their families of origin. Trust is believing that certain behaviors can be expected when interacting with people. Destruction of trust is one way of describing a collision with norms that are not beneficial. Making the experience even more damaging was the realization that they were expected to return to colluding with the Whiteness norms with the full knowledge that doing so was harmful to themselves and to their children. This realization can destroy not only the mother's trust in school employees; it can destroy her trust in the social fabric itself. In destroying her trust, the experience also creates a crack in the mother's sense of reality. While these experiences were emotionally charged and often frightening, the cracks in reality also created openings for these mothers to begin to see what they had been taught previously to not see. As disequilibrating as the collisions were, they were necessary steps to be able to develop a more comprehensive and complex understanding of the ubiquitous ways that race is used in social situations.

The sections in this chapter are organized around similar kinds of interactions. Again, I use these section headings only to organize the mothers' stories. The chapter subheadings are not themes that I am highlighting from the mothers' experiences. Additionally, the section headings are not used here to suggest that they contributed to nor caused the experiences of the mothers. They were places and situations that revealed the collisions, collusions, and contentions that these mothers experienced.

SENDING CHILDREN TO SCHOOL

When I [address] race related stuff I find myself being so much more careful about what I say—careful in the sense that I want to be responsible about what I am saying and what I am putting out there, not that I am not careful about other things but if it is about my son and what he did during the day, that is one thing, but [race is a] sensitive social issue. What if I say the "wrong" thing, what if people say "Oh my god that's the wrong thing—you can't be a White mother of biracial kids and think that!"

Karen, one of the mothers interviewed.

By the time she sends her child to kindergarten, a mother likely has interacted with hundreds of adults when her child was with her. The previous chapter explored many of those types of interactions and experiences of White mothers of daughters and sons of color. Those experiences laid the groundwork for her interactions within the school system. Those previous experiences with mothers, friends, doctors, or strangers in public were the interactions in which each mother had the opportunity to practice (whether she realized it or not) how she will interact with school personnel regarding her children.

Sending one's children to kindergarten can be viewed as similar to sending them to preschool; alternatively, it can be viewed as the demarcation between two worlds. In one world the mother has influence and oversight and the second world she relinquishes her child to a system. Some mothers refuse to fully relinquish their children. Landeros (2011) found mothers in her study who participated in school functions daily to an extent that she labeled those mothers as "entitled-minded" because they "place[d] themselves above teachers on the educational hierarchy" (p. 260). While some of the mothers in my study participated in the children's schooling more than others, none of the mothers in my study fit that description. All of the mothers in my study referred to the schools where their children attended in ways that reflected their acceptance of the school employee's authority over their children. Mothers do not simply send their children to school once the child enters kindergarten. Mothers send their children to school anew each year with hopes and fears about their teachers and their classmates. Mothers also send their children to school every day. Every day, then, is a relinquishing of her child.

This section is about mothers' experiences related to relinquishing their children to an education system. Their stories address the many ways that these mothers grappled with this challenge. Not all the mothers grappled with this as a challenge at the same time. Each mother came to see and understand the challenges she was facing with the Whiteness norms embedded in the school system in her own way. So the stories in this sections do not all address children entering kindergarten; however, they do address the collisions, collusion, and contentions that the mothers began experiencing with the Whiteness norms enacted within the schools where there sons and daughters attended.

One of the mothers I spoke with, Abigail Banker, told me about a conversation she had with another mother discussing their children entering school. This was one of the many collisions and contentions that Abigail described with the Whiteness norm that *there is no reason to acknowledge nor examine structural or systemic racism. It is not the responsibility of White people to educate themselves or their children about race-based oppression. It is acceptable to be recognized as an educated person and claim ignorance about race-based oppression.* Abigail briefly described a conversation she had with a White mother of a White son who attended the same school as her son.

> **Abigail:** It is a very progressive school—it's an alternative education, uhm—and even there anytime I ask [other parents], "Have you brought up slavery with your son?" Now—which is first grade. And it's, "Nah, I don't want to do that—it will make him think poorly of his brown friends." Is an interesting response.

This mother told Abigail that teaching her son about slavery will "make him think poorly of his brown friends." What does the White mother Abigail spoke with think about slavery that allows her to conclude that her White son will think poorly of his brown friends when he understands slavery? Possibly she is confused in her own cursory understanding of slavery. Recent history textbooks are not helping. Many history textbooks inaccurately argue that the secession of the Southern States was due to their concerns over states' rights rather than the issue of slavery (Loewen, 2007). Loewen (2007) explores these "culture-serving distortions" (p. 26) in U.S. history textbooks whose editors explained to him that they intentionally portray the United States as a meritocracy where individualism reigns. The editors are loathe to present any material in their textbooks that does not position the United States as a place where every person has the opportunity and responsibility to pull themselves up by their bootstraps and be successful. Acknowledging the brutality of slavery and its long shadow that remains in the United States flies in the face of such a strategy. Recent examples of publishers whitewashing slavery in U.S. history have made national headlines. Last fall, the publisher, McGraw Hill Education struggled to explain why its ninth grade World Geography textbook referred to enslaved people as "workers" (Wang, 2015) and promised to revise the wording in its supplement and future editions. A few months later, Scholastic similarly scrambled to recall their children's book *A Birthday Cake for George Washington* (Ganeshram, 2016) in response to public outcry. It depicted a chef named Hercules, enslaved by President Washington, happily baking him a birthday cake. Scholastic's statement recalling the book the explanation that "without more historical background on the evils of slavery than this book for younger children can provide, the book may give a false impression of the reality of the lives of slaves and therefore should be withdrawn" (Scholastic, 2016, p. 1). These and other inaccurate presentations in public school educational materials mirror some of the concerns that Abigail has. Abigail asked another White mother how she is teaching her White children about systemic racism. The mother responded in a way similar to the other mother mentioned above shifting the focus away from any responsibility on her part to educate her children appropriately regarding race.

> **Abigail:** Uhm and then I met a mother of four kids—has she talked about slavery, Jim Crow laws, and racism? And she said, "Well we put our—the other two [children] are in diverse schools." And I'm like, I put [my son] in a diverse preschool and that did not help him—that did not educate him.

In this conversation, the mother Abigail spoke to argued that since she did not put her children in school where all the students were White, her children were covered. Her argument implied that her White children were benefitting simply by being around students of color. But how could they learn the things Abigail asked about in classrooms with White female teachers who lack racial literacy skills in schools using inaccurate textbooks? That notion that White people can only learn about race and racism from people of color was also in the explanation that the pediatrician-in-training gave Betsy that was discussed in the previous chapter. He also drew on the excuse that growing up in a city whose population was predominantly White was to blame for his lack of knowledge. This argument shifts the blame for the lack of professional knowledge onto people of color.

There is a stark contrast between Abigail's questions to White parents and their questions to her as is revealed in this description.

> **Abigail:** You know I had one mother actually say to me "You haven't experienced any racism with [your son] have you?" And I was

like, "Ahhh—ah—Yes." And I went on to describe some things that have come up and she was just appalled. But they look at [my son] and see this cute little boy—who could say something wrong to him—you know—even if it doesn't exist in their world.

In this exchange, the White mother of White children was incredulous. Her starting position with Abigail was that it was impossible for Abigail to experience racism with her son. The way she phrased the question revealed that she could not believe that Abigail had such experiences. Abigail, on the other hand, is resigned to not only the experiences themselves, but also the incredulity of White mothers of White children because she has collided a number of times with the Whiteness norm that *racism is only a problem because there are some overtly racist people. Good White people do not behave in overtly racist ways.* In response to her repeated collisions, Abigail took steps to educate herself about systemic racism. Then she began practicing ways to contend with not just these individual enactments of Whiteness norms that she was familiar with, but she sought ways to address the underlying structures and processes as well by developing and conducting her own racial literacy workshops. She offers her workshops in her community and works with school staffs to assist in their racial literacy advancements.

Abigail made it clear that she is resigned that no school will be perfect in her eyes and she is working with what is available. Her efforts to contend with Whiteness norms enacted in school settings contrasts with many of the mothers' stories in which they only referred to teachers as helpful and caring. However, in their stories, these mothers described things that their children's teachers did that were not helpful nor caring. However, the mothers did not characterize the teacher's action as such. Many of the mothers were incapable of positioning teachers as people that could harm their children. For example, Geneva Hanover told a story about her son's first grade teacher who told her to keep her son out of the standardized testing session that was going to take place to determine which students qualified for the gifted and talented programs. The teacher told her to "go ahead and just sign him out because it is just going to frustrate him to take the test." Geneva was not interested in the gifted and talented program at the time, but her son did take the test. He scored the highest in the class. Geneva recalled that the "teacher couldn't believe it and they retested him and he did it again." Geneva and her husband chose not to put their son in the program "because it would mean switching schools." She explained that it was a few years later that she wondered, "Why did that teacher suggest that my son would be frustrated ... other than that he's Black? I have no idea. Why would she suggest that?" I asked about the re-testing and she explained that "they do a re-test to see if it was just a fluke." Immediately after offering that explanation, she stopped and wondered aloud in the interview "if they always do that." In the interview, when she wondered aloud whether their practice of re-testing students was their standard practice, Geneva again collided with the Whiteness norm *White female teachers and school administrators can be trusted to take care of the students in the school. They work for the best interests of all children by following a color-blind approach.*

Laura Moritz explained that she wanted to be prepared for similar experiences at her daughter's school. Laura described her approach to being prepared for racialized experiences. She mentioned her plans to talk with her daughter about two important topics before her daughter starts at her next school because she believed her daughter needed to be prepared for interactions with other students. This is a continuation of the story Laura shared in which a White woman asked Laura where she "got" her daughter that was discussed in the previous chapter.

> **Laura:** … that was a while back because [my daughter] was probably three—three and a half maybe when that happened so I'm like—she's taking all of that stuff in and I wonder what she's doing with it. She's never—she's never said anything—I—I wait—I figure—I either wait until she raises things up like that or if I feel like it's gonna happen like if—when she starts public school, we're gonna have to have a conversation about being Black <she made air quotes>—you know—because she doesn't call herself Black. You know—she calls herself brown—she's brown skinned—her dad is dark brown and she is light brown and I'm White. And a couple of times I've said Black, not really thinking and she said, "I'm not Black, Mama, my skin is brown." And so she has NO idea about the cultural references to Black people or Blackness or what it means to be Black—it's going to be mind-blowing.

Laura's own life experiences have shaped her understanding and meanings around race and they also shaped the ways in which she viewed her daughter's experiences. From her position as a White mother of a Black daughter, she concluded that it was going to be "mind-blowing" for her daughter. Laura did not want her daughter to be "made fun of" for not understanding that the term "Black" is used to categorize people not based on their actual skin color.

The other thing Laura planned to discuss with her daughter was slavery so that her daughter "knows where she fits into that piece" when the topic comes up because "that would never have been her because her brown skin side of the family all came from" an African country recently "and they were never slaves." Here, Laura was colluding with the Whiteness norm that *there is a hierarchy of races involved and types of relationships in which White women mother children of color. The circumstances will be valued differently. It is best to be recognized as belonging to the highest level group possible. The ideal to strive toward is that of a White mother of White children. Be like White mothers of White children as much as possible.* Laura plans to explain to her daughter that her ancestors on her father's side were not enslaved people in the United States. This distinction matters to Laura. This is a status indictor to her and her actions are similar to Hannah's and Cathleen's discussed in the previous chapter. All these mothers are jockeying to distinguish themselves among other White mothers of children of color. They were all selecting characteristics of their circumstances to distance themselves from lower status positions.

Jockeying for position is a type of competition as is selecting a school for one's child. Amy wants to identify the best school for her daughter. When she started to explain how she is approaching that challenge, she got side-tracked and told me stories about her long relationship with her husband and how it impacted her interpretations of the racialized meanings of her daughter's interactions in school at the time of the interview.

> **Amy:** And so, I think that has helped me just in when there has been small incidents at school or where other children are making comments about skin color or like this year we had—uhm as the kids are getting older—my daughter's five and she in a Montessori school which is pretty much the most progressive liberal school in the city. And it's a wonderful school with a lot of consciousness on the part of the teachers and uhm—the parents—and so she's in a class and she's the youngest in the class and it's five to seven year olds. And uhm—so there have been some times when the kids are just starting to come into awareness about color—and—where we live—is a very White city in terms of—ahhh—you know it's really the majority and there are not that many African Americans—I think it's less than 10%—and uhm—but in her little class, there are three biracial kids, including her. And then there is one girl that's Latina, and one girl that's Indian. And so my daughter identifies the five of them as the brown kids. Uhm. But anyway—there was some talk at the beginning by some older girl about that "I like White skin better than brown" and <pause>. You know, just talking in that way—trying to think what else—what other things she said. There was a couple of different things that were said. And while I was not happy with that—and—uhm—you know we did all kinds of things with the school and the class—uhm—I was able to see that that's just part of our culture.

Amy was "not happy" when these early race-based incidents occurred in her daughter's classroom, so she "did all kinds of things with the school and the class." It sounds as if she took action to modify an unhealthy situation for her daughter. However, in her last statement about it she revealed that she "was able to see that that's just part of our culture" which sounds like she was resigned to collude with the dominant norms. As she continued the conversation, her next story focused on her daughter and alternative ways to interpret her daughter's comments about her skin color by suggesting that her daughter's comments were not really about race.

> **Amy:** You know, she was probably was saying things you know to make herself feel better for one and in the same way that the girls are like "I like my pink dress better than your blue dress." Uhm. Which my daughter is perfectly willing to be one of the ones that might say, "My favorite is pink, I like—" You know to really be competitive about things. And so—I don't know—I felt like we were able to handle it really well and without getting completely hysterical when that was going on, because there were a couple of different incidents. Uhm. So. And then also to assume that everyone <u>wants</u> to learn. Everybody really wants to be kind and loving and are if given the opportunity they will be able to reach cross culturally.

Amy's last two sentences above conflict with each other. She emphatically stated that "not everyone wants to learn." Then followed that statement with an assertion that everyone "wants to be kind and loving if they are given the opportunity." Amy's references to people were similar to all my interview conversations. The race of the unspecified people to which the mothers referred was understood to be White and I discuss this more in chapter five. The notion of being given the opportunity implies that White people want to be kind and loving, but they just aren't always given the opportunity. Who or what gives them the opportunity? What or who is holding them back? Are they holding each other back? Are their continual collusions with Whiteness norms hindering their ability to see the opportunities that exist?

Amy returned to her thoughts and expectations about the school years ahead for her daughter when she referred to her husband's background in a pattern similar to the way Laura differentiated her daughter's father earlier in this chapter.

> **Amy:** That's what I learned from the whole getting married piece and so—and also—you know my husband comes from a culture where he—you know—Black people were the—uhm—what is

it called—the majority. And uhm—and he came from—from
a family that was really prominent—and uhm—so he—you
know—I don't—we don't want to teach her to fear people or to
assume that people are going to be against her—uhm.

Here Amy referred to the fact that her husband emigrated from Sierra
Leone and that his family was a "prominent" family there to distinguish her
daughter from children of color whose fathers do not share the same background. Amy positions his heritage as the reason why she wants to teach
her daughter that just because she is Black, she should not fear people
or believe that people are "against her." Amy does not refer to her own
heritage; she leaves that unspoken. All of this is part of her collusion with
the Whiteness norm that *there is a hierarchy of races involved and types of relationships in which White women mother children of color. The circumstances will be
valued differently. It is best to be recognized as belonging to the highest level group
possible. The ideal to strive toward is that of a White mother of White children. Be
like White mothers of White children as much as possible.* Like Hannah, Cathleen,
and Laura, Amy differentiates her daughter from other Black children.

The next section includes stories from mothers who were satisfied with
the schools where their children attended and the teachers there. These
mothers' stories are about their experiences with school personnel or with
other parents and they revealed the Whiteness norms that appeared in
those interactions.

VIEWING TEACHERS AND THE SCHOOL POSITIVELY

*Like nothing, like really stands out to me—uhm—the kids don't have any issues in
school, they've got lots of different races as friends from Black to African to Indian to
Iranian to—uhm—so I have not had any issues with them at the school.*

Ina, one of the mothers interviewed.

More than one mother told me that she and her family had no problems or
no issues with their school. "Wonderful!" I responded in the interviews and
I explained to them that I wanted to hear about all kinds of experiences
and that I was not interested in only certain kinds of experiences. Telling
me first that they didn't have any problems with the schools that their sons
or daughters attended revealed something about their expectations for
my study. I explained that I was interested in all manner of experiences to
counter their impression that my study was only interested in problems.
The invitation for my study stated, in part, "My study will interview White
mothers of sons and daughters who are not White across the United States
to examine their experiences with the staff at the schools where their chil-

dren attend." The mothers who immediately told me that they had no problems with their schools were attempting to counter a dominant narrative of White mothers of students of color who have problems with the schools where their daughters and sons attend. Ina Jefferson was one of the mothers who started the interview telling me that she didn't think she had much to offer that would relate to my study.

> **Jennifer:** I'm going to be talking with moms across the country and asking them to characterize their experiences however they characterize their own experiences. Does that make sense?
>
> **Ina:** Sure, that makes sense. Uhm—so I'm not sure that I have a lot to—to offer in this area it's so culturally diverse that we really haven't run into any issues or any—uhm—problems whether it be in school or in sports or anything with the kids—uhm—I mean one thing that stands out just from a conversation is really just my son and one of his buddies—uhm—who is a White boy—my son is clearly mixed—uhm—they were talking about Martin Luther King and how had he not done what he did that maybe their two friends—they couldn't play together—that—you know—back—back in the day. They may not have been able to be friends, but other than that—like nothing like really stands out to me—uhm—the kids don't have any issues in school, they've got lots of different races as friends from Black to African to Indian to Iranian to—uhm—so I have not had any issues with them at the school. Sports, my son's played in sports since he was four years old and has had multiracial teams—uhm—so I'm not sure if I can give you really good examples or situations where race may have been an issue or we would have had—you know—one thing happen or another. So.

Ina said, "the kids don't have any issues in school, they've got lots of different races as friends from Black to African to Indian to Iranian to—uhm—so I have not had any issues with them at the school" as if the reason that she does not have any problems at their school is because her son and daughter have "got lots of different races as friends." This sort of shorthand way of referring to the norms operating where one lives was evident in many of the interviews. Ina made references to where she lived several times in the interview underscoring the fact that she lived in a large metropolitan area where the hub city had a population that was predominantly Black. She referred to her location as the explanation for why her experiences unfolded as they did. However, if simple population racial percentages were the cause, then it would be reasonable that mothers who lived in other areas populated predominantly with people of color would have reported experiences similar to Ina's. That was not the case. Ina's explanation that her son and daughter had several friends of various races and that she did not have any problems with the school seemed to imply that the school employees must be doing fine. Because she cannot see any problems, none exist. In this way, Ina colludes with the Whiteness norm that *White female teachers and school administrators can be trusted to take care of the students in the school. They work for the best interests of all children by following a color-blind approach.*

But there was more going on in the interview with Ina. When Ina and I talked, she never seemed to relax with me and talk about things in an unrehearsed sort of way. I don't mean that everything she said was actually rehearsed. But we all have stories we have told many times and in that way we have rehearsed them. They are our "go to" stories that we use to respond to questions or conversations that we have been in over and over. Another factor impacting all my interviews was that the practices that the mothers developed for thinking of their race and of race in their families occurred over the years. I was attempting to tap into that without asking about it directly, so as I mentioned before, I followed the lead of the mother in almost all of the interviews. Meaning, I did not try to press the mother. In that sense, my conversation with Ina was a normal conversation between middle class educated White women in which niceness is highly valued. The notion of niceness was evident not only in my interviews, but also in the narratives that the White preservice teachers shared in previous research (Case & Hemmings, 2005; Fasching-Varner, 2012; Low, 2009; Pennington, Brock, & Ndura, 2012; Picower, 2009). "Niceness is about keeping things clean, orderly, homogeneous, and controlled ... but it is also a way of maintaining whiteness" (Low, 2009). My conversation with Ina was polite and it stuck to surface level topics and never strayed into anything outside a safe arena. This example also exposes an example of conversational contours that exist for White mothers when interacting with White women school employees. Those conversations are governed by the same rules of niceness to avoid topics such as race. The same rules were also evident in the conversations between many of the mothers interviewed and their own mothers. All these conversations are seemingly mundane and insignificant because the participants are colluding with a Whiteness norm to keep the conversations away from discussing race.

The purpose of the conversation with Ina seemed to be to reinforce that we both are operating within the norms for good mothers and we were symbolically gently patting each other on the back, saying, "You're a good mom." That ritual requires that we both join the performance. One cannot expect to receive the pats on the back if one doesn't also give the other pats on the back. So in that sense, Ina and I both colluded with the norm of Whiteness to keep the conversation nice in her interview. Ina claimed everything was good and I assured her that I was not surmising otherwise. By skating along the surface of the topic, we both enacted our roles. So by the time Ina mentioned that she could never live anywhere but where she lived, implying that the racism that exists elsewhere would bother her, I didn't follow it up to probe into what her thoughts were about other locations.

I include my reflections on my interview with Ina as an example of how powerfully Whiteness norms structure conversations. I was annoyed with myself and ashamed that I had wasted an opportunity. "How did I let that happen?" I asked myself. I was prepared with the theoretical knowledge and prepared for my interviews and yet I abandoned my plan to discover something new with Ina and we plodded along a well-trodden path of banality. The norms of White women conversations explored by Franken-berg (1993) and Kendall (2006) were evident in my conversation with Ina and after the interview I could have listed and cited them. But what did I do in the conversation and what didn't I do that contributed to that? I reviewed the interview recording many times and analyzed my participa-tion. It was my first interview and I used the experience to reflect on the experience and improve my interviewing practice. I suspect many White mothers can recognize the kind of conversation that Ina and I had, swap-ping stories in a self-congratulatory way. No one went out on a limb, and we aligned ourselves with the norms that define a good White mother therefore reinforcing those norms. We were, after all, both White mothers of sons and or daughters of color sharing our motherhood stories.

Riley's stories about her parents appeared in chapter two. In the inter-view, Riley also described differences between her daughter's and her son's personalities as we shared our motherhood stories. She referred to her daughter as a "people pleaser" and she also said that she was preparing herself for calls from the school for her son being the class clown. She said that her daughter was more like she was when she was younger, con-cerned about following rules and not getting into trouble. In the following vignette, Riley described her approach for being involved and supportive of her children's educations.

Riley: The times I've been at the school and volunteered for things—to sell carnations for Valentine's Day—so we sit in the cafeteria for all three lunch periods and it's just <moves her hands together and then apart from each other> it's not like it's just Hispanic people here and Black people here. But she'll say, "I have my Black friends and I'll have my Hispanic friends and my White friends and Asian friends." And then I'm like, "Well, you don't really need to categorize them—necessarily—but I know what

you're trying to tell me—I know what you mean." And stuff—
so—but. I've had good experiences with her school—and they
seem very helpful in regards to learning and whatnot and so—
for—they want every kid to succeed there too. And then it's
a lot to do with—I guess parents as well I saw a little bit of
that just subbing long term as an assistant in the classrooms—
just every parent's different. Some parents put the burden on
the school—I don't know if it's how I was raised, but I always
wanted to be on the same page classroom-wise—at home—cuz
I want her to learn and I don't expect them to—for her to learn
it all while she's in class—so I take that responsibility at home
to reinforce whatever she's learning.

Riley wanted to back her daughter's teacher to reinforce what her daughter was learning in class. That was Riley's path to helping her daughter
succeed in school and a pathway to being a good mother. Riley described
how she colluded with the Whiteness norm operating at the school because
she believes the employees there had her daughter's best interests at heart.
That Whiteness norm was *White female teachers and school administrators can
be trusted to take care of the students in the school. They work for the best interests of
all children by following a color-blind approach.* I asked Riley to talk about her
interactions with teachers and suggested she could tell me about a recent
parent teacher conference.

Riley: They've all been good. I would say normal. Uhm— particular conferences that stand out in elementary school when she
was in second grade her—she had co-teachers, so one spe-
cialized in math and—reading—er—in different subjects—but
they each had their own teacher and the room was open so
one teacher would come teach the subjects and the other one
would come teach the other. But they <u>asked</u> me to come in for
a conference and uhm—no not that time—that time I asked to
go in because her homework and I couldn't figure out how they
solved the math cuz it's different than the way I learned it and
we were having a hard time at home getting homework done so
I went in so they could show me how they taught it so I could
help her at home.

Riley trusted the school employees. She wanted to be on the same page as
them and implement the same norms that are reinforced at the school so
that her daughter can succeed at school. Embedded in her collusion is the
belief that this was what was best for her children. She acted on that belief
and was rewarded by the school employees for colluding with them.

Riley described the interaction she had with the school employees in which they strongly suggested that her daughter might have a diagnosable condition that could be identified by undergoing psychological testing. Riley told this story as a positive interaction she had with the school employees. Her emphasis in the story was the surreptitious manner that the school employee used to suggest the testing to her.

> **Riley:** And they [the teachers] are like, "You know" And they are winking "We can't tell you to—have her tested because we can't—we can't tell you—but there's no rhyme or reason to [her inconsistent scores on tests]. And then finally I said, "Well a year ago—or however long ago it was that I found out that I'm ADHD, so I will certainly have her tested." [The school employee replied] "Well that's very good, but we can't tell you" And they are winking at me. Nodding and winking. "We can't tell you that." So they were very helpful and I like the fact they actually called me in and said come in.

Riley perceived the way that the teachers and staff positioned her daughter as being worthy of their help as a positive thing. This is only one student, but there is a national trend that students of color are identified in school systems to be in need of special services (Ralabate, 2007) at higher rates than White students. Riley comfortably colluded with the norms of Whiteness in order to obtain what she believed were helpful services for her daughter.

In analyzing the collisions that the mothers described in the interviews, it seemed that each mother had a threshold number of collisions before she began to seek out additional information about the processes impacting her and attempting to contend with the norms. In that sense, it is possible that Riley had not yet experienced her threshold number and type of collisions necessary to prod her to seek information about the systemic forces operating against her children in their school.

Ellen Franklin described positive experiences with the school employees where her sons and daughters attended over the years. She described one collision with one of the norms of Whiteness that occurred when her oldest son graduated high school, but this collision did not seem to lead to anything further for Ellen. In a conversation, a friend made statements about why her son was awarded his full scholarship. Bonilla-Silva's (2010) research demonstrates that this type of race-based explanation is commonly used to support Whiteness norms.

> **Ellen:** So when my oldest, who is in college now, was in high school—he had several peers that were all in high school and—uhm—he's

coming to graduate and my son—he was very smart—he graduated as the valedictorian of his high school—uhm and he got a full ride scholarship and I did have one person comment about him, "Oh well he just got that just because he's Hispanic." I did take great offense at that—because—No—it was his work that got him those scholarships. I mean he was graduating at the top of his class—uhm—and so that was very frustrating that they would say, "Well, no it was just his race that got him that." There's just no way! You know it was just grades, his SAT scores—uhm whether or not that helped at all I will never know, but none of his scholarships came from Hispanic foundations so uhm—that was probably the most blatant thing someone has said to me and they were frustrated because their child was having a very hard time competing for different scholarships. So I think that is an underlying frustration people have and it kind of shocked me how quick they were able to just bounce it off of that—so I of course said, no. I hadn't let other people know that he was graduating at the top of the class like that, but I let <u>her</u> know <chuckles> uhm—because he definitely earned that by his work, not by his background.

Ellen used the word "shocked" to describe how she felt. She did not point to the fact that it was a friend that said it. She pointed to how quickly or easily the friend turned to a race-based explanation for her son's success. That shocked her and her shock revealed her collision with the Whiteness norm that *if a person can identify as White, do it, it will be beneficial to identify that way. But sometimes special opportunities are provided for people of color that they can access simply because of their race.* Ellen also told me about her years of involvement in her sons' and daughters' educations. Ellen described her role as the person managing the process.

Ellen: I think what stands out the most to me is how welcoming and open, really, so many of the principals were to my kids. I always made it point of going in and meeting them whenever we moved—wanted them to know that we didn't see them as primary responsibility for educating our kids, but rather a tool—that's just how I looked at school, that it was a tool that I was utilizing and so that they knew that I was always behind them 100% in whatever they needed. I found that several school systems have excellent communication with the parents and I felt like I could really stay on track whether it was—uhm—using a computer based program where I go on and see what homework assignments were due and what grades my kids were getting done—uhm—on their assignments or if they were turning things in late, that was so helpful—uhm—to other areas where there was really just a good, especially here in [state where she lives now] there is a really good parent community here supporting the school and so I like to see that that involvement is encouraged. They even encourage the parents in the upper grades to take some of the similar type coursework that our kids are taking—it's a classical based—ahh—public school.

In this exchange, Ellen positioned herself as an educated mother who has taken charge of her children's educational journeys rather than leaving them up to the school system. After doing this with her son's education for 12 years, her educated and worldly position contrasts with her shocked reaction that someone attempted to negate her son's scholarly accomplishments by stating that he only received the scholarship because of his Hispanic heritage. Because she classified her interactions with school employees on the whole as positive and beneficial for her children, Ellen did not pursue advocating for changes to the structural forces that maintain inequities and thus she colluded with the Whiteness norm that *White female teachers and school administrators can be trusted to take care of the students in the school. They work for the best interests of all children by following a color-blind approach.*

Every parent has their own reactions and responses to their children's educational experiences. Their own memories of their experiences and their expectations for their children in conjunction with their own identity as they respond in each situation. The mothers I interviewed also created their stories of their experiences using the dominant narratives at hand.

Paige Qually relied on dominant narratives in her stories. Paige was active in the parent teacher organization (PTO) at the school where her daughter attended and she described some of her efforts with the PTO. Paige's description of her involvement in the PTO and their outreach efforts and ways in which parents interact included her overall beliefs about becoming American.

Paige: You hope that those new families coming in—uhm—become committed—uhm—and you can <u>get</u> them committed and bring them into the fold and get them set up and started

Jennifer: So does your PTO have kind of like an outreach?

Paige: Oh absolutely.

Jennifer: Like where you have this whole strategy of—ok new families.

Paige: And trying to get—trying to get—and we talk openly about it—we talk at meetings about it—uhm—ah—trying to get families from <u>different</u> communities within the [school]—uhm—we have—ah—we have a si- we have a good representation from our White and Black communities at our PTO and a poor representation from our—ah—from our Spanish speaking—whether they are Hispanic or Mexican or whatever—from our Spanish speaking and—uhm—what do I want to say—is - - - all other. Any Asian or uhm—like we have a community of—ah—ah—Ethiopian families, we have never—I don't think a single one of them—they may be members of the PTO, but they don't actually come to the PTO meetings. . You know and so we have this—you know, <shaking her head> we have this outreach program— I mean and we just <hand by her mouth in a side whisper> you know, <moves to sit forward and lean toward me> when so-and-so comes in the building to pick up their kid and they're all sitting at the table in the lobby <pause> and I understand—I—I have read the literature—I understand the whole connection to your—your like—ah - <wavering hand motion> - you know—people <sitting back in her chair and whispering> but—"That's her, make friends—and tell them <u>come</u> to the meetings!" You know because we want their input. They have kids. They have a whole community of kids. And our kids—obviously see the difference. My daughter obviously sees the difference—uhm. <pause>

Paige explained that their tactic was to target each mom, befriend her, and try to get her to join the other moms who are already participating in the PTO. Success was viewed mainly by the numbers of parents who participated and participation meant showing up at the school for events. Showing up demonstrates that one is "involved" and thus is a good parent. In this way, Paige was colluding with the norm of Whiteness that *good White parents value education so they get involved in the children's schools*. In Paige's explanation, it was obvious that she valued parents who are not "involved" less than the involved parents. However, research (Hill & Tyson, 2009) has shown that the type of parental involvement most strongly correlated with student success is not the type that Paige was advocating. In other words, parental participation in school activities is not correlated with student academic success. The type of parental involvement that Hill and Tyson (2009) found to be most important for student success was what they called academic socialization. Academic socialization includes parents making their expectations for education and its value known to their children, linking schoolwork to life outside of school, encouraging their children's educational and occupational aspirations, assisting with strategies for succeeding at school, and preparing for the future (Hill & Tyson, 2009). None of those activities requires participation in the PTO or frequently showing up at school functions.

There are other reasons that mothers dedicate their time in their children's schools. Some mothers are investing their time in their children's schools to satisfy their own status desires (Landeros, 2011). While all the mothers in my study whose sons and daughters had attended school described some kind of interaction with the school staff and some of the mothers referred to volunteering for events, Paige's disdain for mothers who did not get "involved" was unique.

Paige continued her comments about race by describing her beliefs about some families whose children attended the same school as her daughter.

> **Paige:** I actually had this conversation last year with—with a parent—who—uhm is an undocumented ah—resident—uhnm—and her daughter—uh—ah—ah—is a U.S. citizen, of course. Uhm—and—ah—I noticed that while her daughter and my daughter—were good friends in kinder and first and second they had kind of grown apart and her daughter had then <making a line or angle motion with her hand angling away from her body> you know—become a part of this other group—of similar situated—where Spanish is the primary language in their community at home and so she's only using English when she comes to school kind of a thing and—you know <shrugs> and they just go <shrugs again> "Hmm. That's the way it is." I'm like <grimaces> ok. <laughs> I mean—how do you—what do you—what do you do? You know—that is a reality. Especially here and I'm not—you know, I'm—that's just—and we—we—I don't want to say we like it that way, but we <u>like</u> it that way.

Paige liked it that the sanctions levied on students of color in her daughter's school were working. Students of color are taught that they must collude with the norms of Whiteness which include speaking English everywhere and abandoning their family culture. Students who did not collude with this norm were not encouraged to maintain friendships with Paige's daughter and the others who Paige included when she said "we." This was one way that Paige colluded with the Whiteness norm that *individual people of color who immigrate to the U.S. can achieve individual success by assimilating to the dominant cultural values. When they do not assimilate they cannot be successful. There is only one definition of success.*

Paige: It's so different than when friends of mine grew up in a similar situation, where their parents—my friends, whose parents were not documented and living in this country back in the sixties <hand flat slapping down on the arm of the chair repeatedly> both fathers and mothers learned English and that's all they spoke. In fact, I have friends who grew up in the sixties here who they can't hardly speak Spanish. They'll say, "Oh, I can understand it—when my mother is talking to me I can understand it, but I can't speak it because <slapping her hand on the chair arm> they would not allow us to speak Spanish in the home. Everybody was speaking English. It's not so anymore. Now they live in a community where the predominant language is Spanish everywhere in the community—in the grocery stores—you know—our—our—the signs are in Spanish—everything is in Spanish. And their kids are living—are now living this dual thing where they don't feel accepted because their English.

Paige did not believe the current situation she described was the way things should be. She thought that families who send their children to the school where her daughter attended should follow the same path of assimilation that includes abandoning one's first language and culture. That kind of assimilation is the path to success in Paige's view. Paige continued colluding with the Whiteness norm that *individual people of color who immigrate to the U.S. can achieve individual success by assimilating to the dominant cultural values. When they do not assimilate they cannot be successful. There is only one definition of success.*

Paige continued making her case for complete assimilation.

Paige: I have, I have a friend whose three daughters—she's undocumented. Three daughters are all U.S. citizens—and—ahh—she still has one in high school, but the first two didn't graduate—saw no reason to graduate—why would you graduate—you don't have—you don't need—what are you—what are you going to do with it—what does it mean to you—as—ahhh—when—ahhh—in your community—what you are supposed to be doing at 17 is being married. You need to be married at 17 and it's just <shaking her head> it irritates me because—even though they went through [the school district]—we don't have an immersion program—by the way—we have English as a second language and they can be in English as a second language all 12 years in school. And they get out and they can speak—you know—English—they can converse <shrugs> I can converse with them—I—ah—but they can't speak English well enough to get a receptionist job—after 12 years of schooling in this city.

Jennifer: Well, they could probably get a receptionist job in a

Paige: in a Spanish speaking—at a Spanish business—at a business that deals with Spanish speaking—But they couldn't go downtown to [name of international firm] and get a receptionist job. Because they can't answer the phone and speak well enough—to speak to people who are calling on from New York City, and LA, and you know Brussels or wherever. <hands flip and crinkles brows> Why—Why is <u>that</u>? <laughs> Why—why is—why do they—why is <u>that</u>?! I mean, Yeah. I don't know. I don't know—it's another thing that I wonder about because—ahh—the—thee <sigh> <pause> <deep intake of breath> Because what happens is—unlike <u>my</u> friends—who have executive jobs with corporations and they're first generation Americans—<u>these</u> people—are still doing—basically the undocumented jobs. The construction, the landscaping, the house cleaning, the childcare, the elder care. So their first generation Americans and that is their—that's—that's where they're going. So have we done a good <u>job</u>? By allowing them <rolling hand motions> I mean is this—is this what we really want?

Jennifer: Well, it depends. Your question depends on who is the "we" in the question, right? And it depends on what is defined as "good." Right? I mean—in terms—when you're saying

Paige: <shrugs>

Jennifer: "Have <u>we</u> done a good job?" It's like—who is the "we" in the question? Are the—is the "we" just—you know—ahhh—middle class White people?

Paige: Right.

Jennifer: Or—is "we" everybody?

Paige: Right.

Jennifer: And what's defined as "good?" If good is defined as just what middle class Whiteness thinks is good

Paige: <head to one side> Aehn. [a sound of disagreement].

Jennifer: Then maybe the answer is no. But if the question gets broadened so that the "we" is larger, and so that the "good" is larger, then maybe the answer is yes.

Paige: Tsk! Yeah—but you know it <laughs> Here's—here's my—ah—when I—if I run through this scenario—because—and don't get me wrong—both of these girls are totally happy—okay—

Jennifer: And that's—you know what—<hand palm up and out-stretched toward Paige>

Paige: <Hand palm down and fingers splayed pointing out toward me> and they

Jennifer: That's the <hands go down>

Paige: They both have multiple kids <hands go down>

Jennifer: And if that's the definition of good?

Paige: They're happy and that's great. Uhm, the fact that both of their husbands might get deported tomorrow and they'd be stuck here with one kid on the one hand and four kids on the other hand, because <palms up and hands out-stretched> he's gone. He's not a U.S. citizen—uhm—yeah—ok yeah—that's happiness <sarcastically said>. Ahh— <laughs> but anyway—we won't go there—but—uhm—but—here's—here's—here's the—the thing that would concern me is the country—the country is—that is—ahh—eh—<deep intake of breath, pause, she put her coffee cup on the floor and held her hands and arms out in front of her with her palms face downward and her elbows wide and her forearms parallel to the floor and her finger tips together> It's the ideal that this country is a country where you can come in and <moving her hands as she speaks> you can quote—better yourself. You can rise up above your station. We don't, we aren't sitting in a caste system—you know

Jennifer: Well that's the

Paige: And—and

Jennifer: That's the illusion

Paige: And—and

Jennifer: that exists here in the United States

Paige: <head to one side> Yeaaaaah—but you know—I mean when you look at—look <sharp intake of breath and opens and closes her mouth to start to speak and stops>

Paige: I understand

Jennifer: That's the story

Paige: That's the promise

Jennifer: That is

Paige: The promise

Jennifer: the promise.

Paige stuck to her belief that if people simply abandoned their own culture and language, they could find success and happiness by following a culture that denigrated them. Paige was arguing that the disparity between immigrant groups was due to individual decisions. She was not interested in analyzing the structures that exist in the United States that we participate in as White women and from which we benefit. Paige was parroting the dominant narrative that there is a level playing field in the United States and those views are also parroted in the education system. These same meritocratic views also are used to shape depictions of U.S. history in textbooks that was discussed above (Loewen, 2007).

Paige argued that since the daughters of her friend are U.S. citizens, they should be following the norms of Whiteness. Those norms include allowing oneself to be discriminated against and tolerating micro-aggressions. Paige's argument also included the notion that things are better now than they were before. Paige sounded upset at the mother and her daughters that she was telling me about for not colluding. How dare they eschew the "opportunities given to them?" How dare they not jump at the chance to subjugate themselves for their entire lives to collude with the American Dream narrative?

Adherence to dominant narratives is a hard habit to break. All the mothers participating in my study were born and lived the majority of their lives in the United States and learned the dominant narratives about America being the land of the free and the home of the brave. That narrative includes stories about immigrants enduring hardships and making a better life for themselves and their families. The illusion of meritocracy includes a false promise that individualism and competition are the pathways for success for everyone willing to put in the hard work necessary. Those narratives allow blaming those who "fail" for their own failures. These were not the only dominant narratives of what it means to be an American that the White mothers interviewed heard and absorbed. They also heard many stories that gave them their place as White American women. Letting go of those dominant narratives is not easy because colluding with them is rewarded and telling counter-stories is penalized. Nor is it always possible to recognize one's own collusion with norms of Whiteness.

The stories in the next section are from three mothers who received notifications from school employees that their sons did something that school employees deemed unacceptable. Their stories reveal how they responded to the situations and the Whiteness norms they experienced. There are some similarities between some of these mother's positioning of the school employees to the experience that Amy described in the first section in this chapter.

DEALING WITH SOMETHING THAT HAPPENED AT SCHOOL

In my heart I didn't want to believe that we were dealing with what my husband and I deemed to be - - - racism.

Vanessa, one of the mothers interviewed.

The sons of three mothers whose stories are discussed in this section are Black and my analysis of their stories aligns with the recommendation from Dumas and Nelson (2016) that "the problems experienced by Black boys must be understood as primarily structural and institutional, rather than psychological and attitudinal" (p. 42). Dumas and Nelson (2016) also emphasize that Black boys deserve "skilled teachers, administrators, and afterschool educators who love them and value their human potential" (pp. 41–42). I chose to focus on this view in my analysis rather than rehash the abundant statistics demonstrating the disproportionality of discipline that school employees mete out on Black boys across the United States because love was the fundamental driver for every mother I interviewed. Every mothers' choices and strategies were enacted out of love. Each mother analyzed the situation as best she could and responded with the resources and capacities she had available. These mothers' love for their sons was fiercely apparent. Love is a powerful motivator. It allows us to persevere in the face of extreme challenges. It encourages us to overlook mistakes and missteps. It commits us to a person for the long-term. Did the school employees in these stories love these Black boys?

Karen Lund described her experiences as a shift when her sons began school. She stated that she shifted from an intellectual understanding of fairness or what was right, to a much more personal concern.

> **Karen:** That for me has been part of that—that shift with my family is that it moves some of these issues from these kind of intellectual, like, "Yeah, that's not fair, that's wrong, you need to do something about it" [thoughts] to like—now it's my kid—now it's—now I'm reading an article and I'm thinking - you know—you know like—ahh—like disproportionality—how uhm—children of color tend to be disciplined more harshly in school than Whites. And I'm like—ok—that could be my child—twelve years old when they get into trouble in the lunch room and now they're in bigger trouble than - - and it's funny—I just had this situation....

As Karen began explaining herself shifting, she referred to the trend across the nation of school personnel meting out disproportional discipline for students of color. But as she continued her story, that was not how Karen framed the situation with her son that she described below. In telling her story, Karen explained that she was not concerned about the relationship between her son and the other boy. Nor was she concerned about her relationship with the teacher. She was concerned about the thoughts that the parents of the other boy had about her; and she never mentioned the disproportional discipline of Black male students again. Karen did not tell her story as an example of disproportional discipline of Black male students even though that was the idea that preceded her story. Instead, she framed it as a story about her combating stereotypes about her son and about her as a mother. Karen's story was about her attempt to combat the negative thoughts that the other parents have about her son and her family.

> **Karen:** He had gotten in trouble at school—uhm—and it was just one of those impulse things—a kindergartner type thing and it involved another child and he just made a few comments to this little boy and it's like—you know—and—every mom's nightmare. He comes home with—like—"the letter"—the typed letter in his school folder because the principal had to get involved and I'm like mortified. So I had him write a letter of apology to the other little boy and we actually wrote a letter to the other boy's parents to let them know how we had handled it and I sent it to the school and asked the teacher to pass it on—and it was like—I was covering all my bases. And I realized that part of my concern is in this case—ah—you know—the little boy—the other little boy—he's six, they get over it type thing, my son and him are like buds again—you know, no big deal. Forgive and forget.

Karen's actions revealed her concerns about how she is positioned. By passing the letter to the other parents through the teacher, rather than meeting with them herself, Karen acquiesced (i.e., colluded) with the position of the school employees as having the power to decide, determine, and frame the truth regarding what occurred. She colluded with the Whiteness norm that *White female teachers and school administrators can be trusted to take care of the students in the school. They work for the best interests of all children by following a color-blind approach.* From Karen's view, the teacher had the principal's backing. That was evidenced by the statement Karen made about the letter being typed and that the principal "had to get involved." Karen's first step to remedy the situation was to have her son write a letter of apology. That positioned her son as a transgressor with regards to the school rules. That also established a precedent that could develop into a habit. Therefore, Karen was in collusion with the very norms that result in the disproportional discipline of Black male students that she fears will adversely impact her sons.

Karen was mortified to think that the White parents of the other student were thinking of her as a bad parent because she is White, her husband is Black, and their son is biracial. The Whiteness norm that Karen collided with is that *good White women mother White children.*

> **Karen:** I think about the other little boy's parents—and all of a sudden it's like, well are they going to be thinking about our son and thinking about our family and somehow in their minds this situation is through a filter of race. Like—it isn't just a six year old who had—doing something silly. It's oh <u>that</u> six year old and his dad's Black and how are they parenting at home and all these assumptions and stereotypes and it was like I'm doing all these things and like writing the letter for them to look at me like—we took this seriously, we're good parents, we are on top of things.

Karen's use of the phrase "all of a sudden" is similar to Yvette's use when she said, "Then, suddenly, I have these children and now ethnicity is always a part of the conversation…" in the previous chapter. Karen did not suddenly become the mother of a six year old Black boy. Nor did the stereotypes and assumptions she was concerned about suddenly appear. Those have existed all her life and long before that. The suddenness that both these mothers referred to was their collisions. They collided with what had been there all along; norms of Whiteness.

The "assumptions and stereotypes" that Karen referred to are the dominant narratives. No one in Karen's situation spoke those dominant narratives. The teacher did not mention them. The principal did not allude to them. It is not necessary for anyone to say them out loud. That is the power of norms. Their very existence as part of the history of the United States gives them power to impact a situation without anyone pointing to them because Whiteness norms slide into social interactions unnoticed.

> **Karen:** And I said to my husband, I'm like, "So am I just being paranoid, that like I worry that when my kids get in trouble other adults are going to—even if they don't say it though—their kind of perception of it is affected by the fact that our kids are Black?" and he's like, "Of course they're going to think that." My husband is like my litmus test—and he's like, "Of course they're going to think that." And it's like, <heavy sigh> No— that sucks!"

In Karen's telling of her conversation with her husband, her dismay, disappointment and disillusionment was evident. She recognized some of the Whiteness norms she had been participating in all her life. Those same norms brought her to where she was as a wife and mother seeing and understanding the odds that are stacked against her sons and all children of color. She faced new realizations when her son started kindergarten. She saw herself as a good mother, but Whiteness norms did not position her as such. Recognizing that how she saw herself as a mother was not how she was positioned by Whiteness norms, Karen concluded "That sucks!" That her experiences are not validated by others in her community disrupted her sense of fairness and also her sense of reality.

Some of the mothers who collided with these Whiteness norms began to see their children's teachers and White parents of White students through new eyes. They began to understand that the problem is not just an individual teacher or individual school administrator because the system itself continually reinforces a set of shifting Whiteness norms that always positions Black male students as culpable. These same forces appear in the mother's story in the next vignette.

Vanessa Wilson used the term racism to label the Whiteness norms that she collided with in her interactions with employees in the school system. That Whiteness norm was that *White female teachers and school administrators can be trusted to take care of the students in the school. They work for the best interests of all children by following a color-blind approach.*

> **Vanessa:** In my heart I didn't want to believe that we were dealing with what my husband and I deemed to be - - - racism. And I really do believe—that we were being—slighted, if you will because our children were African American, and—on top of that they were out of the foster care system. But they were—I mean—by the time we got to the point where I pulled them out, they had just been adopted. They were our children. They had <u>our</u> name.... It didn't even occur to me to extend beyond having to re-train my family because here I'm dealing with professionals and professionals should be good— shouldn't they? They should be understanding, they should be empathetic despite what their personal upbringing may be—professionally they've been trained to know that's ridiculous. And we didn't experience it at the [other program] with the teachers there. They were very welcoming—it—wasn't a problem. But when we got to this school it was a problem.

But in her interactions with the school employees, Vanessa did not use the term racism. She colluded with the Whiteness norm that *good White people do not behave in overtly racist ways. Identifying the impact of someone's behavior as racist when they did not intend to be racist is not fair and should be avoided.*

> **Vanessa:** I think because I challenged it—I put it in a letter and I said this is ridiculous. This—this—the racism needs to stop now. And I put it in such a way that it wasn't even <u>calling</u> it racism. I was alluding to it and it was obviously pretty good because they stood up and the next thing you know not only did they hire the assistant superintendent who also happened to be the special ed director—but he was African American— figuring that would soothe me that first year when he [her son] was in kindergarten. And it didn't. And then when we brought it up again and there were all these troubles—I said, "You know, nothing's changed." And then they hired—as we left and pulled out our kids—it was almost simultaneous- ly—because we were creating a bunch of—you know <hand making a rotating motion> - - - noise, if you will. Then the diversity trainer came in—the director of diversity. And she was responsible for developing—staff development.

By avoiding the word racism when interacting with the school employees, Vanessa positioned herself within the bounds of nice White woman behav- ior and advocated for her son and daughter from that position. Many of the mothers interviewed also positioned themselves in this way. Their behavior is understandable because the view that these mothers had of themselves is that they were still in the nice White women group. However, not all the other nice White women with whom they interacted perceived them in the same position. Sometimes, those in the nice White woman group posi- tion women who reveal the racial inequities of the system (by advocating for children of color) as outside the nice White woman group. Those in the group do this because advocating for children of color by identifying systemic racist practices embedded in public school processes is not some- thing that nice White women normally do.

Vanessa also told me about how her involvement in the education system started to shift from one as a parent concerned about her children's educa- tions to her desire to know more about how the education system operates. That drove her decision to go back to school and get an advanced degree in education so that she could advocate from within the system. She referred to having to "re-train her own family" and she said she didn't think she would need to do that with "professionals." She expected professionals to be appropriately equipped and she found that they were not. Thus, she collided with the Whiteness norm that *there is no reason to acknowledge nor examine structural or systemic racism. It is not the responsibility of White people*

to educate themselves or their children about race-based oppression. It is accept-
able to be recognized as an educated person and claim ignorance about race-based
oppression. Vanessa also admitted that she did not handle everything she
experienced the way she would have wanted to admitting her own collusion with the same norm. So for Vanessa, racial inequities in the school
system was one of the many facets that she wanted to address more fully by
increasing her education.

Vanessa was focused on not only getting a good education for her son,
but also on keeping him safe. Again, keeping children safe was a common
topic in the interviews. The idea of being safe requires an understanding
of the source of danger. Where is the danger? As mentioned earlier, several
of the mothers found it difficult to accept that danger for their children
could come from the very people they trusted to care for their children.

In the next interview excerpt, an interaction with a school employee
influenced Wendy Weston's perception of her son. This mother also viewed
the school employees as helpful and concerned for her children's educations. In explaining the incident, Wendy described her son's rigid sense of
right and wrong. His views are common for all children at that age according to Kohlberg (1984). However, Wendy explained that her son's view of
right and wrong stemmed from his race.

Wendy: I just had [my son] and I took him to my work with me and
he was part of like a class there and—uhm—he just like had
this sense of—ah—in—in—like—justice—like things just had
to be right and fair at two years old and he was out on the
playground and I would—and if somebody was messing—if
somebody said something to his friend, he was right there like,
"You don't do that to my friend." You know—and uhm—I just
remember—uhm—him just kind of always—the teachers would
say that he just had this sense of things needing to be fair and
right—you know in the world—so like I see that even now in
him—you know—and just—as they—as he—so this was kind
of like a childcare center so then once we went into the public
school system—uhm—he still just had that—that quality. And
I don't recall any of the other teachers bringing it up to me so
much, but in second grade—they talked about Martin Luther
King Day—and they talked about—how schools were segregated and somebody said to [my son] "Does that mean [her son's
name] would not have been part of our school?" and that was
the very first time, I think, of all of the kids school that we kind
of realized that, you know, how this—that would affect them if
we didn't talk with them about it.

Wendy connected her memories of her son at the age of two expressing a rigid sense of right and wrong with an experience later when he was in second grade learning about segregated schools. She was stitching together an understanding of why her son was the way he was. Part of the meaning she wove in was that her son was Black and thus, the "because he is Black" became part of her explanation for his rigid sense of right and wrong at the age of two. And then she saw it playing out years later as well. Wendy was not reporting what actually happened, she was telling a mother's story. She was creating her understanding of her son.

> **Wendy:** In second grade when that happened and [my son] with his—his like—that sense of you know—justice, things have to be fair and right. It was really hard on him when that was brought up in class and I really felt as a mom that I failed him there a little bit because the teacher felt bad and in my conversation with her she was, "Oh I just—I really brushed it off and I told [your son] I—that we love him—once—we would never let that happen—you know so that he knew—you know that this is a history lesson and not how things are now—uhm—and so—I just—I think—that has always just stuck out in my head <heavy sigh> as a mom and—and seeing how that affected him.

Wendy felt like she failed her son because it was solely her job to deal with the situation. The teacher "brushed it off" and refused to engage in a meaningful conversation with all her students regarding race. Absolving her son's White female teacher of all responsibility was how Wendy colluded with the Whiteness norm that *White female teachers and school administrators can be trusted to take care of the students at the school. They work for the best interests of all children by following a color-blind approach*. She continued her story.

> **Wendy:** We've—just—kind of been in touch with the kids on those things you know our conversations with them have been—you know—stressing to them that God created us—everyone equal and that we're learning about these things because we don't want to repeat these things—you know—these are things that happened and this is how far we've come and—they're part of your history—you know—they're part of how awesome things can be now.

Wendy said she and her husband stress that "God created us—everyone equal and that we're learning about these things because we don't want to repeat these things—you know—these are things that happened and this is how far we've come and—they're part of your history—you know—

they're part of how awesome things can be now." When Wendy said "your" history, not "our" history, she was colluding with the Whiteness norm that *White people are the norm. There is no need to depict or display people of any race but White. A White person can be displayed and it will be understood that it represents a raceless human in books and advertising.* Whiteness norms position White people as raceless, so race only applies to people who are not White; and the history of the United States that includes genocide, labor camps, and enslavement of people of color is not part of Wendy's history as a White woman. Wendy colluded with those norms when she did not position herself in the history to which she referred. She spoke as if the history that she referred to included her children's and her husband's ancestors, but not hers.

Wendy: Yeah—we just realized—I think that uhm— <pause> maybe that we needed to talk about it more and not just—you—know—notice—make the— <pause> see the differences and acknowledge them but to <u>talk</u> about it more—and that was the year I—that stands out in my brain—you know we've always been—of the Christian faith you know where we are constantly just tell the kids God loves them—Jesus loves you—you know—no matter <u>who</u> you are—but once we got to that second grade it was more like okay, now I think we need to—you know just talk a little more about this because—you know my fear was that [my son] had something inside him that he wasn't telling us or that he felt like he couldn't tell us. I just didn't want him to have feelings like he felt like he couldn't share. <Sigh> and I—I don't know why that was my main concern but you just know that sometimes kids will keep those things bottled up you know and—I could just see it in his face that day that he kind of—you know with that sense of justice in him, knowing—or realizing like—it was kind of a big huge blow to him that you know that—this would actually be like this according to the color of your skin. And we talked about it more and I did talk with his teacher and she felt really, really badly that [my son] would feel bad—you know, she said, "I really tried to do everything I could—uhm—to make him understand that it is <u>not</u> like that anymore and that we are a better society in many ways because that—and so—uhm—so what we just did is we just kind of talked with [my son] about the history a little more and asked if he had any questions about it—uhm—he, of course, didn't quite understand, I don't think he will ever totally grasp—why it was like that—which I think a lot of us are like as well—uhm—but yet it was good to have that—conversation with him where as his parents we could explain you know—you know—uhm—this is—this is how we see you—in this—in this world.

Wendy said it was a big blow to her son "that this would actually be like this" again referring to his race and not her own. She was not describing a realization about herself and about White people and her position in the social dynamics in which she enacts (i.e., colludes with) Whiteness norms. Wendy referred to the passage of time again. The passage of time was referred to by several of the mothers as the reason why things are better now. This is a specious argument. The narrative they are referring to is simple. Things were bad in the past, but they are better now. How did things get better? Time passed. This narrative may be especially appealing because it seems to mirror the human developmental process. Children are born. They cannot do very much. They improve over time. What makes them improve? It appears as if they improve because of the passage of time. However, that is not why they improve. They developed, they grew, they changed, and they learned. While there are philosophical discussions over whether time alone can cause change (Le Poidevin & MacBeath, 1993), it is recognized in social science that time is not a causal agent. The purpose of science is to identify causal agents.

I stay with Wendy for a little while longer even though the next story of hers did not happen at school. It was something that her children were not directly involved with and yet it impacted them profoundly. I include this story because it emphasizes Wendy's position as a White mother of children of color and it ties back to her strategies for keeping her children safe. In talking about where she and her family lived, Wendy said, "It's been good, you know, obviously you are going to have issues anywhere you go." Then she told me a story in which an individual's actions led her and her husband to address the topic of overt racism with their children. I include this story in this section to stress that the impact from these types of experiences occurring outside the school setting are carried by the mothers as they come into the school setting. The collisions and collusions Wendy experienced in the interactions described below are not isolated from all her actions as a mother, nor are they isolated from her interactions with the school employees where her children attend school.

Wendy: Something else that is, kind of, like, happened <pause> recently. Uhm. Is something that happened with my husband and that was uhm—we had gone to a benefit that was at like a bar and grill and we had just popped in to say hi and you know show our support uhm—and this is again in small town, this is actually such a small town and there was somebody who was pretty intoxicated there that made some comments to my husband and I don't think he was <u>trying</u> to be a jerk, but he—he was <chuckles>. And so we left—cuz we didn't want to—we just didn't want to be around it and it was time to go so we left.

Wendy and her husband left the social event after the drunk White man said something overtly racist to Wendy's husband. Their children were not with them and they had no plans to discuss the event with their children. By excusing the White man's action because he was not intending to be a jerk, Wendy colludes and collides with the Whiteness norm that *good White people do not behave in overtly racist ways. Identifying the impact of someone's behavior as racist when they did not intend to be racist is not fair and should be avoided.* The excuse that the intention of the individual committing the offensive act is more important than the harm caused is a common one and is illogical. It argues that the harm caused can be ignored because the person causing the harm did not intend to cause it. A common response to assist people to recognize this lack of logic is a simple description. Suppose there is one person who accidentally stepped on another person's foot and broke a bone in the process. The person with the broken foot is in pain and in need of medical attention. The person who broke the foot begins weeping and wailing that they are sorry and what a terrible thing to have happened to them. Many would agree that the useful thing to do is to assist the person with the broken foot in obtaining the assistance required. The argument advanced above emphasizing intent over impact would have the bystanders attend to the person weeping about their misfortune because they broke someone's foot while ignoring the person who actually is experiencing the broken foot.

In Wendy's story, the incident was not over. Even though she and her husband had not planned on discussing the incident with their children, they were in effect, forced to.

Wendy: And then the family of the—that the benefit was for had gotten word that this had happened—and the mom who had cancer and it was for her was deeply <heavy sigh> they felt <u>so</u> bad about it all, where we had kind of moved on you know. And they—they came here the next night—her and her two daughters—and—and apologized for what had happened even though it wasn't their fault at all, but they apologized. So our kids were all here and my husband had shut the doors to the living room and told them, "Just stay here for a little bit." So we had our conversation with the people who came to apologize. And then the kid were all questions, "What's—why were they here—what's going on—what happened?" And then—so we kind of used it as a teachable moment and kind of had you

know a little talk with the kids and we didn't really go into detail as to—as to what was said. But we just told the kids pretty
much—anytime you hear anything—uhm—that doesn't sit well
with you that makes you feel awkward or wrong or if somebody
uses a word that doesn't sit well with you—you just need to tell
us right away—just be open with us and not hold that inside—if
it's not making you feel right, please tell us. And uhm—and
you know again, we stressed how you know people were just not
smart <chuckles> or they were stupid about certain things and
that some people still are stupid and I hate to use that word,
but it's—you know they just are ignorant and so many things

Here, Wendy colluded with the norm of Whiteness that *racism is only a
problem because there are some overtly racist people. Good White people do not
behave in overtly racist ways.* She asked her son and her daughters to be sure
to tell her and her husband when they experience racial harassment. Wendy
did not divulge what she and her husband planned to do in response to the
racial harassment their children experience.

Wendy: And then we stressed too it's not just—it's not just African
Americans—it's you know—you need to be—because we've
had—in our school district, we've had several Mexican children
that started coming to the school and the kids are welcoming
to them and—and it's like—you know if you hear something
that's not for—er—ah—you know—for them—you know these
are things we have to keep open in our conversations with each
other and not discount it—I guess is what we're trying to let the
kids know because I just don't want them thinking that they
have to hold any bad feelings inside. You know—even if they
don't understand why they feel that way—to just bring it up
with us—uhm. So I guess that's the last experience that we've
kind of had as a family—uhm. And as a mom and I'm sure
you hear this from all the moms you're talking with—is you
just—you want so badly to protect your child from those kinds
of people in this world. And that is I think, the biggest thing for
me, but I know I can't always be there.

Wendy connected her desire to protect her children from "those kinds of
people" with her role as a mother by referring to providing protection as
a normal process that any mother would do. As mentioned in the previous chapter, several of the mothers interviewed referred to themselves as
protectors. Wendy's focus was on individual acts by individual people. Additionally, she placed the responsibility onto her children to notify her when

protection was needed. Wendy's strategy was not addressing the reality that individual racist acts are not the only race-based social processes impacting her children. Wendy did not describe feeling a need to protect her children from the impact of systemic or structural racism. Those systemic forces are less visible and yet they could be the "anything" that makes her children "feel awkward." Nor did Wendy identify interactions with teachers, principals, and police as being sources of those awkward feelings. As Wendy wrapped up this part of our conversation, she returned to the idea of wanting to protect her son.

Wendy: I'm just, as I have gotten older, I feel like I just want to do that more—I just—I—er—cuz going back to that second grade with [my son] and how bad I felt as a mom that I couldn't protect him from that and I felt like I failed, and I didn't prepare him— I didn't—I was so busy trying to make sure that they didn't feel this—you know—difference—or whatever—that I just felt like I—I don't know. So I think since then we've just <pause> and I wish I could actually do it more often and I feel like—but—you know—you just get busy with everyday life and you just live your life and you don't want to always—be like—you know— you know you just always want us to be of the same because we are. You want to just go on and live your life—and enjoy <u>everyone</u> and what they bring to your relationships and—you know—have a really good relationship.

In this wrap up, when Wendy positioned herself as having tasks and responsibilities that she would not have if her children were White, she was colluding with the Whiteness norm that *it is more work for a White woman to mother a child of color than for a White woman to mother a White child.* When she referred to being busy "with everyday life" and wanting to "just go on and live your life" she was referring to a life of escaping the realities of race and living as if it does not exist. Wendy was not the only mother to express such desires. Several of the mothers expressed frustration and weariness with their repeated attempts to educate the people around them so that their realities were understood. For example, remember Yvette in chapter two who kept working to get her mother to understand why it was not a compliment to refer to her grandchildren's eyes as "squinty eyes." However, their weariness and frustration need to be understood in the larger context. Framing their experiences as weariness and frustration only makes sense because these mothers' lives as White girls and White young women led them to expect that they would not experience the racialized experiences that they have been experiencing. The dominant narrative of White girlhood includes a future White man and future White children and all the Whiteness norms with which these mothers are now colliding.

The mothers' stories in the next section all address the idea of intentionally moving to a new school to benefit their children. Some of the mothers' stories address moving to a new home in order to attend a new school and some address just changing schools. In addition to these stories, several other mothers described moving their children to a new school. They all sought out something that would provide more benefits for their children.

MOVING TO A NEW SCHOOL

You know it's kind of—it's almost like—I don't know—It's just—It's kind of more like a feeling. It's not like it was any huge thing that happened, if that makes sense. It's more like—yeah—it just—I always just had a feeling like—like we weren't welcome there <shaking her head> like I don't know how else to say it. Like—and I—and it wasn't just the teachers—it was like a lot of the other parents ...

Nancy, one of the mothers interviewed.

The view that the ideal teacher is like the ideal mother has been intentionally cultivated in elementary school pedagogy (Steedman, 1985). Thus, mothers may have expectations that their sons and daughters will be loved as they learn at school. Some of the mothers I interviewed collided with norms of Whiteness in their early interactions with school personnel because their sons and daughters were not valued there. Some of those mothers decided that the school was flawed and that moving to another location would allow them to find a school without those flaws. Those mothers were operating on an assumption that the problem was with the specific school or the specific teacher. However, the problems that these mothers encountered were not unique to those schools. Whiteness norms are enacted in all school districts (Leonardo, 2009) and the mothers who move to escape them will encounter Whiteness norms at the new school they choose.

When Quinn initially registered her daughter for school, she was told she could only select one race identity. Quinn told me that her interaction with the school system regarding this one fact confirmed, for her, that she was not going to stay in that location and raise her daughter "where she would always be the only kid of color or one of the few." So Quinn moved from a small city in the North to a large metropolitan area in the Southeast. Quinn explained that her decision to move involved more factors than racial demographics. However, the story she told about her move positioned her as a mother removing her daughter from an environment where her daughter would be seen as one of the few. Their departure also created a situation with one less student of color at the school they left behind. That resulted in the remaining students of color standing out even more, exacerbating the very issue for those students that Quinn wanted her daughter to escape. Thus, she was colluding with the Whiteness norm that *locations with low percentages of people of color are not good places for people of color to live. It is better for people of color to live in areas with higher percentages of people of color.*

Amy's stories were included in the first section in this chapter. She described a strategy she was holding onto to deal with a future serious collision even though she did not use the word collision. Because she worried that her daughter would be treated "like an exotic flower," she explained that if too much happened that worried her, she and her family would move. She did not have plans for where she would move to or when she would move. She was holding onto the option of moving in case everything is not "ok" for her daughter. She struggled to describe what it was that she would look for as evidence that "everything's ok."

> **Amy:** I'm afraid of all that unspoken piece. I'm worried about that and I think—I think I would be worried about that regardless because I know how—I think I know how people act. You know—but. And I also work a lot with—like worked with children and teens so I also see all the trauma that they talk about from middle school—and—so our plan right now is to have her be in this school, we are going to try kindergarten and see if we like the school and if the diversity issue is not—uhm damaging to her and if—if everything's ok, we'll stay here at least through elementary school, but if it were not, we would move to a place that would—that was more diverse. Or close to a school that was better for her—cuz we're not going to stay put in a school system that we—we feel is emotionally damaging. I wouldn't do that. But I'm hopeful that it's going to work out.

Amy's contingency plan in case her optimistic plan doesn't work out is to move. That is an all or nothing type of plan. She and her family either move or they don't. Her plan was to continue colluding and tolerate collisions until they reach a certain threshold point. The option to escape by moving to another location is not available to everyone. Believing that it is an option is related to one's financial resources, career choices, and one's sense of agency. Here, Amy was colluding with the Whiteness norm that *locations with low percentages of people of color are not good places for people of color to live. It is better for people of color to live in areas with higher percentages of people of color.*

Amy was not the only mother I spoke with who referred to the strategy of moving to a "better place." What is it that makes one place "better" than another? Is it merely population percentages? Was it simply because a location where more people of color lived would allow their children to blend in that appealed to the mothers? It is possible that the locations that appealed to the mothers are places where people of color have invested in social justice actions in their communities for decades and that investment is noticeable. If that is what the mothers I spoke with were seeking, then by their actions to escape the unhealthy environment and move to a "better" environment for their children, they re-inscribed and enacted a commoditizing process of Whiteness. In other words, the mothers were treating a location where racial justice work has been led and accomplished by people of color resulting in appealing community features as a commodity that they can purchase. They can purchase racial justice benefits for their children of color by moving rather than working within their existing communities toward racial justice goals. Additionally, their desire to move is not simply to benefit their children. They are also escaping their own painful collisions rather than examine their collusions.

Olivia Preston's collisions and her way of escaping differ slightly from Amy's story described above. Olivia moved to be closer to her family of origin. After moving, her experiences with her daughter's school eventually led her to remove her daughter from public school and homeschool her instead.

> **Olivia:** When she went to public school part of the issue was simply a transition from—uhm—the Montessori style to public school style. The other component of that was that I think they assumed that because she was Black, she was going to be Southern Black, which would be the—uhm—hyper—uhm—obedient— and you know—yes ma'am and no ma'am and uhm—part of that is Southern, but there's a different kick to Southern Black where—uhm—you know the child is not going to—uhm— they're just going to be very, very obedient. And that's not how she was raised. If she were White, they would have thought she was bright and inquisitive. And they were complaining about her behavior because when she was done with her work, she would hop up and help the other kids. Well, that's because she's a Montessori kid. Because that's what you do. Okay?

Olivia explained one aspect of her collision with the Whiteness norm that *White female teachers and school administrators can be trusted to take care of the students in the school. They work for the best interests of all children by following a color-blind approach.* Her collision stemmed from her perception that Black students in her daughter's school were expected to behave in accordance with social norms that Olivia referred to as being "very, very obedient." Olivia described her daughter as "bright and inquisitive" and explained that she did not raise her daughter to be hyper-obedient and meek. So Olivia's first steps were to work within the school's structures and have her daughter assigned to a different teacher. But even with that change, Olivia saw pervasive behaviors at the school that she deemed unhealthy for her daughter whether the behaviors were directed at her daughter or not. Simply being there was not healthy for her daughter.

Olivia: So part of that was—just a few cultural uhm—things combined—that collided—and I just kept getting—uhm—she needs to do this and she needs to do that. I finally had to—uhm—So I uhm—I—it took a while—you know—but—I was able to get her—you know even in kindergarten—I was able to get her moved from one teacher to another which still put it with the expectations that she was going to be uhm—you know—here it was—you know "Mom got me moved." Or whatever, so that—ah—that ended up being a little bit of a problem. But got over that. And uhm—they had it where—you know you could pop in during the kid's lunch and eat with them. And my work schedule was such that—I mean I never knew when I could do that. So, in which case, I would show up—and what I saw in the lunchroom was—uhm—here it was—where the teachers in the—you know—uhm—the—other staff that were in there—essentially policing the children—were you know—uhm—they [the teachers] are on the best behavior when a parent's there—and their best behavior was atrocious. They would correct—uhm—a kid of color—particularly boys—they—it was very harsh. They—uhm—the commands that were given to the kid—they were like—three words—like, "Do this now." "Sit down Johnny." Uhm—I mean, just very—uhm—very disrespectful. Because you wouldn't talk to an adult that way. Uhm—and—you would get the same behavior—of you know—not sitting still or you know fiddling with their food—or flipping a tater tot across the table or whatever—you like playing with paper as if it were a football—or what have you—uhm—and—you know if a White kid did it was like, "Oh, Susie, would you please stop that?" And uhm—I mean—it brought me to tears. And I'm sitting there and I'm like, "Ok—putting her in public school was the worst decision I have ever made in my entire life—for my kid." So—uhm—from that point it took me about 18 months to be able to shift in different jobs—what—how to make things work—so that I could essentially work from home. And I pulled her out of public school at Christmas break for first grade. And have been homeschooling her since.

Olivia noticed disparate treatment by teachers with students based on the race of the student that she was unwilling to allow her daughter to be subjected to or witness. Students see how the adults in the school treat students. From those observations, they learn who the acceptable targets are in their environment. Students learn who the kids are that it is okay to bully, ignore, or otherwise discriminate against. In other words, the adults' treatment of students contributes greatly to the establishment of the pecking order (Conley, 2005). Furthermore, teachers are not the only adults in a school setting whose behaviors are closely observed by students. Parents are frequent participants in the daily activities with students in some schools, especially at the elementary level where parental presence is higher. Thus, students and school employees also teach parents who the legitimate targets are in the school setting through comments like, "He is always getting sent to the principal's office" or "We just don't know what we are going to do with her." Olivia chose to remove her daughter from what she perceived was a toxic environment for her daughter.

Nancy O'Keefe also tried working within the structures at her son's school, but after two unsuccessful years trying, she moved her son to a new school. She explained that while she didn't move far geographically, there were big differences between the levels of acceptance of racial diversity. She loved her son's new school. She explained that she "didn't like how the teachers interacted with" her or her son at the previous school. Her son had the same teacher for two years at that school. Nancy explained her discomfort with the previous school that her son attended.

> **Nancy:** It's more like—yeah—it just—I always just had a feeling like—like we weren't welcome there <shaking her head> like I don't know how else to say it. Like—and I—and it wasn't just the teachers—it was like a lot of the other parents and I mean especially people that are older I would just get looks and just—you know—I guess—I don't know—they would just assume I guess that I'm on welfare and—you know—yeah, my son's father was not in the picture, but you know I just think that—I just get so irritated by that stereotype—and—I just—I can never place—you know you can't say "Well, they're just racist." You know—but I mean—that's just the feeling that I got. And I— like I said—I can't ever—you know I can't prove it—it's just a feeling that you get and—I mean—my son—I mean—everybody thinks this of their kid, but he just has—he's so cute, but

he just has the best personality, like he's so sweet, he's always happy, he's always smiley and he—it was like—he was not like that there. It wasn't horrible but he just wasn't himself and I just couldn't—I couldn't understand like how can these people not love my kid? Like most people that are around him are like "He's so sweet, he's—you know—he's got the best personality, he laughs all the time." So—you know—I just think that when people are like that infectious. So like for me—I always thought it was odd that they weren't like that with him.

Nancy explained that she never felt welcomed in her experiences with the school personnel and with the White mothers of White students at the previous school. There wasn't one large collision that Nancy experienced in her interactions with the school environment, there were many small collisions. Nancy repeatedly collided with the Whiteness norm that *White female teachers and school administrators can be trusted to take care of the students in the school. They work for the best interests of all children by following a color-blind approach.* Nancy also collided with the Whiteness norm that *good White women mother White Children.* In the interactions she had with the White mothers of White students at the school when she volunteered for events, Nancy explained that they would not speak with her or sit near her. It was the combination of the way Nancy felt she was treated at the school and the impact the school was having on her son that led her to move to a new school. The contrast that Nancy described between her son's previous school and his current school was subtle yet powerfully impacting his mood and his excitement for learning.

> **Nancy:** And uhm—they just—he really struggled in school—he really struggled. And I mean they were constantly calling me in for meetings telling me he's not keeping up and that kind of thing and now that he's at this school—I mean—it is like night and day. They are amazing here. He's reading now—I mean—he is just completely turned around from where he was at the other school and he went there for two years. So—I mean—yeah— it's just been a huge difference. Uhm—but you know—I just— I don't—I don't have any—really specific—uhm—things that I can say that you know—was like a horrible experience—it was—it just never felt right if that makes sense.

Nancy reiterated that she could not quite put her finger on what it was about that environment that created her discomfort, but she actually described it extremely well. Her description referred to the way she always felt; she said it was that she did not feel "welcome." While she volunteered for school trips and projects, the interactions with the other moms volunteering weren't welcoming, the interactions with the teachers weren't welcoming, and the interactions with the school staff weren't welcoming. The school staff and the White mothers of White students positioned Nancy as a deviant mother and they did not welcome her. Positioning White mothers of children of color as deviant was enacting the norm that *good White mothers mother White children*. From their perspective, those White mothers of White children were not being mean or unkind to Nancy. They were colluding with the Whiteness norm, thus, they were behaving in accordance with the social rules to maintain them. Nancy collided with that Whiteness norm repeatedly and then responded by escaping an environment that she saw as unhealthy for herself and her son. She did not try to combat that narrative of herself. She escaped.

Moving to escape collisions was a strategy that several of the mothers mentioned they had already done, would like to do, were planning to do, or would do if certain things occurred. While the mothers did not use the word escape, safety was one of the dimensions the mothers referred to when discussing where to live. The concept of safety also appears in discourses that reinscribe Whiteness norms (Leonardo & Porter, 2010) because safety is something that White people feel entitled to. Thus, spaces are racialized and safety is a racialized term when describing spaces. Mothers keeping their children safe was also a topic that arose in the interviews.

In my interview with Caroline, the subject of changing locations and schools came up again. Caroline was trying to set her daughter up for success by moving so her daughter can attend a better school.

> **Caroline:** To keep tabs with and knowing all the teachers—it's kind of hard this year because my daughter it was just her first year here. So it was a big difference because you'd know [previous school] school district I know a lot of the teachers, I knew all the office people—you know some of the secretaries are good friends with my mother. So it was kind of hard going to a new place, but I kind of wanted to move her out. I'm still in [name of county—she lives in the same county as previously] where I am now, but I'm a little bit further away. More in a suburb that's not—because I feel like [name of city where she lived previously] was getting a little—too— <pause> racy for me and I'd rather move a little further away and have to commute a little further to make sure my—my kids have a better opportunity—as I would say.

Caroline explained that she had moved from an area with a higher percentage of people of color to an area with a lower percentage of people of color because that move was advantageous for her and her family. All the mothers described moving their family in ways that sounded beneficial for their children. None of the mothers told me that they moved to benefit themselves and that their kids just had to deal with it. That is not how mothers, in general, explain the rationale for the decisions they make. They frequently explain their actions in terms of how it benefits their children, whatever the action is. That is part of following the norms of being a good mother. McMahon (1995) argues that becoming a mother for middle-class White women is a process that effects a "moral" transformation in their self-conceptions providing a symbolic resource that mothers use to structure their identity. Therefore, mothers create explanations for all their actions drawing from a narrative of benefit for their children. The interviews with mothers who discussed moving to benefit their children were the ones in which this type of moral structuring was most readily apparent.

Geneva's stories about her son when he was young appeared in the previous section. At the time of the interview, Geneva had recently moved her teenaged son to an all-boys school. She described the abundance of "nice White women" that were in her son's life before that. She speculated that not all of her sons needs were being met.

> **Geneva:** Everywhere you work there's an—everywhere you look there's an abundance of nice White women ready to help. And I think—with my son, I realized it was just kind of the excess it wasn't necessarily—whether—you know—it was— uhm—how he relates to me—and he was relating to them that way or if it was just—uhm—you know—he knows how to work with nice White women. He knows what they expect and uhm we may not be meeting his needs.

Geneva referred to the "abundance of nice White women ready to help." Like Geneva said, these nice White women work in the school system, they work in social services, they work in healthcare, and they work in childcare. They can be found everywhere enacting the norms of Whiteness. Geneva was attempting to contend with those norms indirectly by putting her son in an environment that she believed had the capacities to help him thrive. She wasn't exactly sure what those capacities were, but she believed that she did not have them, nor did any of the other nice White women she referred to.

Laura recently transferred her daughter from one school to another and initially stated that it had nothing to do with race. Later, she said that "it wasn't the big reason that she transferred schools." At the previous school, her daughter was one of a few students of color. In planning for the next school for her daughter, Laura used the same explanation that Quinn used that was discussed above. Laura wanted her daughter to "feel like she's not the only one." Laura explained that she could "find a school easily that had a dominant brown skin population" but those schools are on the "crappy side of town" and are "the worst schools in town." Laura said that she does not want to "sacrifice, you know, her schooling, just because of race." Laura did not refer to education as something where she can care about and attend to the complex intersections of race with other dimensions such as class. She characterized her options as conflicting opposites. She could place her daughter in a school with a large population of students of color or she could place her daughter in a good school. By characterizing her options the way she did, Laura defends her choice as appropriate and good and she was colluding with the Whiteness norm that *White female teachers and school administrators can be trusted to take care of the students in the school. They work for the best interests of all children by following a color-blind approach.* Educational processes and practices are not race-neutral and Laura's and Caroline's insistence that their decisions criteria for choosing a good school only focused on educational excellence belies their collusion with this norm.

The next section includes stories from mothers I interviewed who are teachers at the schools where their children attend. Their participation in school processes provided a unique perspective, and yet they each used their position as a teacher in different ways to participate with the Whiteness norms thriving at their schools.

WORKING IN SCHOOLS

My relationship with that teacher isn't especially great because she doesn't appreciate me calling her out but—uhm, yes, I would say that, you know, it definitely influences my work as a teacher.

Tenna, one of the mothers interviewed.

Tenna Ushmore was a teacher at the same school where her children attended. She described how her role as a mother influenced her actions as a teacher. Tenna collided repeatedly with the Whiteness norm that *White female teachers and school administrators can be trusted to take care of the students in the school. They work for the best interests of all children by following a color-blind approach.* In her story below, she described a sequence of events that revealed how systemic racism played out to disenfranchise a group of Black female students.

Tenna: Well, I certainly think that having a biracial daughter influences—you know—the way that I think and, you know, the decisions that I make. Uhm—and I certainly have found—you know—myself calling people out at school and, you know, like. I had a student who graduated this year—she was—ah—basically—like her and this other group of kids had offered to—you know—help plan the prom and then these three girls who happened to all be White and this student didn't and the other group of kids happened to all be Black—uhm—you know—they [the three White students] were like, "Oh we don't need your help." And they [the Black students] were kind of upset. And they [the Black students] were like, "Ok, we're going to help with this other fundraiser, we're going to help with the [name of the event] because we do dancing and this is how we are going to be involved our senior year" So they were like—they sort of put the other thing behind them and you know waited for this event to come up. And the event comes up and then all of a sudden they had called in this old alumnus to do it all and said we don't need your help. Of course we know the alumnus is White and all these girls [who are going to help with it] are White. And you know—like are they consciously excluding the Black kids. And so of course [the student who recently graduated] went and called racism on Twitter—which—wasn't the most you know—effective means of communication—but—so—then we [school staff] had meetings about it and so my perspective is certainly—you—their—advisor you know—blonde cheerleader lady—like obviously my perspective and hers were very different. She was like—we—well—you know—she was sort of condoning this racist behavior—and therefore—you could be a little bit racist yourself. You know—and there were statements like "We think you guys [the Black girls] would be distracting." And I was like—ok—are we stereotyping much? You know—like the loud Black girls would be too distracting. You know—and—so we had several meetings and this other lady was like, "I think she [the Black student who posted on Twitter] should receive some punishment for posting that on Twitter!" And I was like—uhm—she didn't threaten anybody, she didn't—there's nothing she did that is punishable—yeah it wasn't the most effective way to communicate—to call them racists on Twitter—but—you know there's nothing that she needs to be punished for we just need to work this out and talk about it and—include them [the Black students].

The other "lady" wanted the Black student punished for calling her actions racist and Tenna collided with the enactment of the norm of Whiteness that *good White people do not behave in overtly racist ways. Identifying the impact of someone's behavior as racist when they did not intend to be racist is not fair and should be avoided.* According to that norm, being called a racist unaccept-able. This norm of Whiteness shifts attention away from the racist actions onto the person making that claim and demands that person be punished for breaching the Whiteness norm. That Whiteness norm dictates that the person identifying actions as racist is the misbehaving individual. Tenna also contended with this norm by convincing the others involved that no punishment was warranted.

The ways in which Tenna contended with Whiteness norms that she encountered in the school where she worked was through a couple of strategies. One of the ways that Tenna contended was by metaphorically holding up a mirror for others to see themselves. Tenna's mirror spe-cifically reflected the Whiteness norms that she observed so that those enacting those norms had the opportunity to see them as well. Another way was through her constant advocating for increasing the number of teachers of color with her principal. Several paraprofessionals of color had been hired recently, but Tenna explained to the principal that because those positions are at a lower structural level than teachers, the positive impact for students will not be the same as having teachers of color. Through these types of actions, Tenna was engaging upstream to make structural changes in the system. Thus, she was contending with the Whiteness norm that *White female teachers and school administrators can be trusted to take care of the students in the school. They work for the best interests of all children by following a color-blind approach.* Her efforts not only provided a counter-narrative to the nice White woman narrative, her active engagement aimed to modify the Whiteness norms themselves. This does not mean that she was also not continually colliding with Whiteness norms, but because she was aware of them and she knew they would keep happening, she was not shocked nor surprised when they occurred. However, Tenna did not simply endure her collisions like Ursula in chapter two. Tenna saw the collisions coming, prepared for them, absorbed them, and moved directly into contending with the Whiteness norm.

Debra Goldson also taught at a school that her sons and daughter attended. She mentioned that employees at the school had asked her several times to speak to potential new employees about her experiences as a White mother in an interracial family. She was not asked to speak to all new potential employees, only the ones whose families were not all White.

> **Debra:** So they were recruiting a new teacher who was White and her husband was Black and she was really leery about coming here—her children and her husband and they asked me if I would talk to her. Just kind of to talk about my experiences and

I could have—I could have taken that in a couple of different ways. I could have been kind of pissed off—like I'm not your token explainer of the—the experiences here. But I chose to instead, just be honest with the woman and I said "Yeah, there's challenges. I mean you're in Whitopia up here in [state where she lives] literally. I don't know if you ever read Benjamin Rich's book, *Whitopia*? Uhm, but he talks about how—the community we live in—the county [name of county] here in [name of state] fits the definition of a Whitopia meaning that—you know—the population of African Americans is so low that it is not even on the radar in terms of this community. You know and in talking to this person who was going to potentially come work here—I was saying, you do need to know you're coming to absolutely White—like—community. Can it work? Yeah—it worked for me. Yeah absolutely. But—you gotta know what you are getting yourself into. You can't come here and think that everybody's going to be like, "Oh! A new African American family! Come on in!" You know—like. Or a biracial family—biracial. So I think I serve a purpose in <u>this</u> community anyway—in kind of—you know—people will call up—hey [her name] I got a—and can you talk to them. It's something that I'm glad to do it cuz I feel like if more people did it then—understanding and acceptance would be a little bit richer.

Debra did not explain how these requests fit into the overall approach or philosophy that her school used to attract and recruit faculty. Debra and I also did not go into great detail on what she meant by "it worked for me." However, she followed that with her statement that "You gotta know what you are getting yourself into you can't come here and think. . . ." If she used that statement with the potential employee, she was revealing some glimpses of what the norms were and where the acceptable boundaries were. Debra told the prospective faculty members that if they move there, they would need to abide by (i.e., collude with) the local norms in order to succeed. Her argument that "I'm glad to do it cuz I feel like if more people did it then—understanding and acceptance would be a little bit richer" is challenging to decipher. She was glad to speak to the candidates and if more people did that then understanding and acceptance would be a little bit richer. Whose understanding and acceptance would be a "little bit richer?" Was it the candidate's understanding? Or her colleague's? How would that richness come about? It is also worth examining the situation she put herself in based on the positional power of the participants. There was the school that employed Debra and the specific individual who asked her to do this and there were the candidates. One way to view these relative positions is that Debra has been co-opted into telling the candidate the rules of the school. Those in power within the school thus avoided a conversation about the racial climate at the school or in the community with the candidate. They asked Debra to do it for them and she agreed. Debra was colluding with two of the Whiteness norms. The first was that *White female teachers and school administrators can be trusted to take care of the students in the school. They work for the best interests of all children by following a color-blind approach.* The second Whiteness norm that Debra colluded with was *there is no reason to acknowledge nor examine structural or systemic racism. It is not the responsibility of White people to educate themselves or their children about race-based oppression. It is acceptable to be recognized as an educated person and claim ignorance about race-based oppression.* I asked Debra about her conversations with other White teachers at her school.

> **Debra:** Uhm—I actually presented at a conference [she gave the name of the conference and her presentation was called about nurturing the multiracial student] trying to kind of—you know educate through that presentation with a colleague of mine at another school—uhm—but yeah the things we've been talking about today and I think in terms of [the kind of school I teach at] in general in looking at the conference, they are predominantly White teachers as well—who have good intentions—absolutely—you know—but they—they just—I don't know if you can't live it, it is really hard to explain it and to understand it—uhm—and—I don't know—er—and—ah—I've had conversations here with other teachers about just kind of the environment that we are living in and—there's kind of an unwritten rule that you adapt to the culture by coming here, that the culture doesn't really adapt to you or your differences and I think that's a constant struggle in education as you try to diversify your student body and your faculty but your—you know—a school built on tradition.

Debra was colliding, colluding, and contending with two Whiteness norms. The first was that *there is no reason to acknowledge nor examine structural or systemic racism. It is not the responsibility of White people to educate themselves or their children about race-based oppression. It is acceptable to be recognized as an educated person and claim ignorance about race-based oppression.* The second Whiteness norm was that *White female teachers and school administrators can be trusted to take care of the students in the school. They work for the best interests of all children by following a color-blind approach.* Debra was contending with these norms by engaging in professional work that provided a counter-narrative to the dominant ones that perpetuate Whiteness norms. But while she did that, she was also ensnared in the illogical argument about intentions discussed above. Debra credited their good intentions but she also recognized that they were falling short of their intentions.

Debra stated that her school is "built on tradition." Tradition is another way of referring to dominant norms. The norms that the school is built on include the norms of Whiteness. Debra was rewarded, as we all are, for colluding. In this next excerpt, Debra described a conversation with another teacher at her school about the school rules that reflect their norms.

> **Debra:** For instance [our school has] a dress code and things and you're asking for diversity and you're asking from all over the world to come here and dress a certain way, even <u>that</u> isn't fully inclusive. Or to dance a certain way—you know school dances—some faculty just get like crazy they are like, "Oh my god, the way they're dancing!" You know. I'm like, "That—that's how they dance where they're from. That's what they do." And they're like, "Oh it's totally inappropriate." It might <u>look</u> inappropriate, but if you take it out of context—you know they are not actually trying to have sex right now—that's how they dance. <laughs> and—er—the—the—that mindset is hard to change and it's hard to accept that someone might wear their pants a different way or might have different dress or ways of saying things—just different things like that and as schools start to diversify and say that that is really a goal of theirs—to diversify and bring in—people from all over the world—and different cultures—I think we all need to be paying attention to what that really means—in an educational setting—what it means for faculty who have taught for 20 years and new faculty coming in and all those kinds of things.

Debra tried to help her co-worker see the commonalities across cultural practices. She was trying to help her co-worker apply a broader lens to what they observed at the dance regarding the way students dress or dance. Debra's role at her school was not related to the school's efforts in bringing students from around the world. Her job was in another area of the school that is unrelated. However, she tried to expand her co-workers understanding by challenging the norms enacted in the moment. That was another way that she contended with the norm of Whiteness that *there is no reason to acknowledge nor examine structural or systemic racism. It is not the responsibility of White people to educate themselves or their children about race-based oppression. It is acceptable to be recognized as an educated person and claim ignorance about race-based oppression.*

School employees enlisting parents into pressuring their daughters and sons to comply with the rules of the school is not an experience unique to White mothers of students of color. This technique is used to garner compliance with all the norms practiced in schools. Some of the mothers acquiesced to the insistent invitations to collude because those invitations were packaged in the ways that nice White helpful women speak. Invitations to collude sound like offers to help because they are offers to help. However, the help is anchored in Whiteness norms. The help comes packaged in phrases like, "This is what is best for your student." "We can help your child." and "Your student needs to follow the rules to get ahead." There is no malice in these offers to help. They are genuine offers to help. The intent is good. However, the impact can include something else entirely.

These offers of help were also one of the ways that the norms are taught to newcomers. People who already know the social norms help newcomers learn the social norms. They offer help through various means and their help teaches newcomers what the social norms are. The social norms are not always referred to or identified explicitly, rather they are accepted as the way things are or sometimes are referred to as best practices. Social norms are taught by school administrator mentors to the principals or teachers whom they guide. Social norms are taught by teachers who model certain behaviors and talk about certain concepts. Thus, social norms are enacted in schools just as they are enacted in corporations and organizations (Fehr & Fischbacher, 2004).

While the intent is good, the impact is something else altogether. The individual mother talking with a teacher or administrator at a school is not likely to be focused on the collective impact of Whiteness norms enacted in schools on students of color across the country. She is concerned about the specifics of the situation for her child. She is focused on her child. She is focused on navigating through the specific situations at the particular school. However, the impact of the Whiteness norms operating at the school results in structural arrangements that make some perceptions, outcomes, and options more likely than others for her children. And she is constantly encouraged to collude with those norms rather than contend with them.

SUMMARY

Many of the Whiteness norms that mothers encountered discussed in this chapter were also experienced earlier. But the most commonly experienced Whiteness norm during the earlier stage of motherhood did not appear for these mothers during this stage. That Whiteness norm was *asking or commenting to White mothers about the physical features of their children who are not White is excusable as curiosity. It is an acceptable way to draw attention to deviant mothers and their children and still claim to be a good person. It is acceptable to ask questions in ways that position the children as objects. It is also acceptable to touch the children as if they were objects.* As their children developed and their interactions with people widened, the mothers experienced different Whiteness norms. In essence, they left some behind and moved on to new ones. Moving on may have generated an initial sense of relief for the mothers, particularly, related to the Whiteness norm specified above. Not having to continually deal with that one was something several of the mothers with younger children longed for. The feeling of moving past a hurdle and onto smoother ground was short-lived however because as the mothers moved into school environments, they encountered new Whiteness norms. The mothers who developed ways of contending with Whiteness norms were the ones who also recognized that escaping Whiteness norms was not possible. Instead of trying to avoid Whiteness norms, those mothers prepared themselves with knowledge and strategies for engaging with Whiteness norms in ways that disrupted them.

It is possible that mothers continue to respond to specific Whiteness norms in the same ways that they did during earlier stages. A longitudinal study could examine that. Table 3.1 summarizes the Whiteness norms addressed in this chapter and chapter five presents all the Whiteness norms.

Table 3.1.   Mothers' Collusions, Collisions, and Contentions With Whiteness Norms Identified During the Mothers and Schools Stage

Whiteness Norms: *Social Processes and Discursive Practices*	*Mother*	*Type of* *Interaction*
White people are the norm. There is no need to depict or display people of any race but White. A White person can be displayed and it will be understood that it represents a raceless human in books and advertising.	Wendy	Collusion
If a person can identify as White, do it, it will be beneficial to identify that way. But sometimes special opportunities are provided for people of color that they can access simply because of their race.	Ellen	Collision
Good White women mother White Children.	Nancy Karen	Collision
Racism is only a problem because there are some overtly racist people. Good White people do not behave in overtly racist ways.	Abigail Wendy	Collison and Contention Collusion and Collision

(Table continues on next page)

Table 3.1.   (Continued)

Whiteness Norms: Social Processes and Discursive Practices	Mother	Type of Interaction
Good White people do not behave in overtly racist ways. Identifying the impact of someone's behavior as racist when they did not intend to be racist is not fair and should be avoided.	Tenna	Collision and Contention
	Vanessa	Collusion
	Wendy	Collusion
Locations with low percentages of people of color are not good places for people of color to live. It is better for people of color to live in areas with higher percentages of people of color.	Amy	
	Caroline	Collusion
	Quinn	
There is no reason to acknowledge nor examine structural or systemic racism. It is not the responsibility of White people to educate themselves or their children about race-based oppression. It is acceptable to be recognized as an educated person and claim ignorance about race-based oppression.	Debra	Collusion, Collision, and Contention
	Vanessa	Collision and Collusion
	Abigail	Collision and Contention
It is more work for a White woman to mother a child of color than for a White woman to mother a White child.	Wendy	Collusion
	Mary	
There is a hierarchy of races involved and types of relationships in which White women mother children of color. The circumstances will be valued differently. It is best to be recognized as belonging to the highest level group possible. The ideal that to strive toward is of a White mother of White children. Be like White mothers of White children as much as possible.	Laura	Collusion
	Amy	

(Table continues on next page)

Table 3.1. (Continued)

Whiteness Norms: *Social Processes and Discursive Practices*	*Mother*	*Type of* *Interaction*
White female teachers and school administrators can be trusted to take care of the students in the school. They work for the best interests of all children by following a color-blind approach.	Karen	Collusion
	Geneva	Collusion and Collision
	Laura	Collusion
	Olivia	Collision
	Ina	Collusion
	Debra	Collusion, Collision, and Contention
	Vanessa	Collision
	Tenna	Collision and Contention
	Ellen	Collusion
	Riley	Collusion
	Wendy	Collusion
	Nancy	Collision
Individual people of color who immigrate to the U.S. can achieve individual success by assimilating to the dominant cultural values. When they do not assimilate they cannot be successful. There is only one definition of success.	Paige	Collusion
Good White parents value education so they get involved in their children's schools.	Paige	Collusion

REFERENCES

Bonilla-Silva, E. (2010). *Racism without racists* (3rd ed.). Lanham, MD: Rowman & Littlefield Publishers, Inc.

Case, K. A., & Hemmings, A. (2005). Distancing strategies: White women preservice teachers and antiracist curriculum. *Urban Education, 40*(6), 606–626.

Conley, D. (2005). *The pecking order: A bold new look at how family and society determine who we become*. New York, NY: Vintage.

Dumas, M. J., & Nelson, J. D. (2016). (Re)Imagining Black boyhood: Toward a critical framework for educational research. *Harvard Educational Review, 86*(1), 27–47.

Fasching-Varner, K. J. (2012). *Working through Whiteness: Examining White racial identity and profession with pre-service teachers*. Lanham, MD: Lexington Books.

Fehr, E., & Fischbacher, U. (2004). Social norms and human cooperation. *Trends in Cognitive Sciences, 8*(4), 185–190.

Frankenberg, R. (1993). *White women, race matters: The social construction of Whiteness*. Minneapolis, MN: University of Minnesota Press.

Ganeshram, R. (2016). *A birthday cake for George Washington*. New York, NY: Scholastic.

Hill, N. E., & Tyson, D. F. (2009). Parental involvement in middle school: A meta-analytic assessment of the strategies that promote achievement. *Developmental Psychology, 45*(3), 740–763.

Hussar, W. J., & Bailey, T. M. (2014). *Projections of Education Statistics to 2022*. National Center for Education Statistics, U.S. Department of Education, Washington, DC.

Kendall, F. E. (2006). *Understanding White privilege: Creating pathways to authentic relationships across race*. New York, NY: Routledge.

Kohlberg, L. (1984). *The psychology of moral development: The nature and validity of moral stages (Essays on moral development)* (Vol. 2). New York, NY: Harper & Row.

Landeros, M. (2011). Defining the "good mother" and the "professional teacher": Parent-teacher relationships in an affluent school district. *Gender & Education, 23*(3), 247–262.

Le Poidevin, R., & MacBeath, M. (Eds.). (1993). *The philosophy of time*. New York, NY: Oxford University Press.

Leonardo, Z. (2009). *Race, whiteness, and education*. New York, NY: Routledge.

Leonardo, Z., & Porter, R. K. (2010). Pedagogy of fear: Toward a Fanonian theory of 'safety' in race dialogue. *Race Ethnicity and Education, 13*(2), 139–157.

Loewen, J. W. (2007). *Lies my teacher told me: Everything your America history teacher got wrong*. New York, NY: Touchstone.

Low, S. (2009). Maintaining Whiteness: The fear of others and niceness. *Transforming Anthropology, 17*(2), 79–92.

McMahon, M. (1995). *Engendering motherhood: Identity and self-transformation in women's lives*. New York, NY: The Guilford Press.

Noel, A., Stark, P., Redford, J., & Zukerberg, A. (2013). *Parent and Family Involvement in Education, From the National Household Education Surveys Program of 2012.*

National Center for Education Statistics, U.S. Department of Education, Washington, DC.

Parsons, T. (1959). The school class as a social system: Some of its functions in American society. *Harvard Educational Review, 29*(4), 297–318.

Pennington, J. L., Brock, C. H., & Ndura, E. (2012). Unraveling the threads of White teachers' conceptions of caring: Repositioning White privilege. *Urban Education, 47*(4), 743–775.

Picower, B. (2009). The unexamined Whiteness of teaching: How White teachers maintain and enact dominant racial ideologies. *Race Ethnicity and Education, 12*(2), 197–215.

Ralabate, P. (2007). *Truth in labeling: Disproportionality in special education.* Washington, DC: National Education Association.

Scholastic. (2016, January 17). *On our minds.* Retrieved from Scholastic: http://oomscholasticblog.com/post/new-statement-about-picture-book-birthday-cake-george-washington

Steedman, C. (1985). "The mother made conscious": The historical development of a primary school pedagogy. *History Workshop, 20*(1), 149–163.

Tschannen-Moran, M. (2014). The interconnectivity of trust in schools. In D. Van Maele, P. B. Forsyth, & M. Van Houtte (Eds.), *Trust and school life: The role of trust for learning, teaching, leading, and bridging* (pp. 57–81). New York, NY: Springer. doi:10.1007/978-94-017-8014-8_3

Wang, Y. (2015, October 5). "Workers" or slaves? Textbook maker backtracks after mother's online complaint. *Washington Post.*

CHAPTER 4

AS SONS AND DAUGHTERS MATURE

No matter the stage of the development of their daughters and sons, mothers are seen and see themselves as responsible for their sons and daughters. "Right or wrong, mothers were held accountable by society and believed that they were responsible for the growth and success of their children" (Francis-Connolly, 2000, p. 288). In Bialeschki and Michener's (1994) study of leisure in the lives of mothers whose sons and daughter were older, they found that even when mothers discussed having more time to dedicate to themselves when their sons and daughters no longer required daily care, they still conformed to the social norms of motherhood in their expressions of what they would do with that time. Thus, regardless of the maturity stage of their daughters and sons, the mothers I interviewed continued to draw from their understandings of themselves as mothers in describing their experiences.

The process of becoming an adult is not merely a physiological one. It is not a straightforward linear process; nor does it happen at one specific time. Mothers assist their sons and daughters in the maturation process throughout their lives. So even while their sons and daughters are in primary school or middle school, mothers' interactions can be seen as part of helping their children mature. Two outwardly recognizable transition events of moving into adulthood, according to Greene, Wheatley, and Aldava (1992) are living responsibly away from and outside the family

Colluding, Colliding, and Contending With Norms of Whiteness, pp. 113–138

home and engaging in meaningful activities which often means attending college or working. Mothers assist their sons and daughters with those transitions, in fact,

> The transition to adulthood can be conceptualized as a *family* project in the sense that goals related to achieving status markers and psychological processes associated with adulthood tend to be jointly constructed between youth and their parents and enacted upon together [emphasis in original] (Domene, Socholotiuk, & Young, 2011, p. 274)

Mothers respond to the various timings and fits and starts their sons and daughters exhibit as they progress in their development. Mothers build from the patterns of behaviors they developed and have used through their relationships with their sons or daughters to assist with the developmental tasks at hand. This chapter examines the experiences of the mothers that I have placed into two categories. One of those categories is the notion of assisting their daughters and sons in maturing. I refer to that as turning over responsibility and the interactions that I placed into this category include experiences from broad timespans. The other category of experiences that this chapter attempts to explore their racialized lives after their sons and daughters no longer live with them.

TURNING OVER RESPONSIBILITY

My son felt like it was racially motivated and I wasn't really sure. So I was like, you got to get me specifics, you know when I go to the school, I got to have dates and times and words and people. I can't go to the school with a—yeah, [my son] thinks. And I said, or if you really think it's just something that you can deal with, then deal—you know. If it's a problem, then I'll go. But, you know, he never brought it back up again.

Faith, one of the mothers interviewed.

There are times when mothers let go of their sons and daughters. They may clasp them back again and love them tightly, but at some point mothers accept that their daughters and sons are responsible for their own lives. That process does not happen all at once and it does not have an official starting time. In a sense, from day one, mothers are preparing their daughters and sons to be responsible for their own lives.

Not all the mothers talked directly about feeling responsible for teaching their sons and daughters how to deal with racism, discrimination, and Whiteness norms. But whether they addressed it or not, some of the mothers I spoke with did not seem to consider themselves directly involved. For example, in the last chapter, Wendy's words below were discussed.

Wendy: We're learning about these things because we don't want to re-peat these things—you know—these are things that happened and this is how far we've come and—they're part of your his-tory—you know—they're part of how awesome things can be now.

Using the words, "your history" conveyed distance between Wendy and her children. It was one of the ways in which Wendy colluded with the Whiteness norm that *it is more work for a White woman to mother a child of color than for a White woman to mother a White child*. Faith Geffers also described experiences in which she colluded with this Whiteness norm. She explained that there were "a lot of times that [my son and daughter] just had to learn to deal with things that I never had to worry about." For example, she described an incident when her son, who was in his late twenties, married, with a child of his own at the time of the interview, came to her about his gym teacher in high school because something happened that he believed was "racially motivated."

Faith: And I wasn't really sure. So I was like, you got to get me specif-ics, you know when I go to the school, I got to have dates and times and words and people. I can't go to the school with a—yeah, [my son] thinks. And I said, or if you really think it's just something that you can deal with, then deal—you know. If it's a problem, then I'll go. But, you know, he never brought it back up again.

In Faith's interaction with her son, her approach was to ask him to deal with the situation himself. While it is true that at the time her son would be on his own in some years and would need to be able to deal with "racially motivated" situations without his mother, it is unclear what guidance Faith provided him. In her story she sounded detached and resigned.

Additionally, the way Faith positioned the school staff regarding submit-ting complaints about teacher behavior hints at some structures worthy of a closer examination. If the school is a place where "racially motivated" actions by teachers are believed to be harmful for students and teachers alike, then one could expect that policies, procedures and practices exist to ensure that such actions are rare, immediately investigated, and not toler-ated. However, if the school is a place where "racially motivated" actions by teachers are not even perceived by the school employees because they are all behaving in collusion with a web of Whiteness norms, then over-whelming evidence would be necessary to force the school employees to even recognize what had occurred. Submitting a complaint would indeed require "dates, times, words, and people." In such an environment, the student's reality is considered invalid because the web of Whiteness norms operating in the school demands proof of specific individual actions of overt racism. Faith understood that to go to the school with a complaint, she would need to comply with the definition of racism that the school used. In a school that does not acknowledge the existence of systemic racism, such experiences by the students is not something that parents nor students are allowed to submit complaints for. Students are expected to handle it, deal with it, and accept it. Parents are expected to collude with these Whiteness norms and to co-opt their daughters and sons into compliance; and that is what Faith did. She collided and colluded with the Whiteness norm that *White female teachers and school administrators can be trusted to take care of the students in the school. They work for the best interests of all children by following a color-blind approach.*

Teaching daughters and sons how to deal with racism and discrimination is part of racial socialization. In Twine's (1999) research, she compared the racial socialization practices of White parents of Black children with the practices of Black parents of Black children in England. Twine (1999) concluded that the White parents were deficient because they did not follow the practices that Black parents followed. This argument employs an essentialist understanding that all Black children require certain parental actions because of their racial identity. This was the same logic that Wendy employed when she concluded her son's rigid sense of right and wrong at the age of two stemmed from that fact that he is Black. This argument also supports the Whiteness norm that *it is more work for a White woman to mother a child of color than for a White woman to mother a White child.* I argue that it is not more work for a White woman to mother a child of color. As I have mentioned previously, these mothers have learned the social norms surrounding race well. Those norms taught these mothers to keep race out of focus in their lives and to ignore the reality that their lives were highly racialized. They were taught to not look at the norms of Whiteness directly while they were taught to inflexibly adhere to them. Thus, these mothers had learned a great deal about race and they were often using the same strategies through which they had learned to teach the Whiteness norms they learned to their daughters and sons.

It was their experiences as mothers that, for some of them, moved race from the periphery of their lives to the center because the rules they learned as White girls no longer benefited them. The dissonance created for them in their collisions also created opportunities for these mothers to reconsider and reshape their beliefs and behaviors. In that way, it is little different than the opportunities mothers have to reconsider their beliefs and behaviors relating to any topic that they allowed to languish in the periphery of their lives before they became mothers. So rather than finding fault with Faith's mothering, I am more interested in how the norms of

Whiteness enacted in the schools influenced her. Parents intent on helping their children succeed in school can search for subtle cues that illuminate the path of success as defined by school employees. Those parents are eagerly lapping up the instructions from the school employees and coaching their children on those subtleties as well. Those subtleties include the norms of Whiteness. What norms of Whiteness were practiced and rewarded at the school that Faith's son and daughter attended?

Mary Norridge was not a stranger to the Whiteness norms practiced in schools. Nor was she unaware of the dangers her son faced at school because of them. She described a conversation with her son in which she was focused on keeping him safe after school.

> **Mary:** I can remember another time in high school, as I'm driving home from work, I'm seeing him walking—uhm—across a field—taking a shortcut to go to the house. And he was walking alongside the back area of a business that had a fence—and he had a—it was a chain link fence—and he had a board or something—you know going along the fence—and hitting it with the stick—you know? And uhm—and I stopped him—I stopped and pulled him right up and just screamed at him, "What are you doing?!" "Nothing." And I said, "That's not what it looks like to somebody—you look like someone who is trying to case the area—to come back later." And he's looking at me like, "Are you insane?" And uhm—I just said, "You can't do that. When you walk home from school, you stay on the sidewalks. And don't take the shortcuts through the field. People will think you're trying to mess with their stuff if you go through their back yards—the back areas—behind fences." And uhm—you know at that point he's just thinking I'm crazy. Even though he knows—he doesn't want to be told that by his mom, you know.

To keep her son safe, Mary instructed him to limit his spontaneous behavior and explained to him that to stay safe, he could not behave in ways that could possibly perceived as threatening to others. Mary wanted to protect her son from danger. What is perceived as dangerous depends a great deal on the perceiver's positioning. For some of the mothers, the source of danger included White teachers, principals and other school employees, police, White students' parents, White students, school culture, the school curriculum, and school policies and procedures. Positioning teachers, principals, and school staff as the source of danger because they are colluding with Whiteness norms is not common in research on teachers or preservice teachers. However, to fully and critically explore the ways in which Whiteness norms operate, this position must be considered. Some of the mothers, like Mary, repeatedly collided with Whiteness norms that were harmful to their children and came to understand that danger can come from teachers, principals, and the police. Mary also described an event when her son was just starting middle school when he was out walking their dog and was stopped and questioned by police officers. Mary was "furious" with herself for not preparing her son before the police stopped him. Mary saw it as her responsibility to instruct him and she was colluding with the Whiteness norm that *it is more work for a White woman to mother a child of color than for a White woman to mother a White child.*

In my conversation with Geneva whose stories also appeared in the last chapter, she discussed some of her strategies within the education system to assist her son and daughter be successful. In devising her strategies, she was navigating through the Whiteness norms practiced at the schools. But she never mentioned a sense of responsibility for teaching her son and her daughter how to navigate safely in racist America. She and I were discussing the changes in the grading scheme used by the school district her daughter and son attended and how complicated it was for parents to be able to decipher the assessment levels. Thinking strategically about grades in high school with an eye toward their impact on college applications was one of Geneva's concerns, but not her main concern. She was equally concerned that her sons and daughter were actually learning.

Geneva: You know because I think that message was somewhere for him—that it was more important that you are engaged and learning and that we understand why your grade might have gone down but that wasn't about—that was about putting your name on the paper—that was about—uhm—ah—you know following a direction. That wasn't really about learning. And Ah, you know my daughter, her—her—one of her classes that I really appreciate right now—ah—is orchestra. She plays the cello—she's getting to a point where—you know—she needs to really pursue it. She's gotten this far a few years into it and I really just hear the improvement—uhm. I think it's the one class right now where the grade system makes sense to me. She has to practice—daily—as much as she can—or up to a certain amount per week. She does a practice chart—she turns it in every Monday or Tuesday. If you don't turn it in Monday or Tuesday, you get a zero. You can't turn it in late. It's one of those—ok—but the point is also the practicing and if you're practicing then you are also improving and then the—you know playing for the teacher, you will get a good grade because you've been practicing and you'll understand it and so you'll get the return from the practice time and that she gets all As.

But on her practice chart—all zeroes. We struggle every week. She fills it out after every practice and she has me sign it and she takes it to school and doesn't turn it in. She just can't—get this down. But there's no mystery of why she's not getting an A [for the class] when her playing is improving. You know and you have to do that. And I can say, well I don't really care about that because I know you're practicing, but you're never going to be able to get that A if you don't follow the directions. You know?

When Geneva referred to the need to be able to "jump through hoops" and get a higher grade, she was referring to a kind of collusion. The collusion she referred to was not only with norms of Whiteness. It was collusion with all the norms performed in schools that perpetuate what Torres (1998) referred to as the myth that education is a neutral and apolitical activity. In Geneva's stories she seemed to be trying to use the education system to benefit her son and daughter without getting stuck in its sticky web. Geneva was concerned that her son and her daughter were really learning; however, she was still concerned about the impact of grades on her son's college opportunities. Geneva's focus in this instance was how to help her son and daughter work the system to their advantage (i.e., collusion) while not losing their passion for real learning. Geneva adjusted her goals and her strategies over the years. She talked about some of the things she did differently with her daughter than she did with her son based on the things she learned about how systemic racism operates and her changes reflected her contentions with the Whiteness norm that *White female teachers and school administrators can be trusted to take care of the students in the school. They work for the best interests of all children by following a color-blind approach.* Using the increased understanding that she gained, Geneva engaged with the school staff where her daughter attended in different ways than she did when her son was very young. She critically analyzed the decisions impacting her daughter and her daughter's interactions with school staff rather than passively accepting them.

Sara Tobin also had a son and a daughter with a similar age gap between them as Geneva's son and daughter although Sara's son and daughter were both several years older. Sara described experiencing differences in mothering them through their school years. Sara explained that her son excelled in middle school and received a great deal of support from school personnel there. Then, she described troubling changes she saw in her son after he started high school. In middle school he had been first chair on the trumpet, lead in the school play, and captain of the basketball team. When he moved on to high school, she explained that there were many more students at that school and that the support that her son had been receiving was no longer there.

> **Sara:** So [my son's] experience was not good at all. But a lot of that was his own—of his own doing. And my daughter's was okay. But you know, not great. I certainly didn't have the same feelings and it seemed to me that when I tried to—ah—get involved there—you know with the school and teachers and whatnot—I wasn't really encouraged to do that. But [my son's situation was] not the fault of the school and I'm not sure that there was something they could have done about any of that. Just too much partying with a lot of students that kind of fell off the - - Now I will say as far as trying to hold him accountable, he was given detentions and he would not serve the detention and there weren't really repercussions from that other than more detentions. I think when he graduated he had something like 340 some detentions—so he was not allowed to walk in the graduation ceremony—well that was fine with him. He didn't care about that. So I don't know what else they could have done. They didn't do a very good job of trying to hold him accountable I guess.

Sara's description focused entirely on the school and she did not share her experiences as a mother. Sara colluded with the Whiteness norm that *White female teachers and school administrators can be trusted to take care of the students in the school. They work for the best interests of all children by following a color-blind approach.* When I pressed her for more details about her feelings during that time, she replied, "Oh—oh—I don't think we want to talk too much about that—it was horrible. It was an awful time. You know. It was really bad. <heavy sigh> Very challenging. But we got through it." She wanted to suppress those memories and not reflect on them. I tried another angle to elicit more about her experiences.

> **Sara:** Hmmm—I remember being protective the way that all moms are protective and feeling that I had to be even more so because of the children being biracial and—uhm—because—ahh—just going into a store—you that people would—ah—follow around my children and wonder about my children because of the way they look—so—uhm—yeah—I definitely remember being real protective about that. Yeah, yeah—I think—ahh—that a lot of people thought that I was—uhm—probably overly sensitive and reading things into situations that weren't there. Uhm. I know they were. <chuckles>. I think they thought, "You're just exaggerating."

Sara declared herself to be protective like "all moms are" but that she had more work to do because her son and daughter were biracial. Thus, she was colluding with the Whiteness norm that *it is more work for a White woman to mother a child of color than for a White woman to mother a White child*. She also referred to many experiences when she noticed things that her friends did not and instead of believing her, they told her that she was imagining things and exaggerating. These were collisions Sara experienced with the Whiteness norm that *many people of color and some White people are "too sensitive" about race. They think every situation has something to do with race when most situations have no racialized meaning whatsoever*. Having her perception of reality repeatedly questioned by people who refused to see what was occurring was tiresome for Sara.

Vanessa told a story about her oldest who was home from college at the time when I interviewed her. He was the same son of hers that she referred to in her story that I discussed in the previous chapter. She shared a story with me about a recent experience he shared with her during the holiday break.

> **Vanessa:** My son [the 22 year old she had spoken of when he was young] had a heartbreak at Christmas. He was dating a girl—a—Caucasian girl—beautiful girl—cute little thing—very genuine—very—they were both on the same page. He had been talking to me, "Mom, I've just been praying, I just want to find the right person and have a full life and for me dating is more than this this and that. Dating is—is a long term thing—I'm doing it specifically—it's not just dating" And—ah. The girl—they're from a small town and her father made her call it off because he is African American. It blew me away. Blew me away. I had asked him about it. I had told him—uhm—I said, "Are you sure her father can accept the fact that you're—African American?" I said, "I don't know why he wouldn't, you're the best guy in the group of friends that you have for her to date. Cuz, you are!"

Vanessa's indignation, surprise, and shock were all indicators of her collision. Vanessa questioned whether White fathers of White women are still insisting that their daughters cannot marry Black men. Vanessa asked her son ahead of time if the woman's father could accept him. Placing that responsibility on her son positioned him as the source of the problem and the one responsible for solving it. Because she framed the situation as a binary set of choices, Vanessa was also colluding with the Whiteness norm that *racism is only a problem because there are some overtly racist people. Good White people do not behave in overtly racist ways*. The father accepts him or he doesn't. The father is either racist or he isn't. The reality of relationships are always more complicated than that.

> **Vanessa:** That was very devastating for him. Because, how do you pre-pare your son for that—that—it—you feel a little guilt—you feel a little blame—did I cause this because he's a part of my family and we're treating him like every other child—no dif-ferences—we see their uniqueness but we don't see them to be—uhm—any different than the next kid. They are loved. Did I now expose him to hardship because he—uhm—adapted so well—and he thinks we're all so normal—but out in the real world—that's not how people see us. I would have liked to say—ok this is 15 years, we've come a long way—is it really still happening? Does it really still exist?

In Vanessa's collision there were elements similar to the ones Karen expressed in the previous chapter. They both were upset about their sons' experiences and both told me their stories in a way that focused on them-selves as mothers. But where Karen's concern was focused on how she was perceived by the White parents of the White student involved, Vanessa wondered if she caused the problem for her son by treating him "no dif-ferent" than her White sons and daughters. In stating that she did not treat her oldest son any differently, Vanessa was referring to the fact that of her ten sons and daughters, two were Black and eight were White. Vanessa perceived herself as interacting with her sons and daughters the same regardless of their race. However, society treats them differently based on their race. Vanessa compared her mothering of her oldest son to her moth-ering for her White sons and daughters and she described it, or declared it, to be no different. Vanessa colluded with the Whiteness norm to *act as if everyone is White. Do not acknowledge that peoples' experiences differ because systemic racism exists*. This is the same norm that White teachers and school administrators collude with when they claim to treat all their students the same regardless of race. The sameness they are referring to includes the set of Whiteness norms with which they are colluding. Those norms do not impact people of color in the same way they impact White people. So while a person's actions are literally the same, the impact is not the same. Thus, those teachers are claiming that because they are enacting the same norms, some of which benefit only White people, with all their students, the students are receiving equal treatment. Refusing to acknowledge the race of individuals and to accept the reality of race in their lives is not treating students equitably. Race matters. Pretending that it does not and claiming to treat everyone the same is colluding with a Whiteness norm. That claim of sameness is also part of the silencing that Leonardo (2013) describes is a key part of keeping Whiteness norms in place.

In the next narrative, there is another example of silencing. Debra talked about the few students of color at the school where she taught. Her sons and daughter also attended that school. She said that the students of color "no matter what color they are" tend to hang out with each other, but her oldest son "doesn't identify that way."

> **Debra:** So—when people would try to draw him in to those groups— you know—he was mostly identifying with White friends. You know, he dates White girls, he—you know—does not—he doesn't play basketball—er—ah—cuz most of the—not most— but a lot of African Americans that come here are basketball recruits or football recruits or whatever—uhm—and so—he has kind of this struggle too—so in terms of where do I fit in? So he wrote his whole senior paper—you know and I cried when I read it—because it's not something you talk about a lot—you know—in day-to-day family life. And finally when your child has to write about it and writes a ten page paper about this kind of like identify struggle it's interesting.

Debra's preparations with her oldest son to assist him in his transition to adulthood did not include regular conversations about racial identity. This was evident because Debra's statement that racial identity was "not something you talk about a lot—you know—in day-to-day family life." Debra stated that she does not discuss race daily. She ignores it daily. This is one of the practices of White women that perpetuates silence on the topic of race (Frankenberg, 1993). That is what allows Debra to cry when she reads her son's senior paper. Instead of daily contending with Whiteness norms by acknowledging and discussing the race-based meanings that impact her life and the lives of her sons and daughter, Debra colluded with the Whiteness norms to *act as if everyone is White. Do not acknowledge that peoples' experiences differ because systemic racism exists.* Then she cried when she read of her son's ongoing struggle with his own racial identity.

According to Root (2004), multiracial identity is fluid and context dependent. Debra had her own challenges coming to terms with her sons' and daughter's racial identities. At another point in the interview Debra connected her recollections of registering her oldest son for school years ago with her thoughts as she was assisting him with his college applications.

> **Debra:** The elementary school that my one oldest son started at was in a very White neighborhood—uhm and I remember registering him for like the first day of school and going into the school

and you have to check off a box and they had the standard boxes cuz this was 13 years ago or whatever and—you know—it was Black, White, Hispanic, Native American, Asian, right—whatever they were and—it was my first kid and I was like—I don't—there was the school secretary—I—ah—I was like, "Can I check two?" And she's like, "No, you can only check one." And I'm like, okay—and I was like, "Well I don't really know what to do." And she was like, "Well, you're White, right?" And I was like, "I am, but my son" And she was, "No, it goes by the race of the mother." <pause> and I was like, "Really? I always thought it went by the race of the father." And we got into this argument about it and like I remember cuz I was uncomfortable with having to choose whether he was going to be labeled White throughout his schooling—once—cuz once you register your kid in public school you can't go back and change it—you know like—and I—and I was really uncomfortable with this secretary saying, "Well you're registering him and you're clearly White, let's just register him as White." And I did it and I just felt really uncomfortable about it because I felt like that's not really what he was—uhm—and that was my like kind of induction by fire if you will—like to—you know this is what it's going to be like to have children—you know—throughout the time.

In Debra's story above, her position advanced the notion that racial identity is fixed. In telling this story that occurred 13 years prior, her emphasis was on getting his racial identity accurately recorded and the confrontation that arose between herself and the school secretary who was a White woman. Debra's story also revealed how she resolved that early confrontation with a school employee. Even though she was uncomfortable with the idea, Debra complied with the structure that the White female school employee provided her. Debra continued her story and connected it to recent events.

Debra: Course when you get—when your kids are older and they're starting to apply for colleges and stuff, you <u>don't</u> want them to be White because there's clearly an advantage if they mark off that they're Black. You know—that's the reality of it there too. You know like—so—you're constantly kind of like—assessing where you are in life and what advantages come from clicking off White or clicking off Black or clicking off Other or whatever it is. Because it's a fluid process because it changes over time of what's best for your kids in a certain situation. So my son is identifying as—you know he's like, "I'm identifying as an African American in college because clearly it's going to help me get in the better schools or the better programs or whatever as an African American kid coming from [the high school] he went to]" You know—like—it's an advantage—it was an advantage for him to be listed as a student of color for college applications <u>clearly</u>—uhm—so anyhow.

In this story, Debra acknowledged that racial identity is fluid as she parroted a commonly held myth about college admissions and affirmative action disproportionally benefitting students of color. She positioned her son's access to a biracial identity as commodity that he can use to further his chances of success in a system based on the norms of Whiteness. She positioned his race as currency he can cash in depending on the situation. Debra's overall approach was colluding with the Whiteness norm *if a person can identify as White, do it, it will be beneficial to identify that way. But sometimes special opportunities are provided for people of color that they can access simply because of their race.*

Quinn described how she involved her elementary school aged daughter in experiences to learn and develop life skills. So for Quinn, assisting her daughter in her transition to adulthood has started already; it isn't something that will start when her daughter is in high school. Furthermore, Quinn's conception of taking responsibility for oneself is part of her faith. She touched on this idea of being a responsible person in her story about her serving her community.

Quinn: Everything I do, I think about her too—for the most part. Like my work with the Women's Center she's [her daughter] a young woman, she's going to grow up in this society and I don't want her to grow up in the way it is, so the things I do—I hope and the things I teach translate into development so it won't be the same. I'm hopeful I guess I should say. So—even with church, when we go do service projects or we do some of the—so that's one of the things we talk about too when we have a missions partner when we go into to do service in [area of the metropolitan area where she lives] but I could easily leave her at the neighbor's house and go do it—but it's the relationships you build when you're doing things too—so she's a part of that. And so <u>she's</u> part of it—she's there serving too. And there are days when she's like "I don't want to go." And I'm like, "Well, it's not about you." <Chuckles> You know—or there'll be days when—and we all have selfish days and "I don't want to bring my crayons and share that with them because they're mean to me." And I say, "Well, you have lots of crayons and not everyone has crayons and everyone likes to color and you know what—not everyone's going to be nice, but you should still be nice." You know so we have lots of conversations on the way there and we invite our neighbors which are her friends so the circles of influence start to connect.

In Quinn's discussion with her daughter about crayons, Quinn explained that she did not want her daughter to grow up in the world as it is. So in everything Quinn did, from something as simple as a discussion about crayons, Quinn interlaced her values and her expectations for her daughter to always be working to improve things into the conversation. Quinn also talked with her daughter about race-based and other systemic inequities and how they are perpetuated. She involved her daughter in community activities in which groups of children explored the same issues.

Quinn: Uhm—but I think the big thing like with the crayons is just talking about—we talk about diversity and one of the really like "make me proud moments" and this was <u>her</u>—we talk about it a lot—cuz she will ask questions and I appreciate that but uhm—and I don't think they are my words—I think they were—so we did—we wrote like "stereotype"—"prejudice"—"diversity" for these kindergartner through third graders to write down what that meant to them. And so she wrote under diversity, "God makes no mistakes." Uhm. And so—I think—bringing that back again—you know like—God created all these people <points to herself> I'm not more special than they are, you're <points out away from herself> not more special than they are—like we're in this together. You may not value them, but God values them. God values you. So you need to—it's bigger than me it's bigger than you. Uhm, we treat people with respect. We value people—they may not be nice—but you don't know what's going on in their life. Mom has bad days and you say things to Mom and I'm like ok. And then I thank her afterwards and I say "I'm sorry I had a bad attitude and that wasn't right." So I think just in a sense that humility and knowing that things are bigger than us.

For Quinn, contending with the norms of Whiteness was larger than just her thoughts about how to deal with specific behaviors when interacting with people. For her, the context was much larger. It is woven into her overall social justice mindset. This was how Quinn contended with the Whiteness norm that *there is no reason to acknowledge nor examine structural or systemic racism. It is not the responsibility of White people to educate themselves or their children about race-based oppression. It is acceptable to be recognized as an educated person and claim ignorance about race-based oppression.*

Quinn told me about an assignment that her daughter brought home from school that required students to indicate their country of origin on a global map. Quinn helped her daughter mark all the countries from which her ancestors came. Quinn described her interaction with the teacher in which the teacher said, "No, you can only mark one." Quinn explained to the teacher that she believed that would be inaccurate. The teacher stated, "We never had this come up before." Quinn responded with, "Good. I work really hard to make sure she is proud of all her different racial, ethnic, and cultural backgrounds." This provides an example of the deftness and smoothness of Quinn's contention. She did not allow her collision to impede her contention with the Whiteness norm the teacher was colluding with that *if a person can identify as White, do it, it will be beneficial to identify that way. But sometimes special opportunities are provided for people of color that they can access simply because of their race.* Quinn contended smoothly with that norm.

Another example of contention that Quinn described was in a conversation she told me about with friends of hers in which someone used the expression "good hair." Quinn positioned the conversation as an opportunity to explore what the person meant. Her genuine interest and curiosity about the other person's perspective allowed her to authentically engage with them and together they explored the use of that term and how its use perpetuates the processes of marginalization. Quinn knew what the expression meant. She also knew what role it plays in marginalizing Black women and girls. In engaging with others who used the expression, she did not attack them for their use of that expression. She used empathy and compassion to engage authentically.

At the core of Quinn's belief was strength and faith that she can make a difference through her persistence and acceptance. That is another way that Quinn contended with Whiteness norms like *there is no reason to acknowledge nor examine structural or systemic racism. It is not the responsibility of White people to educate themselves or their children about race-based oppression. It is acceptable to be recognized as an educated person and claim ignorance about race-based oppression.* She anticipated collisions before they occurred and she accepted the person who was enacting Whiteness norms in the interaction rather than feeling indignant and offended. By accepting the person, she engaged with them without anger or indignation.

Quinn's manner of contending with Whiteness norms was integrated with every part of her life. It was not simply part of her intentional actions as a mother. Additionally, her acceptance that collisions occur seemed key to her ability to contend effectively. She did not talk about collisions as shocking to her, she didn't say that they drive her bananas, nor did she talk about feeling bothered or irked by them.

This section provided examples of mothers' experiences in preparing their sons and daughters to live independent of them. Each mother's experiences fit into an intricate mosaic unique to her family depending on innumerable variables including the number of sons or daughter each mother had and their ages. But once all her daughters or sons have left her house, what is next for her?

WHITE WOMEN ONCE AGAIN?

Everyone says "You're so non-traditional." Like that's supposed to be offensive and I'm like, "Yep!" You know, it doesn't bother me like—I'm used to fighting for the things I really—there's just certain things....

Quinn, one of the mothers interviewed.

The mothers I interviewed whose sons or daughters had grown and begun lives of their own as adults had come to where they were through their individual paths. Those paths included enjoying their family triumphs and tackling challenges. Whatever they learned along the way and whatever ideas and strategies they developed, they were shaped by their circumstances and their personalities. The representation I am creating in organizing the chapters the way I have is not meant to imply that White mothers of daughters and sons of color share a core set of characteristics, nor a set of common experiences, nor are they traveling a common path. The mothers of young children I spoke with could only address their experiences with their youngsters, while the mothers of grown sons and daughters looked back through years of experiences when they recollected the days when their children were small. To be sure, there are some differences between the way that race as a subject is addressed in U.S. society today and the way it was addressed two or three decades ago. In telling their stories from years ago, both the dominant narratives that impacted the mothers at that time and the current dominant narratives are influencing their stories.

At the time of my interview with Faith, her daughter was at college and her son was married with a son of his own. Faith's description of encounters with strangers challenging her mother relationship with her son and daughter when they were young mirrored many of the stories that the younger mothers told me. All these mothers described incidents in which their motherhood was questioned. So this type of experience has not significantly changed in the United States over several decades. White mothers of children of color are still positioned as deviant.

Faith had been married for over 10 years when she got divorced and she parented her daughter and son alone after that. She described her thoughts about herself when she was recently dating a White man and compared those thoughts to her memories of when her children were young.

Jennifer: You mentioned something about—this sense of being in "no man's land" and then you said—you said something about—I don't know if it was tied directly to that or not, but—I remember you saying "until I was in my forties" and so can you tell me a little more about what you were referring to there?

Faith: Ahhhhh—In my—when I was forty I met and dated the very first White man I had ever gone out with. That's when I started to—even—after my divorce—I would not even entertain the idea of dating White men because I didn't trust them with my children. Ahhh—I just didn't trust them not to see or say something—not see, but say something—innocently—that I was going to be offended or they were going to be offended or to really truly accept them unconditionally—I never trusted them. So I always shied away from White men. Uhm—when I was forty I dated my very first White man for almost two years. And—I kind of—he was also with my kids—and I kind of credit him with helping me to become more comfortable with who I am and my racial identity. Because at the end of the day, no matter how many Black friends I have or how many Black organizations I might belong to or how many Black people I socialize with—at the end of the day I'm still White. And in the same way that I didn't want my children to have a self-concept that was not what society saw them because I thought it was setting them up for trouble, I have kind of had that concept myself. For a while I didn't feel White. I knew I wasn't Black, but I didn't feel White. So I got to give him credit for helping me find my racial identity. Weird isn't it?

Faith explained that for decades, she did not reap the rewards that a White woman who colludes with the norms of Whiteness does, therefore, she did not "feel White." Regardless of the Whiteness norms with which she was colluding, there were always benefits denied her because she was a White mother with a son and a daughter of color. However, when dating a White man in her forties, her public image was different than when her children were young. With her son and daughter out of the picture, she could slide into a new identity and she did. Thus, she revealed her collisions and collusions with the Whiteness norm *if a person can identify as White, do it, it will be beneficial to identify that way. But sometimes special opportunities are provided for people of color that they can access simply because of their race.*

> **Faith:** Well, I think it was for the first time since I was a teenager because I got married so young—I was in a relationship with someone and we could go anywhere and no one questioned us. You know—we encountered no problems, we didn't—we weren't stared at—we weren't—you know we weren't kind of slighted in any way shape or form we didn't get different service at the restaurant. And that was my first time experiencing that. I think in a relationship I always looked for the—is that waiter ignoring us you know—I think that waiter is ignoring us type thing or I got so used to people staring at me that I got—I just quit noticing people staring at me. And so for the first time in my adult life I got to be comfortable with who I was and it kind of carried over—uhm once I got there and it's something I should have experienced as a very young adult but I didn't because of the situation I was in. So for the—yet—I mean I was forty before I got comfortable with who I was—yeah.

In Faith's explanation, she seemed to contradict herself. First she claimed that she became so accustomed to things like poor service or people staring at her when her children were young and with her that she quit noticing. Then she argued that years later without her son and daughter with her, while dating a White man, she experienced for the first time being comfortable with who she was. The discomfort that Faith referred to was her ever-present awareness that society marked her as deviant. In Faith's statement, "It's something I should have experienced as a very young adult" she positioned comfort as something of value to which she was entitled. Examining the unearned benefits of being White in U.S. society as privileges identifies comfort as one of the benefits of White privilege (Kendall, 2006; Rothenberg, 2012). In a study of 11 White mothers married to Black men, O'Donoghue (2005) focused on what she referred to as their loss of White privilege. I argue that characterizing White mothers of biracial children in this manner is too limiting. While some statements by some mothers reflect a sense of loss, a critical examination is necessary to understand how a sense of loss is created. Such examination reveals that these mothers reflect a sense of loss when they superficially compare their real lives to their imagined lives if they had had White children. Or in other words, they compare their actual lived experiences to a dominant image of what their lives were supposed to be. That dominant image is not one they created; it is one that society has thrust upon them. That dominant image is reified as the ideal. So in their comparisons of themselves to the ideal, they identify the things they do not have as things they have "lost." The things they have lost include naively teaching their White children to collude with Whiteness norms with no awareness that they are doing so. Therefore, framing their experiences as having lost White privilege supports the Whiteness norm that *it is more work for a White woman to mother a child of color than for a White woman to mother a White child*.

> **Faith:** Because I was so young and my family kind of turned their backs so and so we immersed ourselves in—in his family—and his culture and his church and everything and I was just immersed in the Black—in Black society. I never socialized a lot with White people—you know work friendships, but I was always afraid to take them any further because, you know, you are going to get rejected again, so. Those are the big fears for a relationship. But. We get older we get wiser and we stop caring what other people think.

Faith referred to the rejection that she thought was imminent when she said "you know you are going to get rejected again" as a norm. When Faith made this normative statement, she was expressing a level of acceptance of that frame of her life. Accepting and expecting the rejection is a form of collusion. Those who transgress the norms and accept the sanctions meted to them without challenging them are colluding with those norms. In effect, they are saying yes, I transgressed and therefore I deserve the sanctions. Thus, Faith was colluding with the Whiteness norm that *good White women mother White children*.

Fran's situation was quite different than Faith's. Some of Fran's stories were discussed in chapter two and those stories included her recollections of when her daughters were very small. Her oldest daughter was in college at the time of our interview. Fran told me at one point that she did not have "any problems" when her oldest daughter began going to college. Yet, she did have concerns for her daughter. Her oldest daughter was studying to become a teacher and Fran told me about one of their conversations in which her daughter shared her concerns.

> **Fran:** Well—I say that—she's kind of a bit discouraged I think with education system and the more that she's gone to school and she sees how things have like never changed—that's frustrating to her. You know? You look and you think this is the way it's always been done—this is the politics of being a teacher and she's just like, "I don't even know if I want to do it." You know. "If things don't change—like—well I don't know if I want to be a teacher in that—in that type of school."

Fran referred to things in schools not changing when describing how her daughter was beginning to express doubts about being able to accomplish her goals within the school system. In part, Fran was referring to the norms that are enacted by school employees regardless of laws, policies, or programs that come and go. The systemic practices and values embedded in schools are the norms; and in U.S. schools, those include the norms of Whiteness (Carnevale & Strohl, 2013; Delpit, 2006; DiAngelo, 2010; Leonardo, 2009). One of those Whiteness norms is that *there is no reason to acknowledge nor examine structural or systemic racism. It is not the responsibility of White people to educate themselves or their children about race-based oppression. It is acceptable to be recognized as an educated person and claim ignorance about race-based oppression.* That realization (i.e., collision) both disappointed and frustrated Fran and her daughter.

I asked Fran to talk about her experiences and she did that by focusing her daughter's experiences. I didn't interpret that to mean she was evading my question, I think that is how she made sense of her experiences, through her daughters' eyes. In any event, Fran framed college as the time when her daughters would become fully themselves. It provided a launching off point for Fran to tell me about an interaction of hers with an older woman she recently met through church. In their first interaction, Fran was offended by what the woman said, and it was Fran's subsequent conversation with her daughter that helped her stay engaged and contend with the Whiteness norms with which she collided.

Fran: The second we get angry, people close their ears. I mean that's a huge challenge for me because—especially when I was younger—I'm getting better because I've learned that lesson. It doesn't mean I do it all the time and it doesn't mean that I don't get angry or that I don't have to sit and some of that stuff sometimes on how I am going to respond to something. Like one day—there's this lady in our bible study and she's older, she's probably—probably my mom's age—maybe a little—maybe she's 60—and so she comes in, she just moved here from [another state] and she tells me after bible study one day that she had a sister that was married to a Black guy that used to beat her up and all this stuff and she—I was like—when I left the conversation, she's like how Black people in [state she moved from] are different and I mean, she said so many racist things in that conversation—uhm—another thing she said she heard this Black pastor on tv one time that said the reason that Black men marry White women is for status. And I said, you know, "You can't believe everything you hear on tv and I can absolutely promise you that's not true." Hey. That's totally inappropriate to say. But I left there, and my daughter—my oldest daughter was with me and I was <u>so</u> stinking mad—I was <u>so</u> mad! And I'm like, "I just want to go off. I'm like I don't understand why I'm always put in this situation—like" And she's like, "Well, that's exactly why it happens because you need to be an example, and you know, you're a positive person that can make change and you are going to learn how to talk to her about it and you're not going to shut her off." And I was so mad though—and it took me a long time and I'm friends with this woman now. She's learned a lot.

In this story, Fran did what several of the mothers I spoke to did in describing the other person she interacted with, she emphasized the person's age when it was someone older than her. Her actions colluded with the Whiteness norm that *some older people do and say racist things. Even though what they do and say is offensive, they are simply reflecting the norms of the time when they grew up and they cannot help themselves. There is a limited number of these people and they will eventually die. So it is best to avoid and ignore them.* This illogical argument again uses the notion that the passage of time alone is all that is required for racism to eventually disappear. The myth argues that older White people are expected to behave in a more racist manner and because of that, they sort of get a pass, so don't be too hard on them because they don't know any better. The conclusion of that incorrect argument is that once all the old racist people die off, the United States will be less racist. This dominant narrative claims nothing needs to be done to improve the situation, time will take care things, and we just need to be patient. While this is a comforting illusion, it also perpetuates and strengthens the very situation that is supposed to be improved by ignoring it. It also provides allowance for everyone's behavior to become increasingly racist as they age. After all, they will be excused for that behavior the older they are.

In Fran's story, she was upset and asked "Why does this always have to happen to me?!" That not only indicated Fran's collision, it also revealed how she tended to view her collisions. Fran positioned the experience as something that "has to happen" to her. That reflected her collusion with it because while she railed against it and thought it was unfair, she still positioned it as a necessary part of life. It was Fran's daughter who responded rationally and calmly by explaining to her mother that she had a responsibility to stay engaged and work on the relationship with the woman from church. I speculate that Fran's daughter had that conversation with her mother because it was the kind of conversation her mother had with her many times over the years. Allowing our sons and daughters to parent us in that way, is a method for allowing them to test their wings. Thus, it is a part of the "family project" (Domene, Socholotiuk, & Young, 2011, p. 274) of transitioning to full adulthood mentioned at the beginning of this chapter. Thus, Fran's frustration and her daughter's calm response was an example of her daughter practicing her own behaviors and beliefs.

Mary's sons and daughters have all completed their transitions to adulthood. Mary's concerns about her son's safety appeared earlier in this chapter. At the time of the interview, Mary worked with one of her daughters in a professional capacity. Her daughter was an assistant principal at a school. Through her work at the school, Mary contended with the Whiteness norm that *White female teachers and school administrators can be trusted to take care of the students in the school. They work for the best interests of all children by following a color-blind approach.*

> **Mary:** My husband and I do a lot of—uhm—well antiracist train-ing and discussion groups and stuff and—uhm—we just did a workshop at the youngest daughter's school, she's an assistant principal at the charter school and uhm—one of the things that we talked with her staff about—you know we tell them that we expect that everybody has bias and prejudice and you may not call yourself a racist and other people may not either but racism is like radioactivity—when it exists, everyone is affected. And everyone has, even if they're unconscious—biases. And we now include in our training, we taken some normal biology courses and we've have John Powell come to speak here and met with him—uhm and he does a lot of the unconscious bias stuff and he—he's saying the—I want to say the amygdala, but it might be a different part of the brain. But the amygdala has already seen somebody—it's met with its committees, it's sent out the memo before the conscious part of your brain even recognizes anything about that person. All the rest of your brain has al-ready made decision and a judgment on who you're coming to or coming up with. So we use brain studies a lot to talk about how people formulate things and how we have a lot of uncon-scious bias just because things are drilled into you daily in this country. You really don't have a choice. I mean you have choices in terms of recognizing them, but you don't have a choice in terms of exposure.

Continually expanding her own understanding of racism from a biologi-cal, social, and psychological perspective to develop her training content, is one of the ways that Mary contended with the Whiteness norm that *there is no reason to acknowledge nor examine structural or systemic racism. It is not the responsibility of White people to educate themselves or their children about race-based oppression. It is acceptable to be recognized as an educated person and claim ignorance about race-based oppression.* Like Quinn, whose quote is the epigraph for this section, Mary identified direct opportunities through her work to help others learn about the complex processes involved. Mary's efforts were directed at impacting the norms of Whiteness enacted in entire school districts. The teachers and other school employees that Mary trained interacted with hundreds of students and parents. Thus, the work she did contending with Whiteness norms impacted more individuals than responding in specific individual collision incidents. That does not mean that Mary no longer collided when she experienced Whiteness norms. The dominant image of White women who have partnered with men of color that positions them as having crossed a line or a boundary is pervasive. It has to be effective at perpetuating norms to influence behavior. The image of having crossed a line helps sustain the actions that position such women as deviant. Mary understood this persistent force that creates collisions with Whiteness norms and through understanding it she could predict when and where collisions were likely to occur and then navigate them effectively.

Using the dominant imagery of a boundary line being crossed might result in an idea that there is an option to re-cross the line in the other direction. For single mothers, or those with White partners, once their sons and daughters are no longer living in their homes, the outward living indications of her interracial family are removed from her immediate vicinity. A dominant Whiteness narrative could encourage a view that their lives return to normal. That storyline includes an understanding of normal that includes colluding with Whiteness norms. This inescapable narrative of White motherhood pervades every story that the mothers I interviewed told me. It oozes out of their stories as phrases and images like a constant series of memes appearing internally for each of us, unbidden.

Dominant narratives are created from the lives of real people, with the details stripped away so that their lives become a simple image, like a children's coloring book outline drawing rather than a photograph. Such simple outlines are void of nuance, uniqueness, and individuality. Simplified images devoid of complexity are reduced to recognizable representations. Loewen (2007) describes this reduction process as "heroification" (p. 1) and I argue that the same process that creates heroes, creates demons. The simplified stories serve as a guide or a description for a person's entire life. But in the simplification process, the uniqueness of the individual is lost and all that remains is an image reflecting the dominant social norms. While such simple bold outline drawings are immeasurably deficient, there are times when individuals use those dominant images and narratives to explain their own lives and to understand the lives of people around them. But a critical stance encourages one to eschew the coloring book outline drawing and allow the eyes to see the real lives of these mothers with all their messy complexities, contradictions, and confusions.

SUMMARY

The motherhood experiences addressed in this chapter did not address all the situations a mother encounters in assisting her daughter's and son's maturation process. There could be many more sections than the two presented here and they could include many more experiences that occur in mothers' lives. I compressed the information here to keep the focus on the Whiteness norms that connect directly or indirectly to the educational sphere. The table below provides a summary of the collusions, collisions, and contentions with Whiteness norms discussed in this chapter and chapter five presents all the Whiteness norms.

Again, as mothers moved into new arenas with their daughters and sons, they encountered new Whiteness norms. Leaving some behind may have provided a brief respite for some mothers, like handling the last diaper. Moving on to new experiences can feel like growth. However, simply moving on from one set of Whiteness norms to another set of Whiteness norms is not growth. Additionally, moving from one set to another set did not seem to impact the ways in which the mothers interacted with Whiteness norms. However, the mothers who developed ways to contend with the norms referred to their repeated collisions with Whiteness norms as contributing to their decisions to increase their understanding of what they were experiencing. Their steps to increase their learning often led them to increase their racial literacy. Their increased understanding then often led them to develop ways of contending with the Whiteness norms. Through contending with the norms of Whiteness, the mothers accepted the reality of the Whiteness norms without colluding with them. Their collisions, then, were less traumatic because they were actively engaged in ways to modify (i.e., contend with) the norms as well.

Table 4.1. Mothers' Collusions, Collisions, and Contentions With Whiteness Norms Identified During the As Sons and Daughters Mature Stage

Whiteness Norms: *Social Processes and Discursive Practices*	*Mother*	*Type of Interaction*
Act as if everyone is White. Do not acknowledge that peoples' experiences differ because systemic racism exists.	Vanessa Debra	Collusion
If a person can identify as White, do it, it will be beneficial to identify that way. But sometimes special opportunities are provided for people of color that they can access simply because of their race.	Debra Faith Quinn	Collusion Collusion and Collision Contention
Good White women mother White Children.	Faith	Collusion
Racism is only a problem because there are some overtly racist people. Good White people do not behave in overtly racist ways.	Vanessa	Collusion
Some older people do and say racist things. Even though what they do and say is offensive, they are simply reflecting the norms of the time when they grew up and they cannot help themselves. There is a limited number of these people and they will eventually die. So it is best to avoid and ignore them.	Fran	Collusion and Collision
There is no reason to acknowledge nor examine structural or systemic racism. It is not the responsibility of White people to educate themselves or their children about race-based oppression. It is acceptable to be recognized as an educated person and claim ignorance about race-based oppression.	Quinn Fran Mary	Contention Collision Contention
It is more work for a White woman to mother a child of color than for a White woman to mother a White child.	Faith Sara	Collusion
White female teachers and school administrators can be trusted to take care of the students in the school. They work for the best interests of all children by following a color-blind approach.	Faith Geneva Sara Mary	Collusion and Collusion Collusion, Collision, and Contention Collusion Contention
Many people of color and some White people are "too sensitive" about race. They think every situation has something to do with race when most situations have no racialized meaning whatsoever.	Sara	Collision

REFERENCES

Bialeschki, M. D., & Michener, S. (1994). Re-entering leisure: Transition within the role of motherhood. *Journal of Leisure Research, 26*(1), 57–74.

Carnevale, A. P., & Strohl, J. (2013). *Separate & unequal: How higher education reinforces the intergenerational reproduction of White racial privilege.* Washington, DC: Georgetown Public Policy Institute.

Delpit, L. (2006). *Other people's children: Cultural conflict in the classroom.* New York, NY: The New Press.

DiAngelo, R. J. (2010). Why can't we all just be individuals?: Countering the discourse of individualism in anti-racist education. *InterActions: UCLA Journal of Education and Information Studies, 6*(1), Article Number 4.

Domene, J. F., Socholotiuk, K. D., & Young, R. A. (2011). The early stages of the transition to adulthood: Similarities and differences between mother-daughter and mother-son dyads. *Qualitative Research in Psychology, 8*(3), 273–291.

Francis-Connolly, E. (2000). Toward an understanding of mothering: A comparison of two motherhood stages. *The American Journal of Occupational Therapy, 54*(3), 281–289.

Frankenberg, R. (1993). *White women, race matters: The social construction of Whiteness.* Minneapolis, MN: University of Minnesota Press.

Greene, A. L., Wheatley, S. M., & Aldava, J. F. (1992). Stages on life's way: Adolescent's implicit theories of the life course. *Journal of Adolescent Research, 7*(3), 364–381.

Kendall, F. E. (2006). *Understanding White privilege: Creating pathways to authentic relationships across race.* New York, NY: Routledge.

Leonardo, Z. (2009). *Race, Whiteness, and education.* New York, NY: Routledge.

Leonardo, Z., & Boas, E. (2013). Other kids' teachers: What children of color learn from White women and what this says about race, Whiteness, and gender. In M. Lynn, & A. D. Dixson (Eds.), *Handbook of critical race theory in education* (pp. 313–324). New York, NY: Routledge.

Loewen, J. W. (2007). *Lies my teacher told me: Everything your America history teacher got wrong.* New York, NY: Touchstone.

O'Donoghue, M. (2005). White mothers negotiating race and ethnicity in the mothering of biracial, Black-White adolesecents. *Journal of Ethnic & Cutltural Diversity in Social Work, 14*(3/4), 125–156.

Root, M. P. (2004). Multiracial families and children: Implications for educational research and practice. In J. A. Banks & C. A. Mcgee Banks (Eds.), *Handbook of research on multicultural education* (2nd ed.). San Francisco, CA: Jossey-Bass.

Rothenberg, P. S. (2012). *White privilege: Essential readings on the other side of racism* (4th ed.). New York, NY: Worth Publishers.

Torres, C. A. (Ed.). (1998). *Education, power, and personal biography.* New York, NY: Routledge.

Twine, F. W. (1999). Bearing Blackness in Britain: The meaning of racial difference for White birth mothers of African-descent children. *Social Identities, 5*(3), 185–210.

CHAPTER 5

CONCLUSIONS

The mothers I interviewed knew a lot about race. They knew the rules and norms of Whiteness and they knew how to collude with them. Collusion includes not making the rules explicit. These mothers were not ignorant about race nor were they lacking exposure to race. They have been exposed to race all their lives and have learned their lessons well. Claims of ignorance and lack of exposure are norms of Whiteness (Leonardo, 2009). Getting caught up inside the very discourses that perpetuate Whiteness norms while trying to examine them is the same challenge Frankenberg (1993) experienced decades ago, "the challenge in talking about white women thinking through race is capturing the correct balance between their 'entrapment' in discourse and their conscious engagement with it" (p. 140). However, I do not argue for a correct balance. I argue for a thorough exploration of both the entrapment in the discourses and conscious engagement with them. So while many of the mothers did not mention their awareness of their collusions with Whiteness, some did, and their awareness frequently came about after collisions with a Whiteness norm. Collisions with Whiteness norms were always more obvious than collusions to the mothers even though they did not label them as such and often struggled to articulate their experiences. They were, however, quite often aware that their experiences represented a "breach of the background expectancies of everyday life" (Garfinkel, 1967, p. 55).

Colluding, Colliding, and Contending With Norms of Whiteness, pp. 139–151
Copyright © 2017 by Information Age Publishing

This chapter provides a consolidated list of the Whiteness norms I explicated in my study. It also presents a review of the model and a summary discussion of the collisions, collusions, and contentions with those norms.

WHITENESS NORMS

Racism is the normal order of things in US society.

(Ladson-Billings, 2013, p. 37)

The table below summarizes the Whiteness norms I identified in my study. This table does not identify the mothers, rather it identifies the motherhood stages (which are the same as the chapter titles) during which these norms were experienced. Some of the norms were apparent in all the motherhood stages and some were concentrated in just one stage. There are some norms with which mothers only experienced in one way, for example, mothers only colluded with the Whiteness norm to *act as if everyone is White. Do not acknowledge that peoples' experiences differ because systemic racism exists*. Additionally, some of the norms were evident in several interviews and some only appeared in one or two interviews. Future research with Whiteness norms can explore these features further.

One of the main conclusions I drew from examining these mothers' experiences with Whiteness norms was that the key to growth and learning was not the specific Whiteness norm that the mother experienced, rather it was the way in which she participated with the norm. There were qualitative differences between the three ways of interacting with Whiteness norms I have detailed. Collisions were instrumental because they fractured the mothers' existing understandings which created openings for new learning. Through new learning, several of the mothers developed ways of contending with the norms of Whiteness.

Colluding unconsciously with Whiteness norm was comfortable for these mothers because it was outside of their awareness. Contrasting with their collusions were their collisions. Collisions were not comfortable experiences. Collisions were noticeably disquieting because they disrupted the mothers' understandings. Revealed in each mothers' description of a collision was how it ruptured her sense of reality. Collisions sound damaging, and yet repeated collisions were the key to opening the door to new learning because in several of the mother's efforts to attend to the fractures, she sought out new information and she expanded her understanding of what occurred. Through increasing her understanding of her experiences (i.e., after increasing her racial literacy) some of the mothers were no longer stuck in their collisions unable to effectively respond in situations. They had moved on to contending with Whiteness norms.

Table 5.1.   Mothers' Collusions, Collisions, and Contentions With Whiteness Norms Identified Across all the Stages

Whiteness Norms: Social Processes and Discursive Practices	Motherhood Stage	Type of Interaction
White people are the norm. There is no need to depict or display people of any race but White. A White person can be displayed and it will be understood that it represents a raceless human in books and advertising.	Becoming a Mother	Collision
	Mothers and Schools	Collusion
If a person can identify as White, do it, it will be beneficial to identify that way. But sometimes special opportunities are provided for people of color that they can access simply because of their race.	Becoming a Mother	Collusion
	Mothers and Schools	Collision
	As Sons and Daughters Mature	Collusion, Collision, and Contention
Act as if everyone is White. Do not acknowledge that peoples' experiences differ because systemic racism exists.	As Sons and Daughters Mature	Collusion
Racism is only a problem because there are some overtly racist people. Good White people do not behave in overtly racist ways.	Becoming a Mother	Collusion and Collision
	Mothers and Schools	Collusion, Collision, and Contention
	As Sons and Daughters Mature	Collusion
Good White parents value education so they get involved in their children's schools.	Mothers and Schools	Collusion
It is best to avoid overtly racist people because they cannot change. If one cannot avoid overtly racist people, tolerate their behavior and do not participate in it. Not participating in it signifies that one is not a racist.	Becoming a Mother	Collusion and Collision
Good White people do not behave in overtly racist ways. Identifying the impact of someone's behavior as racist when they did not intend to be racist is not fair and should be avoided.	Mothers and Schools	Collusion, Collision, and Contention

(Table continues on next page)

Table 5.1.   (Continued)

Whiteness Norms: Social Processes and Discursive Practices	Motherhood Stage	Type of Interaction
Good White parents do not approve of their White daughters partnering with men of color.	Becoming a Mother	Collusion and Collision
	As Sons and Daughters Mature	Collusion and Collision
Good White women mother White children.	Becoming a Mother	Collusion and Collision
	Mothers and Schools	Collision
	As Sons and Daughters Mature	Collusion
When interacting with interracial couples, focus on the White person. Direct your questions to that person and look at that person.	Becoming a Mother	Collusion and Collision
Asking or commenting to White mothers about the physical features of their children who are not White is excusable as curiosity. It is an acceptable way to draw attention to deviant mothers and their children and still claim to be a good person. It is acceptable to ask questions in ways that position the children as objects. It is also acceptable to touch the children as if they were objects.	Becoming a Mother	Collusion and Collision
White grandparents who accept and love their grandchildren of color are doing more work than White grandparents of White grandchildren.	Becoming a Mother	Collusion
Adults who become parents make sure their races match. People whose race matches go together. People whose races do not match, do not belong together.	Becoming a Mother	Collusion and Collision

(Table continues on next page)

Table 5.1. (Continued)

Whiteness Norms: Social Processes and Discursive Practices	Motherhood Stage	Type of Interaction
It is more work for a White woman to mother a child of color than for a White woman to mother a White child.	Becoming a Mother	Collusion
	Mothers and Schools	Collusion
	As Sons and Daughters Mature	Collusion
There is a hierarchy of races involved and types of relationships in which White women mother children of color. The circumstances will be valued differently. It is best to be recognized as belonging to the highest level group possible. The ideal to strive toward is that of a White mother of White children. Be like White mothers of White children as much as possible.	Becoming a Mother	Collusion and Collision
	Mothers and Schools	Collusion
White people can and do harm Black people who are innocent.	Becoming a Mother	Collision
There is no reason to acknowledge nor examine structural or systemic racism. It is not the responsibility of White people to educate themselves or their children about race-based oppression. It is acceptable to be recognized as an educated person and claim ignorance about race-based oppression.	Becoming a Mother	Collusion, Collision, and Contention
	Mothers and Schools	Collusion, Collision, and Contention
	As Sons and Daughters Mature	Collision and Contention
It is collectively the responsibility of people of color to teach White people how to behave because there is no other way for White people to learn to behave in respectful ways with people of color.	Becoming a Mother	Collusion

(Table continues on next page)

Table 5.1.   (Continued)

Whiteness Norms: Social Processes and Discursive Practices	Motherhood Stage	Type of Interaction
White female teachers and school administrators can be trusted to take care of the students in the school. They work for the best interests of all children by following a color-blind approach.	Becoming a Mother	Collision
	Mothers and Schools	Collision, Collusion, and Contention
	As Sons and Daughters Mature	Collusion, Collision, and Contention
Locations with low percentages of people of color are not good places for people of color to live. It is better for people of color to live in areas with higher percentages of people of color.	Becoming a Mother	Collusion
	Mothers and Schools	Collusion
	As Sons and Daughters Mature	Collusion
Individual people of color who immigrate to the U. S. can achieve individual success by assimilating to the dominant cultural values. When they do not assimilate they cannot be successful. There is only one definition of success.	Mothers and Schools	Collusion
Some older people do and say racist things. Even though what they do and say is offensive, they are simply reflecting the norms of the time when they grew up and they cannot help themselves. There is a limited number of these people and they will eventually die. So it is best to avoid and ignore them.	As Sons and Daughters Mature	Collusion and Collision
Many people of color and some White people are "too sensitive" about race. They think every situation has something to do with race when most situations have no racialized meaning whatsoever.	Becoming a Mother	Collision
	As Sons and Daughters Mature	

Not every mother in my study shared contending experiences, but for those that did, their experiences were often described as calm and matter-of-fact interactions. The emotional turmoil of the collisions subsided. Those mothers could still see their collisions, but because they understood them, they could see the signposts alerting them that a collision was imminent. Then they experienced their collisions more like efficiently negotiating a speed bump rather than crashing into something. They knew where the collisions were likely to occur and they knew how to navigate them. It was the combination of repeated collisions <u>and</u> increasing their racial literacy that prepared these mothers to move into contending behaviors that disrupted Whiteness norms. Therefore, I argue that collisions are a necessary step toward learning. The collisions were filled with emotion and cognitive dissonance because they provided a view of reality that did not fit the mothers' customary views. For the mothers who learned how to contend with norms of Whiteness, facing those realities repeatedly allowed the mothers to absorb the reality and accept it. Then they were able to develop strategies to contend with that reality.

This learning route that the mothers forged is also available to White female teachers, preservice teachers, principals, administrators, and other school employees. Because they work in environments where these and other Whiteness norms are enacted every day, it is feasible that they could experience collisions with those Whiteness norms in ways similar to the collisions that the mothers experienced in my study. White female teachers and preservice teachers who similarly repeatedly collide with Whiteness norms who then acquire new learning to increase their racial literacy could expect to reap benefits similar to the mothers I interviewed. This implies that the learning process for White female teachers and preservice teachers would not be smooth nor comfortable. In the existing Whiteness research with White female teachers and preservice teachers, much focus has been on identifying their collusion with Whiteness norms (Case & Hemmings, 2005; Fasching-Varner, 2012; Lensmire, 2012; Pennington, Brock, & Ndura, 2012; Picower, 2009; Sleeter, 2005; Yoon, 2012). Therefore, I suggest that expanding the focus to include collisions and contentions with Whiteness norms will be more productive in future research. Such a focus also supports Fasching-Varner's (2012) argument for more rigorous teacher candidate evaluation processes at universities because the learning path identified here requires White female teacher candidates who have the capacity to repeatedly undertake collisions with Whiteness norms in order to learn.

MODEL

My model depicting collusions, collisions, and contentions with social norms presented in chapter one is provided in Figure 5.1. Social norms operate in all societies and each society or social group has many social norms for all sorts of social interactions. Norms are taught to newcomers to the social group through modeling, direct instruction, and through sanctions (Sherif, 1965). Sanctions include reinforcing the adherence to norms through providing or withholding benefits. Additionally, sanctions do not need to be applied every time for the norm to be maintained and reinforced (Nelissen & Mulder, 2013).

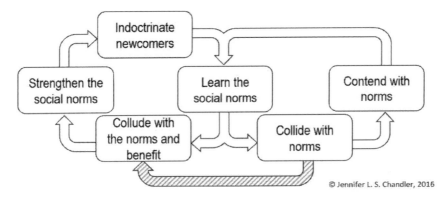

© Jennifer L. S. Chandler, 2016

Figure 5.1.   Model of colluding, colliding, and contending With norms.

When we collude with the dominant social norms of a situation, we are signaling to the other participants that we want to be valued as one who belongs and one who cooperates (Druzin, 2013). However, more than one social norm applies to any given social interaction. Additionally, norms shift and evolve over time. Assessing the situation and choosing which norms to collude with is something people do in all social interactions. Understanding and acknowledging how norms operate and that norms shift over time may help some people relinquish their emotional connection with the enactment of the specific norms in place and ease their transition to new norms.

The norms of a society are transmitted through narratives. Narratives are archetype storylines used to explain and justify behavior. "Discourses that become dominant do so because they serve the interests of those in power" (DiAngelo, 2010, p. 3). Organizations or individuals who operate with only one dominant narrative limits them. When dominant stories are the only ones used, they become the only narrative through and against which everyone must craft their individual stories. Those narratives play a central role in shaping our identities. It is not comfortable countering those narratives. When we counter the dominant narrative we are also refusing to conform to a norm. The narratives are the unwritten scripts and the unsaid assumptions that mold social interactions. It is often easier to slide silently into performing in accordance with the dominant scripts and storylines. It is easier and more comfortable to collude. However, because it is expected and accepted, collusion is less noticeable that the other two ways of interacting with social norms. Therefore, the discussion that follows starts with collisions because they are the most obvious.

Collisions

Members of interracial families become candidates for racial literacy projects during those moments when they become conscious of the ruptures or gaps between the realities of their lives and the assumptions made about their White lives by others. (Twine & Steinbugler, 2006, p. 360)

Collisions are the ruptures and gaps that the mothers interviewed described. Some of the mothers interviewed experienced collisions that included a realization that their beliefs about their families, their friends, their professional service providers, or about the society in which they live were not true. For a few seconds, Cathleen could not believe that the White man sitting next to her in a public space slapped her toddler while he sat in her lap. She described the experience "the most insane feeling." At first, Vanessa could not believe that the White father of the White girl that her son loved prohibited his daughter from seeing her son. These were just two examples and several of the mothers described similar collisions that included their feelings of disbelief. Applying Garfinkel's (1967) constructs to their experiences, they were reacting to a "breach of the background expectancies of everyday life" which produce "bewilderment, uncertainty, internal conflict, psycho-social isolation, acute and nameless anxiety" (p. 55). Most of the mothers interviewed described collisions and those collisions were often revealed by their indignation, shock, anger, annoyance, irritation, and discomfort. Some of the mothers used their own euphemisms for those experiences, such as Yvette who said that it "drives me bananas!"

Some of the collisions the mothers experienced were interactions in which the norms of Whiteness were specifically targeting the mothers as deviant. Examples of those kinds of experiences were when strangers asked where the mothers "got" their children or asked a variation of "what is she?" about their children that positioned their children as odd objects available for public inspection. These kinds of public actions serve an important function for the dominant group in that they publicly identify deviants. Those actions also assert the authority of the Whiteness norm itself at the same time. "Designation of culturally legitimate behavior as deviant depends upon the superior power and organization of the designators" (Gusfield, 1968, p. 61). Thus, the strangers asking those questions are fulfilling a function in perpetuating Whiteness norms. They are not simply curious. The strangers were colluding with the norms of Whiteness which govern who is a legitimate target for such questions (Cassilde, 2013).

For the person colliding with a Whiteness norm, the focus during and after a collision is initially on the emotions triggered by the experience. Among the mothers interviewed, one strategy for responding to collisions was to seek solace until the emotional commotion subsided. Sometimes, the mothers returned to colluding while also seeking ways to avoid future collisions. That pathway is depicted as the shaded arrow in my model above. One example of an avoidance strategy in action was Cathleen's description of her plan to never put herself in a situation like the one she experienced with her son when the White man slapped her son. She explained that she never planned to travel with her son without her husband again. Her son is two years old. She chose a strategy that will restrict her movement in public because she believed it can help her reduce the likelihood of a similar future collision.

Collusions

It is certainly possible for whites not to act out of [the] dominant frame, as many periodically do. Yet, most whites, at least much of the time, live their daily lives unreflectively out of some version of that white racial frame. Important elements of that frame control much societal interaction and communication, even for otherwise savvy whites, because these elements are omnipresent and considered "normal." Most whites do not even realize they routinely operate from some version of this dominant frame. (Feagin, 2013, p. 199)

Colluding with a norm means complying with it. It does not mean agreeing with the norm or liking it or valuing it. Collusion comes from understanding the norm and complying with it, thereby reinforcing it with others by modeling it. People learn from behavior modeled by those around them without any direct instruction (Sherif, 1965). Collusion is expected. Collusion is normal. When they were White girls, the mothers in my study experienced thousands of enactments of the norms of Whiteness modeled around them and they learned from those experiences. So did the White women who work in schools across the country.

In the mothers' stories, their collusions were not simply occurring because they had learned how to collude and had come to accept collusion as normal. At times, they were colluding because they believed it would benefit their children. For example, Riley appreciated hints from the teachers to have her daughter take tests that could lead to her receiving a designation in school that would give her access to additional services. Riley believed her daughter's success in school depended on her daughter getting that designation. I am not arguing that Riley and her daughter either benefitted or were harmed by the process of getting tested. Whether or not an individual student receives something that can be perceived as beneficial when that student's mother colludes with the norms of Whiteness is a separate concern from the Whiteness norms themselves and the ways in which White mothers and White school employees participate in perpetuating those norms.

Just as collisions will continue, so will collusion. Moving from a culture where collusion with Whiteness norms is expected and rewarded to a culture where collusion with healthy norms that are thoughtfully and collaboratively chosen is a worthy goal that is discussed in the next chapter. Examining the existing contentions with Whiteness norms will also assist in that effort.

Contentions

As women, we have been taught either to ignore our differences or to view them as causes for separation and suspicion rather than forces for change. Without community, there is no liberation … the master's tools will never dismantle the master's house. (Lorde, 2003, pp. 26–27)

In my model, contending with the norms of Whiteness includes more than refusing to collude. It includes engaging with processes that perpetuate social norms further upstream to influence the form of the social norms themselves. Challenging norms of any kind takes energy and preparation. Getting oneself prepared also takes knowledge and determination. It is also intentional; being prepared just doesn't happen. Intentional thinking, planning, learning, discussing, and developing strategies are all part of contending with Whiteness norms. Contention can encourage people to critically examine the norms they are colluding with. For example, Quinn's invitations to collude with new norms mentioned above were a way of contending with the existing Whiteness norms. In those situations, Quinn's engagement in a conversation about hair with her friends was a way of moving the engagement upstream. She was not indignantly confronting strangers in the act of reaching out to touch her daughter's hair. She was enacting a critical thinking norm rather than a Whiteness norm in her conversations with friends when they began identifying who had good hair and who did not. She gently and firmly pushed her friends to move beyond the simplistic binary of good and bad.

Another example of a mother moving her engagement upstream in her personal sphere was the way in which Hannah decided to stop ensuring that she wore her wedding ring whenever she went out in public. Hannah realized she was colluding with a norm of Whiteness when she differentiated herself from single White mothers of biracial children whose fathers were Black. Hannah stopped colluding with the Whiteness norm and began speaking about it in her personal sphere as part of her ongoing exploration of the role that race plays in her life. When Hannah stopped differentiating herself from other White mothers of children of color she might be more likely to invest energy working together with them for gains that benefit all their children.

Hannah's and Quinn's contentions are examples of individual actions engaging upstream. Mary contended with the norms of Whiteness in her professional life. She engaged teachers and other school staff members in professional development contexts when she conducted training that addresses systemic racial oppression. Helping school employees recognize their behavior patterns of pretending not to see race is one way that Mary contended with norms of Whiteness. These mothers' contentions with the norms of Whiteness can be seen as contributing to a collective school transformation project.

Debra's and Tenna's actions can be imagined as part of such a collaborative project as well. Debra described her school in this way, "There's kind of an unwritten rule that you adapt to the culture by coming here, that the culture doesn't really adapt to you or your differences and I think that's a constant struggle in education." The constant struggle Debra referred to is part of how she viewed her contentions with the norms of Whiteness operating within her school. She presented at conferences on how teachers can support multiracial students in schools like hers. Tenna is also a teacher. Her stories revealed her personal contentions with the norms of Whiteness at her school. Tenna pushed her principal to hire more teachers of color, for example. Like the mothers mentioned above, these teachers are individuals pursuing their racial justice goals in their unique ways. What effect might these mothers' efforts have if they were a part of a collaborative effort to replace Whiteness norms perpetuated in a school or across a school district with equity norms?

REFERENCES

Case, K. A., & Hemmings, A. (2005). Distancing strategies: White women preservice teachers and antiracist curriculum. *Urban Education, 40*(6), 606–626.

Cassilde, S. (2013). Where are you from? In *The melanin millennium: Skin color as 21st century international discourse* (pp. 115–138). New York, NY: Springer.

DiAngelo, R. J. (2010). Why can't we all just be individuals?: Countering the discourse of individualism in anti-racist education. *InterActions: UCLA Journal of Education and Information Studies, 6*(1), Article Number 4.

Druzin, B. H. (2013). Eating peas with one's fingers: A semiotic approach to law and social norms. *International Journal for the Semiotics of Law, 26*(2), 257–274.

Fasching-Varner, K. J. (2012). *Working through Whiteness: Examining White racial identity and profession with pre-service teachers.* Lanham, MD: Lexington Books.

Feagin, J. R. (2013). *The White racial frame: Centuries of racial framing and counter-framing* (2nd ed.). New York, NY: Routledge.

Frankenberg, R. (1993). *White women, race matters: The social construction of Whiteness.* Minneapolis, MN: University of Minnesota Press.

Garfinkel, H. (1967). *Studies in ethnomethodology.* Englewood Cliffs, NJ: Prentice Hall.

Gusfield, J. R. (1968). On legislating morals: The symbolic process of designating deviance. *California Law Review, 56*(1), 54–73.

Ladson-Billings, G. (2013). Critical race theory—What it is not! In M. Lynn & A. D. Dixson (Eds.), *Handbook of critical race theory in education.* New York, NY: Routledge.

Lensmire, A. (2012). *White urban teachers: Stories of fear, violence, and desire.* Lanham, MD: Rowman & Littlefield Education.

Leonardo, Z. (2009). *Race, Whiteness, and education.* New York, NY: Routledge.

Lorde, A. (2003). The master's tools will never dismantle the master's house. In R. Lewis & S. Mills (Eds.), *Feminist postcolonial theory: A reader* (pp. 25–28). New York, NY: Routledge.

Nelissen, R. M., & Mulder, L. B. (2013). What makes a sanction "stick"? The effects of financial and social sanctions on norm compliance. *Social Influence, 8*(1), 70–80.

Pennington, J. L., Brock, C. H., & Ndura, E. (2012). Unraveling the threads of White teachers' conceptions of caring: Repositioning White privilege. *Urban Education, 47*(4), 743–775.

Picower, B. (2009). The unexamined Whiteness of teaching: How White teachers maintain and enact dominant racial ideologies. *Race Ethnicity and Education, 12*(2), 197–215.

Sherif, M. (1965). *The psychology of social norms.* New York, NY: Octagon Books.

Sleeter, C. E. (2005). How White teachers construct race. In C. McCarthy, W. Crichlow, G. Dimitriadis, & N. Dolby (Eds.), *Race, identity, and representation In education (critical social thought)* (2nd ed., pp. 157–171). New York, NY: Routledge.

Twine, F. W., & Steinbugler, A. C. (2006). The gap between Whites and Whiteness: Interracial intimacy and racial literacy. *Du Bois Review, 3*(2), 341–363.

Yoon, I. H. (2012). The paradoxical nature of Whiteness-at-work in the daily life of schools and teacher communities. *Race Ethnicity and Education, 15*(5), 587–613.

CHAPTER 6

RECOMMENDATIONS

There are two sections of recommendations in this chapter. The first section focuses on using the model in change efforts within schools and school districts. Because my model is a process model, it can be used to frame and understand the complexities involved in transforming the organizational culture of a school or a school district. Transformation itself is not a concrete set of steps. It is likely to move forward and lurch back in an organic way depending on the investments of the people involved. Those people could use my model to help establish their goals, to understand the chaotic change process itself, and to help them identify the Whiteness norms they are enacting at their school. The second section in this chapter addresses using the model in future research. Expanding beyond simply gathering data to conclude that White teachers and preservice teachers are colluding with Whiteness norms is a new avenue of research. Examining the multiple ways in which people interact with Whiteness norms can help push the research in this area appreciably forward. This research extends far beyond the scope of public schooling in the United States. The model would prove useful in any culture in examining any type of social norms.

Colluding, Colliding, and Contending With Norms of Whiteness, pp. 153–161
Copyright © 2017 by Information Age Publishing

CHANGING NORMS IN SCHOOLS

The White female teacher inherits and inhabits a social position that originates, as they all do, in the past. She embodies the ideal of the "true woman," benevolent protector of a moral state with a will and duty to domesticate children.

(Leonardo & Boas, 2013, p. 321)

This section does not focus on race-based inequities present in the U.S. education system. The structural forces and the ways in which they influence behaviors and outcomes for the U.S. education system have been presented elsewhere, for example, see Carnevale and Strohl (2013). This section provides an overview of how the conclusions from my study can be used by those who are undertaking change initiatives in schools.

Public school employees are rewarded for colluding with the norms of their organizations and those rewards are granted by those who were also hired, given merit pay, and promoted within those norms. This process applies to teachers, support staff, administrators, and other school employees as much as it does to those in consulting firms, military squads, or co-op collectives. People enforce and uphold the norms at the same time that their behavior is also governed by those norms (Sherif, 1965). The degree to which individuals act to shape and modify the norms of the groups with which they participate varies with the person and the group. White female teachers share some similarities with the mothers I interviewed. They all can find themselves enmeshed in the same dominant narratives regarding their lives and the lives of children of color. Leonardo (2009) argued that while frameworks used by White educators to structure their understanding of their lives, their students, learning processes, and society are not determined by the fact that they identify as White, it is White educators who enact and perpetuate frameworks dominated by Whiteness norms more frequently than educators of color.

Participation with Whiteness norms varies. People are not always colluding with norms of Whiteness. Nor are they colliding with Whiteness norms all the time. At times, they are contending with Whiteness norms and not all contentions are equal. I argue that developing effective contentions involves an acceptance of what Sullivan (2014) refers to as "a different set of virtues, a different *ethos* for their racial justice efforts, one that is not centered on dominant, liberal understandings of moral goodness" (p. 147). In a school environment, places and structures that allow, encourage, and support the two groups of White women (teachers and mothers of children of color) to come together with parents and community partners to discuss their collisions, collusions, and contentions can develop shared understandings of the Whiteness norms operating in their school that would be productive.

Given that school environments are places where Whiteness norms are perpetuated, this section addresses how using my model of collusion, collision, and contention can assist in tackling the following four objectives below within school environments. While these four objectives apply to organizations beyond schools, the focus will be on the school environment because that was one of the consistent locations where Whiteness norms impacted the mothers in my study.

1. Identify, analyze, and define the Whiteness norms operating.
2. Choose which Whiteness norms to replace.
3. Identify and implement new norms.
4. Track progress.

The activities involved in accomplishing each of the four objectives listed above are general processes used in a variety of change management approaches so this section does not provide a detailed explication of them. Rather this section provides some cautions and some broader suggestions regarding the use of the model.

First, because they are filled with emotion, collisions are noticeable and memorable and that makes them a viable place to start the analysis necessary to uncover the Whiteness norms operating in a school environment. Collisions are the indicators of places for deeper analysis. While collisions can occur for school employees, based on my study, examining the collisions that occur for parents of students is a fruitful place to begin the analysis. However, the goal is not to immediately focus on eliminating collisions. The goal is to first collect information about the collisions and analyze that information. Schools that provide and support a robust suggestion and complaint process have mechanisms in place for gathering some information that could lead to identifying existing common collisions. Analyzing collisions to decipher the Whiteness norms operating is not an easy undertaking. It is emotionally taxing and intellectually challenging. It will take a considerable investment of time and concentrated effort by people who possess the skills and experience to do so.

There is another kind of collision that needs to be discussed here even though this type of collision was infrequently apparent in the stories of the mothers interviewed. Collisions can occur for anyone with any set of norms that differ from their expectations. For example, Quinn described interactions in which some people with whom she was conversing collided with her norms of equity and inclusion. Likewise, Mary also described some interactions in which the school employees with whom she interacted were colliding with her norms of racial justice. When a person abides by norms of racial equity and is not colluding with norms of Whiteness, people who <u>are</u> colluding with Whiteness norms may notice and have a collision with those racial equity norms. Those collisions can result in the same kinds of reactions of indignation, shock, and anger that the collisions the mothers I interviewed experienced. Other researchers (Bonilla-Silva, 2010; Case & Hemmings, 2005; Gordon, 2005; Yoon, 2012) have also discussed the frustration, silence, and incoherence that is common during these kinds of collisions. In school environments, these types of collisions will also illuminate areas for further analysis. They can indicate locations to begin identifying Whiteness norms.

I am suggesting that the steps I outlined in the beginning of this section can assist in transforming a school from one where Whiteness norms are perpetuated and reinforced to a school where staff, students, and families engage in racially just behaviors that are supportive and respectful. The goal of the transformation process I am suggesting is not to provide a method of identifying individuals who are engaged in collusive behaviors. Following such a path is not likely to be successful because discussing the process of collusion can sometimes evoke notions of guilt and blame. Kendall (2006), Sullivan (2014), and Trepagnier (2010) have explored guilt, shame, and blame that arises when addressing Whiteness norms and I direct readers to their work for strategies and recommendations for handling those reactions. Using my model allows those involved in a transformation process to focus on changing the norms, rather than changing individual people. All sorts of groups change their norms. Sometimes the groups stay intact as the norms change. Sometimes group members depart and new members join while norms are shifting. Sometimes the changes come rapidly in response to other influences and sometimes slowly (Sherif, 1965). The model can provide a broader context to serve as a roadmap during the transformation.

Second, readers must keep in mind that using the model does not dictate the new norms an organization chooses. New norms more harmful than the existing Whiteness norms could conceivably be selected and implemented. My model does not preclude that. Using the model provides a structure; it does not dictate choices made by individuals using the structure. The choices are always up to the people in the organization. They have the capacity to modify the norms they follow and whether they choose to do so, is up to them. For school transformation projects using the four steps listed above, identifying and analyzing existing Whiteness norms and developing norms to replace them as a collaborative project that includes staff, students, and parents can also provide a space where participants practice the new norms. Embodying the new norms will require people to model the new norms and they will require support. Tracking progress of the adoption and reinforcement of the new norms and the decline of collusion with the Whiteness norms selected for replacement can be incorporated into teacher and staff evaluations. All while these efforts are ongoing, collisions will continue to occur and will remain important indicators. Rather than attempting to dissuade parents or staff from reporting their collisions as disruptive and non-productive, an atmosphere that accepts them will contribute to the transformation process. Transformation requires more than a couple of hours of training for staff and it includes more than modifying policies and procedures. Transformation is more complex than that.

Third, I recommend using collisions as the major signpost to locate starting points for analyzing experiences to uncover the Whiteness norms that are operating in a school. I recommend this because the challenges in analyzing collusions can easily overwhelm the effort. One reason for this is because collusion is ordinary. There is nothing remarkable occurring when everyone is colluding with a norm and that makes collusions difficult to spot for the people inside the cycle of collusion. Another reason it is challenging to use collusions as the entry point for analyzing Whiteness norms is because places where everyone is colluding are also usually places where the organization appears successful. Tasks are getting accomplished and goals are being met. No one is likely to want to disrupt those locations and unsettle business as usual. This is ironic because it is precisely those areas where collusion with Whiteness norms is occurring that the school transformation effort will be altering. However, to begin there is probably too challenging. Therefore, coming at collusions from another angle is what I recommend.

There is a way that understanding how collusion works can be beneficial to a transformation project. Colluding with Whiteness norms is not often overtly demanded, it is expected. In my study, the sanctions for non-compliance with the operating Whiteness norms were not immediate, nor were they always threatening. Rather, collusion was elicited through behavior expectations. Many times the behavior expectations were communicated through what I call invitations to collude. An invitation to collude is akin to someone asking another person to dance. The invitation includes a set of expectations and assumptions because both people are at the dance and the dancing is observable. The person being asked to dance assumes the individual asking knows how to dance in the manner demonstrated by the other dancers. The one asking assumes that there is a good chance the one being asked will accept the invitation. The one who is asked to dance weighs the consequences of refusing the invitation. Thus, the two people are involved in a complex set of moves based on social norms before they even reach the dance floor. In this way, invitations to collude can be deliberately enlisted to invite people to collude with the <u>new</u> equity norms that are selected. This is a form of modeling the new norms. This is a basic behavior modification tactic (Bandura, 1969) and teachers already use this tactic in helping their students learn. In order to begin inviting people to collude with a new norm, the one doing the inviting must understand what the new norms are. They must also understand what collusion with the new norms looks like so they can recognize when those they are inviting begin colluding with it. It is through this sideways avenue that the transformation group can use their understanding of collusions to assist the transformation project. Quinn's conversations with her friends can be viewed as invitations to collude with new norms. Instead of castigating her friends, she invited them to join with her in critical thinking to examine the narratives about "good hair" and "bad hair."

Fourth, while I intentionally avoid suggesting specific replacement norms, I strongly recommend that people involved in school transformation projects do not simply eschew their existing Whiteness norms and plan to replace them with nothing. Selecting new norms is the responsibility of those participating in such transformative projects. Transformation means moving from what currently exists to something new. It does not mean creating a void. Furthermore, leaders will benefit from understanding the selection process as something more complex than a simplistic binary that configures the old norms as bad and the new ones as good. As I mentioned above, transformation is not a quick replacement of norms; transformation requires development, growth, and learning. During that growth and learning, collisions will continue. They are occurring now whether or not people are aware of them. New collisions can be expected to be triggered during a transformation project. Those new collisions will include those experienced by people who expect the Whiteness norms (that are being replaced) to continue untouched. That type of collision is sometimes referred to as resistance and Kendall (2006) provides five strategies for individuals working on their own resistance and those involved with school transformation projects may find them useful.

Applying the collusion, collision, contention model supports a nonlinear understanding of interpersonal and organizational change because accepting that everyone can collude, collide, and contend with Whiteness norms helps move the focus out of the realm of binary thinking. Binary thinking can lead to arguing over whether or not something someone did was racist. Binary thinking concentrates attention on deciding who is right and who is wrong. Binary thinking creates boundary lines and then everyone's energies are expended on policing those boundaries. A process model like mine can help most when those using it do not fixate on determining if the interactions were collusions or collisions. Accepting that collisions will be frequent during the transformation process and devising healthy and supportive responses and structures that fit the organization will be more useful places to invest energies.

Lastly, contentions can play a vital role in the implementation and track progress steps. Contentions are part of the strategies to help implement new norms. Regardless of the content of a norm, replacing an existing norm with a new one is not a straightforward activity like replacing an existing information system with a new one for a school district. In that scenario, once the existing system is replaced, employees no longer have access to the old system, so no matter how uncomfortable it is learning the new technology, employees with no access to the old system are forced to use the new one. Social norms are not that easy to replace. People are highly skilled in agreeing in principle to new norms, but unconsciously repeating the old norms. That is where contentions come in. When those leading the transformation project contend with the norms of Whiteness in observable ways that uncover the Whiteness norm itself, their actions redirect people's attention. Continued contention like the efforts described by the mothers I interviewed will also help others to enact the replacement norms. Thus, contention serves as a learning reinforcement during implementation when students, teachers, administrators, families, and community members begin practicing new behaviors.

Contention is challenging for everyone involved because collisions do not cease. The mothers who described adept contentions still collided first with the Whiteness norm. Even though their collisions in many cases were like smoothly navigating a speed bump, if one is not prepared for it, damage can still result. So for those enacting contention in a school transformation effort, continual preparations are necessary so that they can see their own collisions coming, navigate them smoothly, and move directly into contending. That will require an adequate resource investment to support those who are contending.

My discussions of collusions, collisions, and contentions throughout the book addresses them as individual processes. It is important to keep in mind that a person can collude with some norms while also experiencing collisions with other norms, and while also contending with yet some other norms. Many people will only begin to see and recognize their collusions after becoming familiar with recognizing collisions. I saw this with the mothers I interviewed.

The next section briefly outlines using my model in future research. Pressing forward is critical for building upon knowledge gained. I will be using my model to complete a meta-analysis of existing studies and in my research on leadership processes. I invite new researchers and veterans alike to apply the model and to share their results in using it.

FUTURE RESEARCH

Constructing whites as knowledgeable about race has two advantageous; one, it holds them self-accountable to race-based decisions and actions; two, it dismantles their innocence in exchange for a status as full participants in race relations.

(Leonardo, 2009, p. 108)

Existing research with White female teachers and preservice teachers has revealed some norms of Whiteness enacted in school spaces by teachers and preservice teachers (Case & Hemmings, 2005; DiAngelo, 2010; Fasching-Varner, 2012; Gordon, 2005; Lensmire, 2012; Parks, 2006; Pennington, Brock, & Ndura, 2012; Picower, 2009; Sleeter, 2005; Yoon, 2012). While many of the norms I discovered align with the norms they uncovered, those research projects were not conducted using a consistent model. I suggest that my model can assist future research by providing a common framework for continuing critical Whiteness analysis within schools. Using my model could assist with collaborative efforts by providing a common language around which to discuss and address the Whiteness norms that are operating.

Using my model also supports the recommendations made by Marx and Pennington (2003) who advocate pushing preservice teachers past their "denials by continuously, but gently and respectfully, pulling attention back to the ways in which their own words implicate them in White racism" (p. 103). The ways in which their own words implicate them in White racism are their collusions with the norms of Whiteness. White teachers of students of color are not the only ones implicated in this way. My model can also assist those following Sullivan's (2014) recommendation that "White people who wish to fight racism must become more intimately acquainted with their Whiteness in order to transform it" (p. 71) because it positions those colluding as responsible for their actions and yet does not position them as bad people by using a scale with binary polarities. Using my model does not impose a judgment on people for their participation in the norms of Whiteness. The model acknowledges that norms always exist, norms are always evolving, and how one engages with norms is a choice.

REFERENCES

Bandura, A. (1969). *Principles of behavior modification.* New York, NY: Holt Rinehart & Winston.

Bonilla-Silva, E. (2010). *Racism without racists* (3rd ed.). Lanham, MD: Rowman & Littlefield.

Carnevale, A. P., & Strohl, J. (2013). *Separate & unequal: How higher education reinforces the intergenerational reproduction of White racial privilege.* Washington, DC: Georgetown Public Policy Institute.

Case, K. A., & Hemmings, A. (2005). Distancing strategies: White women preservice teachers and antiracist curriculum. *Urban Education, 40*(6), 606–626.

DiAngelo, R. J. (2010). Why can't we all just be individuals?: Countering the discourse of individualism in anti-racist education. *InterActions: UCLA Journal of Education and Information Studies, 6*(1), Article Number 4.

Fasching-Varner, K. J. (2012). *Working through Whiteness: Examining White racial identity and profession with pre-service teachers.* Lanham, MD: Lexington Books.

Gordon, J. (2005). White on White: Researcher reflexivity and the logics of privilege in White schools undertaking reform. *The Urban Review, 37*(4), 279–302.

Kendall, F. E. (2006). *Understanding White privilege: Creating pathways to authentic relationships across race.* New York, NY: Routledge.

Lensmire, A. (2012). *White urban teachers: Stories of fear, violence, and desire.* Lanham, MD: Rowman & Littlefield Education.

Leonardo, Z. (2009). *Race, Whiteness, and education.* New York, NY: Routledge.

Leonardo, Z., & Boas, E. (2013). Other kids' teachers: What children of color learn from White women and what this says about race, Whiteness, and gender. In M. Lynn, & A. D. Dixson (Eds.), *Handbook of critical race theory in education* (pp. 313–324). New York, NY: Routledge.

Marx, S., & Pennington, J. (2003). Pedagogies of critical race theory: Experimentations with White preservice teachers. *International Journal of Qualitative Studies in Education, 16*(1), 91–110.

Parks, M. W. (2006). I am from a very small town: Social reconstructionism and multicultural education. *Multicultural Perspectives, 8*(2), 46–50.

Pennington, J. L., Brock, C. H., & Ndura, E. (2012). Unraveling the threads of White teachers' conceptions of caring: Repositioning White privilege. *Urban Education, 47*(4), 743–775.

Picower, B. (2009). The unexamined Whiteness of teaching: How White teachers maintain and enact dominant racial ideologies. *Race Ethnicity and Education, 12*(2), 197–215.

Sherif, M. (1965). *The psychology of social norms.* New York, NY: Octagon Books.

Sleeter, C. E. (2005). How White teachers construct race. In C. McCarthy, W. Crichlow, G. Dimitriadis , & N. Dolby (Eds.), *Race, identity, and representation In education (critical social thought)* (2nd ed., pp. 157–171). New York, NY: Routledge.

Sullivan, S. (2014). *Good White people: The problem with middle-class White antiracism.* Albany, NY: State University of New York Press.

Trepagnier, B. (2010). *Silent racism: How well-meaning White people perpetuate the racial divide* (2nd ed.). Boulder, CO: Paradigm Publishers.

Yoon, I. H. (2012). The paradoxical nature of whiteness-at-work in the daily life of schools and teacher communities. *Race, Ethnicity and Education, 15*(5), 587–613.

APPENDIX A

The Study

PARTICIPANTS

The mothers interviewed lived in locations across the United States. Some lived in the same area for a number of years, and some lived as children in areas different from where they live as adults. The location references in the short biographical introductions for each mother below are based on the following categorization:

Northeast: Maine, Vermont, New Hampshire, Massachusetts, Connecticut, and New York.

East: Pennsylvania, New Jersey, Delaware, Maryland, West Virginia, Virginia, and Washington, DC.

Southeast: North Carolina, South Carolina, Georgia, and Florida.

North: North Dakota, South Dakota, Minnesota, Wisconsin, and Michigan.

Central: Nebraska, Iowa, Kansas, Missouri, Illinois, Indiana, Kentucky, and Ohio.

South: Texas, Oklahoma, Arkansas, Louisiana, Missouri, Tennessee, and Alabama.

Colluding, Colliding, and Contending With Norms of Whiteness, pp. 163–171

Southwest: Arizona and New Mexico.

West: California, Nevada, Utah, Colorado, and Wyoming.

Northwest: Washington, Oregon, Idaho, and Montana.

The following section provides details that the 30 mothers shared with me about themselves. All the names used are pseudonyms and I omitted details here and in the interview excerpts to obscure their exact locations and other specifics about their lives. Table A.1. below lists the mothers by their pseudonyms and indicates where they lived at the time of the interview and the race identification of the parents of her children. The table does not include a column to describe each mother's partnership situation. Those details are in the brief bios that follow.

Table A.1. Study Participants

Pseudonym	U.S. Region	Mother Relationship	Race Identification of the Parents of the Child(ren)	Number and Age of Child(ren)
Abigail Banker	South	Adoptive	Mother Black; Father, Black	4
Betsy Caruthers	Central	Biological	Mother, White; Father Black	2
Caroline Danforth	North	Biological	Mother, White; Father Black	10
		Biological	Mother White; Father Native American	18
Darlene Eckard	North	Biological	Mother, White; Father Black	16
Ellen Franklin	Southwest	Biological	Mother, White; Father Mexican	20, 17, 15
		Adoptive	Mexican and Black	10
Faith Geffers	Southwest	Adoptive	White and Black	26
		Biological	Mother, White; Father, Black	22
Geneva Hanover	Northwest	Biological	Mother, White; Father, African	17 & 12
Hannah Isling	Central	Biological	Mother, White; Father, Black Haitian	2 children under 4

(Table continues on next page)

Table A.1.   (Continued)

Pseudonym	U.S. Region	Mother Relationship	Race Identification of the Parents of the Child(ren)	Number and Age of Child(ren)
Ina Jefferson	East	Biological	Mother, White; Father, Black	13 & 15
Jane Kopfeldt	Southwest	Biological	Mother, White; Father, Black	2
Karen Lund	East	Biological	Mother, White; Father, Black	2 children under 5
Laura Moritz	South	Biological	Mother, White; Father, from Sierra Leone	5
Mary Norridge	West	Adoptive Biological	Mother Black; Father, Black Mother, White; Father, Black	40 30 & 26
Nancy O'Keefe	Central	Biological	Mother, White; Father, Black	6
Olivia Preston	South	Adoptive	Mother Black; Father, Black	11
Paige Qually	South	Biological--	Mother, White; Father Black Caribbean	9
Quinn Resin	Southeast	Biological	Mother, White, Latina; Father, Black	1 in elementary school
Riley Stevenson	South	Biological	Mother White; Father, Black	13 & 3
Sara Tobin	North	Biological	Mother, White; Father, Black	28 & 24
Tenna Ushmore	Northwest	Adoptive Biological	Mother, White; Father, White Mother, White; Father, Black	15 6
Ursula Vale	West	Biological	Mother, White; Father, Costa Rican	3 & not yet 1
Vanessa Wilson	North	Adoptive Adoptive Adoptive	Mother, White; Father, White Mother, Black; Father Black Mother, Black; Father Black	8 children in middle school or high school 1 college age 1 high school age

(Table continues on next page)

Table A.1.   (Continued)

Pseudonym	U.S. Region	Mother Relationship	Race Identification of the Parents of the Child(ren)	Number and Age of Child(ren)
Wendy Weston	North	Biological	Mother, White; Father, Black	12 & 8
Yvette Zanders	West	Biological	Mother, White; Father, Filipino	3 & not yet 1
Amy Kaster	South	Biological	Mother, White; Father, from Sierra Leone	5
Beth Danforth	North	Biological	Mother, White; Father, Moroccan	Not yet 1
Cathleen Dillard	North	Adoptive	Mother, Black; Father Black	2
Debra Goldson	Northeast	Biological	Mother, White; Father, Biracial (Black & White)	1 graduating high school, 1 in high school, & 2 in elementary school
Emma Matthews	Northwest	Biological	Mother, White; Father, Black	2 in elementary school
Fran Johnson	South	Biological	Mother, White; Father, Black	1 graduating high school, 2 in high school

Abigail Banker lived in a large metropolitan area in the South region. Abigail identified herself as White. She lived in many locations in the United States growing up including the Northeast, the Southeast, and the South. She also lived in more than one South American country growing up. After trying to have children when she was married, she learned that she could not carry a child. Abigail's husband (who she identified as White) did not want to adopt. Sometime after her 16 year marriage to him ended, she was in a relationship with a woman and they both wanted to become mothers. They pursued donor avenues for Abigail's partner to become pregnant and that did not work. They negotiated with a woman to adopt her baby she was carrying and that arrangement ended with the mother deciding to keep her child. Another adoption attempt fell apart when Abigail's mother became ill and Abigail assisted her. Abigail's mother died. She felt that she was through trying to adopt, when a friend contacted her about a situation with a nine month old boy. The result was that in a very short time Abigail adopted him. Abigail identifies her son as Black. He had just turned four when I interviewed Abigail.

Betsy Caruthers lived in a large metropolitan area in the Central region. She grew up in a small rural town in the same region where she lives now. Betsy identified herself as White. Betsy was married and their biological daughter was two. Betsy identified her husband as Black. Betsy described the area where she grew up as being "very White." She lived in the same house all throughout her childhood until she went off to college where she met the man she married. She was in graduate school and she referred to herself as a "part time PhD student" when we spoke.

Caroline Danforth lived in a large metropolitan area in the North region. Caroline grew up in the same area where she now lives. She was single at the time of the interview. Caroline identified herself as White. Her biological son was 18 and Caroline identified his father as Native American and her biological daughter was 10 and she identified his father as Black. This mother's son went to the same school district that she attended and Caroline's mother recently retired from that school district as well. Caroline recently moved out of that school district.

Darlene Eckard lived in a large metropolitan area in the North region. Darlene grew up in the same area where she now lives. Darlene identified herself as White. She had been married for seven years and she identified her husband as Black. That marriage ended in divorce and she moved back to the city. Darlene was not married at the time of the interview. Her biological daughter was 16 years old at the time of the interview.

Ellen Franklin had recently moved to a large metropolitan area in the Southwest region. Ellen lived in the West and the Southwest growing up. Ellen identified herself as White. At the time of the interview Ellen had been married for over 20 years and she identified her husband as Mexican. She and her husband had two biological sons, one age 20 (in college) and one age 15 (in high school) and one biological daughter age 17 (in high school) and one adopted daughter age 10 (in elementary school). Their adopted daughter is biracial (Black and Mexican). Ellen and her family have lived in over 10 different locations around the world as they moved when her husband was assigned to various locations as he served in the military.

Faith Geffers lived in a large metropolitan area in the Southeast region. Faith grew up in the same area where she lived at the time of the interview. Faith identified herself as White. Faith married when she was 17 and had been married for 15 years when she and her husband divorced. She identified her husband as Black. She and her husband adopted their son when they had been married for 10 years and had been unsuccessful trying to have a child. After adopting their son, they had a biological daughter. At the time of the interview, Faith identified her son as biracial (Black and White) and he was 26 old and had married a White woman and they lived in another state with their biological son. Faith's daughter was 22 years old and was in college.

Geneva Hanover lived in a large metropolitan area in the Northwest region. Geneva identified herself as White. Geneva was married at the time of the interview and identified her husband as African. Their biological son was almost 17 and their biological daughter was almost 12 at the time of the interview.

Hannah Isling recently moved from a large metropolitan area in the West region to a small metropolitan area in the Central region which is the area where she grew up. Hannah identified herself as White. She was married and identified her husband as Black Haitian. She and her husband had two biological sons both under four years old. She, her husband, and their two boys were living with her parents at the time of the interview. Her grandparents live in the same city and her siblings live nearby as well.

Ina Jefferson lived in a large metropolitan area in the East region. Ina lived in the Northern, the Central, and the Eastern regions growing up. Ina identified herself as White. She was married for about 20 years and she identified her husband as Black. Their biological son was 15 and their biological daughter was 13.

Jane Kopfeldt recently moved from a large metropolitan area in the Northwest region which is where she grew up in a large metropolitan area in the Southwest. Jane identified herself as White. Jane was single and identified the father of her two year old biological daughter as Black.

Karen Lund lived in a small city in the East region. Karen lived in several Eastern states and one Southeastern state growing up. Karen identified herself as White and her husband as Black. They had two biological sons both under five years old.

Laura Moritz lived in a large metropolitan area in the South region. Laura lived in the Northeast and the South growing up. Laura identified herself as White. She was single and she identified the father of their biological five year old daughter as from Sierra Leone.

Mary Norridge lived in a large metropolitan area in the West region. She had lived in the South and the West while growing up. Mary identified herself as White. Her oldest son was 40 and he was adopted. She identified him as Black. She and her husband, who she identified as Black, also had two biological daughters ages 30 and 26. Mary and her husband divorced and she is remarried. She identified her current husband as Black.

Nancy O'Keefe lived in a large metropolitan area in the Central region. She lived in the Northwest, the West, the Southeast, and the Central regions growing up. She identified herself as White and the father of her biological son as Black. She was single and her son was six years old. The area where she lived is on the state border and she had recently moved across that border.

Olivia Preston lived in a large metropolitan area in the South region. She had moved there recently to be closer to family. She had lived in the North region growing up. She was single and her adopted daughter was 11 years of age at the time of the interview. She identified her daughter as Black.

Paige Qually lived in a large metropolitan area in the South region. Paige grew up in Germany and in the area where she lived at the time of the interview. She identified herself as White. Paige was single and she identified the father of her nine year old biological daughter as Black Caribbean.

Quinn Resin recently moved from a small city in the North region to a large metropolitan area in the Southeast. She was divorced and she identified her ex-husband as Black and identified herself as White, Latina. Their biological daughter was in elementary school at the time of the interview.

Riley Stevenson lived in a large metropolitan area in the South region which is the same region where she grew up. She and her husband, who she identifies as Black have a biological daughter who was 13 and a biological son who was three. Riley and her family lived with her parents at the time of the interview due to her husband's extensive travel for his job.

Sara Tobin lived for some time in a small city in the North region and for some time in the large metropolitan area in the North where she grew up. Sara lived in that large metropolitan area with her husband, who she identified as Black, until their biological son was eight and their biological daughter was four. Sara's son was 28 and her daughter was 24 at the time of the interview. Sara identified herself as White. She and her husband divorced. Sara moved to the small city where she raised her son and daughter. She remarried and her second husband, who had died years before the interview, was White.

Tenna Ushmore lived in a large metropolitan area in the Northwest region which is the area where she grew up. Tenna was single and she had lived in the East while attending college. Tenna identified herself and her 15 year old adopted son as White and the father of her six year old biological daughter as Black. Tenna and her sister have lived together for the last 10 years. Tenna's sister's two children, whom she identified as White, also live with them. Tenna indicated that her children and her nieces refer to each other as sisters. Tenna's son lives away at boarding school.

Ursula Vale lived in a large metropolitan area in the West region. She lived in the Southeast growing up and in the North during college. Ursula identified herself as White and her husband as Costa Rican. Their two biological sons were three and not yet one.

Vanessa Wilson lived in a small city in the North region. She lived in a large metropolitan area in the North region growing up. Vanessa identified herself and her husband as White. They adopted ten sons and daughters, two of whom they identified as Black—one son who was in college and one daughter who was in high school at the time of the interview.

Wendy Weston lived in a very small village in the North region near her parents and it was the same area where she grew up. She lived in a slightly larger, but still small city in the North region while attending college, which is where she met her husband. Wendy identified herself as White and her husband as Black. Their biological son was 12 and their biological daughter was eight.

Yvette Zanders lived in a large metropolitan area in the West region. Yvette was married and identified herself as White and husband as Filipino. They had a three year old biological son and a biological eight month old daughter. She grew up a few hours away from where she lived at the time of the interview.

Amy Kaster lived in a large metropolitan area in the South region. Amy explained that she and her husband, who she identified as being from Sierra Leone, had been together for a long time before they had their daughter who was five years old at the time of the interview. She grew up in the South region.

Beth Danforth lived in a small metropolitan area in the North. She grew up in the North region and had lived for a while in the South and she had also lived in Italy for a while as well. That is where she met and married her husband. She explained that he was from Morocco. Beth and her husband had one biological son who was 18 months at the time of the interview.

Cathleen Dillard lived in a large metropolitan area in the North. She identified her husband as White and their adopted son as Black. Their son was under two at the time of the interview. Her husband had a daughter from a previous relationship who did not live with them regularly, but who was involved in their lives. Cathleen did not indicate a race identification for her step daughter. Cathleen lived in the East region for her first ten years, then in the North region, then in the South region, and now she lives in the North region again.

Debra Goldson lived in a small metropolitan area in the Northeast region. Her oldest son had graduated from high school and was preparing for college. Her next oldest son was in high school, her daughter and her youngest son were in elementary school. She and her husband were in the process of getting divorced at the time of the interview. She identified her husband as biracial (Black and White). She lived in the East and Southeast regions growing up.

Emma Matthews lived in a large metropolitan area in the Northwest. She was single and had two biological daughters who were in elementary school. She identified their father as Black. She grew up in the Northwest region.

Fran Johnson lived in a large metropolitan area in the South. She identified her husband as Black. She and her husband have three biological daughters—one who was in college, one just graduating from high school and one in high school. Fran grew up in the Central region.

METHOD

My interest was to explore how social processes were reinscribing or maintaining Whiteness norms in the lives of White mothers of children who are not White. In depth interviewing allowed me to hear the mothers' stories about their interactions with family, friends, healthcare providers, childcare providers, teachers, and with strangers. I asked the mothers to tell me any stories they wanted to tell. Some of the mothers struggled in the beginning as they tried to guess what kinds of interactions I was interested in. I repeated that I was interested in any interactions that they wanted to share. So while I did not direct them to talk to me only about interactions they had with people in which race was a factor that is an area all the mothers addressed

Although I did not ask the mothers about their education, many of the mothers referred to their time in college and from other details mentioned, I got the impression that every mother I spoke had attended college. I didn't ask about their employment either and a few mothers mentioned or referred to their employment, but I didn't develop any impressions about their employment as a whole. If pressed, I would say that all the mothers I interviewed were middle class, but that is not based on any rigorous data collected or objective criteria. That is just my sense. I didn't ask the mothers about their current or prior marital or partner status either, but all the mothers addressed the subject of their partner status themselves. I didn't ask the mothers about their families of origin and yet, many of them discussed their families of origin. After asking about where they grew up I explained to each of them that I expected that each conversation would meander across topics and that was to be expected. Each mother I interviewed told me the race of the father of their daughters and sons. I never asked. I also did not exclude anyone from the study based on what she told me was the race she identified with or the race she identified for the father. I conducted some of the interviews face-to-face and some of them through audio and visual online communication methods. A small number of the interviews were conducted on the phone. I recorded all the interviews and used the original recordings for all my analysis.

APPENDIX B

Virginia 1691, Act XVI

LAWS OF VIRGINIA, APRIL 1691.—3D WILLIAM & MARY
ACT XVI. *AN ACT FOR SUPPRESSING OUTLYING SLAVES*

WHEREAS many times negroes, mulattoes, and other slaves unlawfully absent themselves from their masters and mistresses service, and lie hid and lurk in obscure places killing hoggs and committing other injuries to the inhabitants of this dominion, for remedy whereof for the future, *Be it enacted by their majesties lieutenant governour, councell and burgesses of this present general assembly, and the authoritie thereof, and it is hereby enacted*, that in all such cases upon intelligence of any such negroes, mulattoes, or other slaves lying out, two of their majesties justices of the peace of that county, whereof one to be of the quorum, where such negroes, mulattoes or other slave shall be, shall be impowered and commanded, and are hereby impowered and commanded to issue out their warrants directed to the sherrife of the same county to apprehend such negroes, mulattoes, and other slaves, which said sherriffe is hereby likewise requred upon all such occasions to raise such and soe many forces from time to time as he shall think convenient and necessary for the effectual apprehending such negroes, mulattoes and other slaves, and in case any negroes, mulattoes or other slaves or slaves lying out as aforesaid shall resist, runaway, or refuse to deliver and sur-render him or themselves to any person or persons that shall be by lawfull authority employed to apprehend and take such negroes, mulattoes or other slaves that in such cases it shall and may be lawfull for such person and persons to kill and distroy such negroes, mulattoes, and other slave or slaves by gunn or any otherwaise whatsoever.

Provided that where any negroe or mulattoe slave or slaves shall be killed in pursuance of this act, the owner or owners of such negro or mulatto slave shall be paid for such negro or mulatto slave four thousand pounds of tobacco by the publique. And for prevention of that abominable mixture and spurious issue which hereafter may encrease in this dominion, as well by negroes, mulattoes, and Indians intermarrying with English, or other white women, as by their unlawfull accompanying with one another, *Be it enacted by the authoritie aforesaid, and it is hereby enacted*, that for the time to come, whatsoever English or other white man or woman being free shall intermarry with a negroe, mulatto, or Indian man or woman bond or free shall within three months after such marriage be banished and removed from this dominion forever, and that the justices of each respective countie within this dominion make it their perticular care that this act be put in effectuall execution. *And be it further enacted by the authoritie aforesaid, and it is hereby enacted,* That if any English woman being free shall have a bastard child by any negro or mulatto, she pay the sume of fifteen pounds ster-ling, within one moneth after such bastard child be born, to the Church wardens of the parish where she shall be delivered of such child, and in default of such payment she shall be taken into the possession of the said Church wardens and disposed of for five yeares, and the said fine of fifteen pounds, or whatever the woman shall be disposed of for, shall be paid, one third part to their majesties for and towards the support of the government and the contingent charges thereof, and one other third part to the use of the parish where the offence is committed, and the other third part to the informer, and that such bastard child be bound out as a servant by the said Church wardens untill he or she shall attaine the age of thirty yeares, and in case such English woman that shall have such bastard child be a servant, she shall be sold by the said church wardens, (after her time is expired that she ought by law to serve her master) for five yeares, and the money she shall be sold for divided as is before appointed, and the child to serve as aforesaid.

And forasmuch as great inconveniences may happen to this country by the setting of negroes and mulattoes free, by their either entertain-ing negro slaves from their masters service, or receiveing stolen goods, or being grown old bringing a charge upon the country; for prevention thereof, *Be it enacted by the authority aforesaid, and it is hereby enacted,* That no negro or mulatto be after the end of this present session of assembly set free by any person or persons whatsoever, unless such person or persons, their heires, executors or administrators pay for the transportation of such negro or negroes out of the countrey within six moneths after such setting them free, upon penalty of paying of tenn pounds sterling to the Church wardens of the parish where such person shall dwell with, which money, or so much thereof as shall be necessary, the said Church wardens are to cause the said negro or mulatto to be transported out of the countrey, and the remainder of the said money to imploy to the use of the poor of the parish.

APPENDIX C
Notes Regarding Transracial Adoption

The realm of transracial adoption in the United States is beyond the scope of this book, however some observations are necessary here because of the variations in the dominant narrative about White mothers of children of color depending on whether she is an adoptive mother or a biological mother. There are variations in the dominant narratives about White mothers of children of color when children are adopted, depending on the race of the father, and depending on whether the parents are or were married. In Chapter two, Cathleen's story when she mentioned her worry of what people are thinking about her when they see her and her son in public and her husband is not with them calls on one of those narratives. It concerned Cathleen to think that some people are assuming that she partnered with a Black man and that her little boy is their biological son. In this way, Cathleen colluded with the Whiteness norm that *there is a hierarchy of races involved and types of relationships in which White women mother children of color. The circumstances will be valued differently. It is best to be recognized as belonging to the highest level group possible. The ideal to strive toward is that of a White mother of White children. Be like White mothers of White children as much as possible.*

The information on the Child Welfare Information Gateway website of the U.S. Department of Health and Human Services, Administration for Children and Families (1999) cites sources all of which are prior to 1994. The following advice appears in a list of seven things that "parents in a transracial or transcultural family should do" (para. 13).

Tolerate No Racially or Ethnically Biased Remarks

As adoptive parents in an interracial or intercultural family, you should refuse to tolerate any kind of racially or ethnically biased remark made in your presence. This includes remarks about your child's race or ethnic group, other races and ethnic groups, or any other characteristic such as gender, religion, age and physical or other disability. Make it clear that it is not okay to make fun of people who are different, and it is not okay to assume that all people of one group behave the same way. Teach your children how to handle these remarks, by saying, for instance, "I find your remark offensive. Please don't say that type of thing again," or "Surely you don't mean to be critical, you just don't have experience with . . ." or "You couldn't be deliberately saying such an inappropriate comment in front of a child. You must mean something else."

Try to combat the remarks while giving the person a chance to back off or change what has been said. This way you will teach your child to stand up to bias without starting a fight—which could put your child at risk. In addition, by being gracious and giving others a chance to overcome their bias/ ignorance, you can help to change their beliefs and attitudes over time. Positive exchanges about race will always be more helpful than negative ones. (Transracial and Transcultural Adoption, 1999, para. 19)

This advice to parents to engage in conversations regarding race does not appear to mirror the approach taken by the U.S. Department of Health and Human Services, Administration for Children and Families. Their training presentation available on their website *Ensuring the Best Interests of Children: Through Compliance with the Multiethnic Placement Act of 1994, as amended* (2009) explains that the subject of race is to be completely avoided. The Multiethnic Placement Act, or MEPA as it is called, was enacted in 1994 and amended in 1996. The training explicitly explains that organizations receiving federal funding may not ask or consider why a family wants to parent a child whose race, color, or national origin is not the same as their own. Nor may an organizational representative ask or consider what a family knows about people who identify with a race, color, or national origin that is not the same as their own. Lastly, a representative may not ask or consider "Whether a family's activities reflect a knowledge of or appreciation for the race, color, or national origin of the child the family wishes to parent" (2009, p. 36).

Briggs (2012) examined the history of transracial adoption by focusing on the politics and noted that "families are where we live our economic and social relations, and in families formed by law the fiction that families are "private," constituted in opposition to the "public," is laid bare as the fairy tale that it is" (Briggs, 2012). The fairy tale that Briggs refers to is the dominant narrative. Additionally, Steinberg and Hall (2000) assert that "our current adoption system is as institutionally racist as every other system in this country" (p. 140). While the precise storyline of the dominant narrative regarding adoption has changed over time, the general image of adoptive parents as benevolent benefactors has persisted. That image coexists with the narrative that White mothers are not capable of fully caring for their daughters and sons of color because their race does not match that of their children. Together, these support the narrative there is quantitatively more work involved for a White mother to care for a child of color than to care for a White child.

REFERENCES

Briggs, L. (2012). *Somebody's children: The politics of transracial and transnational adoption.* Durham, NC: Duke University Press.

Steinberg, G., & Hall, B. (2000). *Inside transracial adoption.* Indianapolis, IN: Prespectives Press.

Transracial and Transcultural Adoption. (1999). Retrieved 2014, from U.S. Department of Health and Human Service, Administration for Children and Families, Child Welfare Information Gateway: https://www.childwelfare.gov/pubs/f_trans.cfm

U.S. Depatment of Health and Human Services, Adminitration for Children and Families, Office for Civil Rights. (2009). *Ensuring the best interests of children: Through compliance with the Multiethnic Placement Act of 1994, as amended.* Retrieved from http://www.hhs.gov/ocr/civilrights/resources/specialtopics/adoption/mepatraingppt.pdf

REFERENCES

Bandura, A. (1969). *Principles of behavior modification.* New York, NY: Holt Rinehart & Winston.

Battalora, J. (2013). *Birth of a White nation: The invention of White people and its relevance today.* Houston, TX: Strategic Book Publishing.

Bialeschki, M. D., & Michener, S. (1994). Re-entering leisure: Transition within the role of motherhood. *Journal of Leisure Research, 26*(1), 57–74.

Bonilla-Silva, E. (2010). *Racism without racists* (3rd ed.). Lanham, MD: Rowman & Littlefield Publishers, Inc.

Briggs, L. (2012). *Somebody's children: The politics of transracial and transnational adoption.* Durham, NC: Duke University Press.

Cabellero, C., & Edwards, R. (2010). *Lone mothers of mixed racial and ethnic children: Then and now.* London, England: Runneymeade.

Carnevale, A. P., & Strohl, J. (2013). *Separate & unequal: How higher education reinforces the intergenerational reproduction of White racial privilege.* Washington, DC: Georgetown Public Policy Institute.

Case, K. A., & Hemmings, A. (2005). Distancing strategies: White women preservice teachers and antiracist curriculum. *Urban Education, 40*(6), 606–626.

Cassilde, S. (2013). Where are you from? In R. E. Hall (Ed.), *The melanin millennium: Skin color as 21st century international discourse* (pp. 115-138). New York, NY: Springer

Conley, D. (2005). *The pecking order: A bold new look at how family and society determine who we become.* New York, NY: Vintage.

Dancy, R. B. (2012). *You are your child's first teacher* (3rd ed.). New York, NY: Ten Speed Press.

Delpit, L. (2006). *Other people's children: Cultural conflict in the classroom.* New York, NY: The New Press.

DiAngelo, R. J. (2010). Why can't we all just be individuals?: Countering the discourse of individualism in anti-racist education. *InterActions: UCLA Journal of Education and Information Studies, 6*(1), Article Number 4.

Domene, J. F., Socholotiuk, K. D., & Young, R. A. (2011). The early stages of the transition to adulthood: Similarities and differences between mother-daughter and mother-son dyads. *Qualitative Research in Psychology, 8*(3), 273–291.

Druzin, B. H. (2013). Eating peas with one's fingers: A semiotic approach to law and social norms. *International Journal for the Semiotics of Law, 26*(2), 257–274.

Dumas, M. J., & Nelson, J. D. (2016). (Re)Imagining Black boyhood: Toward a critical framework for educational research. *Harvard Educational Review, 86*(1), 27–47.

Dweck, C. S. (2007). *Mindset: The new psychology of success.* New York, NY: Ballantine Books.

Erikson, K. T. (2003). On the sociology of deviance. In D. H. Kelly, & E. J. Clarke (Eds.), *Deviant behavior: A text reader in the sociology of deviance* (6 ed., pp. 85–92). New York, NY: Worth.

Fasching-Varner, K. J. (2012). *Working through Whiteness: Examining White racial identity and profession with pre-service teachers.* Lanham, MD: Lexington Books.

Feagin, J. R. (2013). *The White racial frame: Centuries of racial framing and counter-framing* (2nd ed.). New York, NY: Routledge.

Fehr, E., & Fischbacher, U. (2004). Social norms and human cooperation. *Trends in Cognitive Sciences, 8*(4), 185–190.

Fine, M. (2015). Resisting Whiteness/Bearing Whiteness. In E. Moore, Jr., M. W. Penick-Parks, & A. Michael (Eds.), *Everyday White people confront racial and social injustice: 15 stories.* Sterling, VA: Stylus.

Fram, M. S., & Kim, J. (2008). Race/ethnicity and the start of child care: A multilevel analysis of factors influencing first child care experiences. *Early Childhood Research Quarterly, 23*(4), 575–590.

Francis-Connolly, E. (2000). Toward an understanding of mothering: A comparison of two motherhood stages. *The American Journal of Occupational Therapy, 54*(3), 281–289.

Frankenberg, R. (1993). *White women, race matters: The social construction of Whiteness.* Minneapolis, MN: University of Minnesota Press.

Ganeshram, R. (2016). *A birthday cake for George Washington.* New York, NY: Scholastic.

Garfinkel, H. (1967). *Studies in ethnomethodology.* Englewood Cliffs, NJ: Prentice Hall.

Garner, S. (2007). *Whiteness: An introduction.* New York, NY: Routledge.

Glenn, E. N., Chang, G., & Forcey, L. R. (Eds.). (1994). *Mothering: Ideology, experience, and agency.* New York, NY: Routledge.

Goffman, E. (1959). *The presentation of everyday self.* New York, NY: Anchor Books.

Goldring, R., Gray, L., Bitterman, A., & Broughman, S. (2013). *Characteristics of Public and Private Elementary and Secondary School Teachers in the United States: Results From the 2011–12 Schools and Staffing Survey.* Washington, DC: U.S. Department of Education.

Gordon, J. (2005). White on White: Researcher reflexivity and the logics of privilege in White schools undertaking reform. *The Urban Review, 37*(4), 279–302.

Greene, A. L., Wheatley, S. M., & Aldava, J. F. (1992). Stages on life's way: Adolescent's implicit theories of the life course. *Journal of Adolescent Research, 7*(3), 364–381.

Gusfield, J. R. (1968). On legislating morals: The symbolic process of designating deviance. *California Law Review, 56*(1), 54–73.

Harro, B. (2013). The cycle of socialization. In M. Adams, W. J. Blumenfeld, C. Castañeda, H. W. Hackman, M. L. Peters, & X. Zúñiga (Eds.), *Readings for diversity and social justice* (pp. 45–52). New York, NY: Routledge

Helms, J. E. (2008). *A race is a nice thing to have: A guide to being a White person or understanding White persons in your life* (2nd ed.). Hanover, MA: Microtraining Associates.

Hening, W. W. (Ed.). (1823). *The Statues at large; Being a collection of all the laws of Virginia from the first session of the legislature, in the year 1619* (Vol. II). New York, NY. Retrieved from http://vagenweb.org/hening/vol02-09.htm

Hill, N. E., & Tyson, D. F. (2009). Parental involvement in middle school: A meta-analytic assessment of the strategies that promote achievement. *Developmental Psychology, 45*(3), 740–763.

hooks, b. (2014). Are You Still a Slave? New York: The New School. Retrieved from http://events.newschool.edu/event/bell_hooks_scholar-in-residence_-_are_you_still_a_slave_liberating_the_black_female_body#.Vgas1t9VhBc

Hughes, D., Smith, E. P., Stevenson, H. C., Rodriguez, J., Johnson, D. J., & Spicer, P. (2006). Parents' ethnic-racial socialization practices: A review of research and directions for future study. *Developmental Psychology, 42*(5), 747–770.

Hussar, W. J., & Bailey, T. M. (2014). *Projections of Education Statistics to 2022.* National Center for Education Statistics, U. S. Department of Education, Washington, DC.

Kena, G., Musu-Gillette, L., Robinson, J., Wang, X., Rathbun, A., Zhang, J., … Dunlop Velez, E. (2015). *The Condition of Education 2015.* Washington, DC: U. S. Department of Education.

Kendall, F. E. (2006). *Understanding White privilege: Creating pathways to authentic relationships across race.* New York, NY: Routledge.

Kohlberg, L. (1984). *The psychology of moral development: The nature and validity of moral stages (Essays on moral development)* (Vol. 2). New York, NY: Harper & Row.

Ladson-Billings, G. (2013). Critical race theory—What it is not! In M. Lynn, & A. D. Dixson (Eds.), *Handbook of critical race theory in education.* New York, NY: Routledge.

Landeros, M. (2011). Defining the "good mother" and the "professional teacher": Parent-teacher relationships in an affluent school district. *Gender & Education, 23*(3), 247–262.

Le Poidevin, R., & MacBeath, M. (Eds.). (1993). *The philosophy of time.* New York, NY: Oxford University Press.

Lensmire, A. (2012). *White urban teachers: Stories of fear, violence, and desire.* Lanham, MD: Rowman & Littlefield Education.

Leonardo, Z. (2009). *Race, Whiteness, and education.* New York, NY: Routledge.

Leonardo, Z., & Boas, E. (2013). Other kids' teachers: What children of color learn from White women and what this says about race, Whiteness, and gender.

In M. Lynn, & A. D. Dixson (Eds.), *Handbook of critical race theory in education* (pp. 313–324). New York, NY: Routledge.

Leonardo, Z., & Porter, R. K. (2010). Pedagogy of fear: Toward a Fanonian theory of 'safety' in race dialogue. *Race Ethnicity and Education, 13*(2), 139–157.

Levin, D. T. (2000). Race as a visual feature: Using visual search and perceptual discrimination tasks to understand face categories and the cross-race recognition deficit. *Journal of Experimental Psychology, 129*(4), 559–574.

Loewen, J. W. (2007). *Lies my teacher told me: Everything your America history teacher got wrong.* New York, NY: Touchstone.

Lorde, A. (2003). The master's tools will never dismantle the master's house. In R. Lewis & S. Mills (Eds.), *Feminist postcolonial theory: A reader* (pp. 25–28). New York, NY: Routledge.

LOVING V. VIRGINIA, 395 (Supreme Court of the United States 1967).

Low, S. (2009). Maintaining Whiteness: The fear of others and niceness. *Transforming Anthropology, 17*(2), 79–92.

Maillard, K. N. (2009). Miscegenation: An American leviathan. *Human Rights, 36*(3), 15.

Marx, S., & Pennington, J. (2003). Pedagogies of critical race theory: Experimentations with White preservice teachers. *International Journal of Qualitative Studies in Education, 16*(1), 91–110.

McAdam, D., Tarrow, S., & Tilly, C. (2001). *Dynamics of contention.* Cambridge, England: Cambridge University Press.

McLaren, P., Leonardo, Z., & Allen, R. L. (2000). Epistemologies of Whiteness: Trangressing and transforming pedagogical knowledge. In R. Mahalingam, & C. McCarthy (Eds.), *Multicultural curriculum: New directions for social theory, practice, and policy* (pp. 108–123). New York, NY: Routledge.

McMahon, M. (1995). *Engendering motherhood: Identity and self-transformation in women's lives.* New York, NY: The Guilford Press.

Miller, T. (2005). *Making sense of motherhood: A narrative approach.* Cambridge, England: Cambridge University Press.

Miller, T. (2007). "Is This What Motherhood is All About?": Weaving experiences and discourse through transition to first-time motherhood. *Gender & Society, 21*(3), 337–358.

Nelissen, R. M., & Mulder, L. B. (2013). What makes a sanction "stick"? The effects of financial and social sanctions on norm compliance. *Social Influence, 8*(1), 70–80.

Noel, A., Stark, P., Redford, J., & Zukerberg, A. (2013). *Parent and Family Involvement in Education, From the National Household Education Surveys Program of 2012.* National Center for Education Statistics, U. S. Department of Education, Washington, DC.

O'Donoghue, M. (2005). White mothers negotiating race and ethnicity in the mothering of biracial, Black-White adolescents. *Journal of Ethnic & Cutltural Diversity in Social Work, 14*(3/4), 125–156.

Onwuachi-Willig, A. (2013). *According to our hearts: Rhinelander v. Rhinelander and the law of the multiracial family.* New Haven, CT: Yale University Press.

Oscars: The Onion Under Fire for Calling Quvenzhane Wallis the C-Word. (2013, February 24). Retrieved from The Hollywood Reporter: http://www.hollywoodreporter.com/news/onion-calls-quvenzhane-wallis-c-424113

Parks, M. W. (2006). I am from a very small town: Social reconstructionism and multicultural education. *Multicultural Perspectives, 88*(2), 46–50.

Parsons, T. (1959). The school class as a social system: Some of its functions in American society. *Harvard Educational Review, 29*(4), 297–318.

Pennington, J. L., Brock, C. H., & Ndura, E. (2012). Unraveling the threads of White teachers' conceptions of caring: Repositioning White privilege. *Urban Education, 47*(4), 743–775.

Pew Research Center. (2013). *King's dream remains an elusive goal: Many Americans see racial disparities.* Washington, DC: Pew Research Center. Retrieved August 23, 2013, from http://www.pewsocialtrends.org/2013/08/22/kings-dream-remains-an-elusive-goal-many-americans-see-racial-disparities/

Picower, B. (2009). The unexamined Whiteness of teaching: How White teachers maintain and enact dominant racial ideologies. *Race Ethnicity and Education, 12*(2), 197–215.

Posner, R. A., & Rasmusen, E. B. (1999). Creating and enforcing norms, with special reference to sanctions. *International Review of Law and Economics, 19*(3), 369–382.

Ralabate, P. (2007). *Truth in labeling: Disproportionality in special education.* Washington, DC: National Education Association.

Rich, A. (1986). *Of woman born: Motherhood as experience and institution.* New York, NY: W. W. Norton & Company.

Root, M. P. (2004). Multiracial families and children: Implications for educational research and practice. In J. A. Banks & C. A. Mcgee Banks (Eds.), *Handbook of research on multicultural education* (2nd ed.). San Francisco, CA: Jossey-Bass.

Rothenberg, P. S. (2012). *White privilege: Essential readings on the other side of racism* (4th ed.). New York, NY: Worth Publishers.

Scholastic. (2016, January 17). *On Our Minds.* Retrieved from Scholastic: http://oomscholasticblog.com/post/new-statement-about-picture-book-birthday-cake-george-washington

SCHUETTE v. BAMN, 12–682 (Supreme Court of the United States April 22, 2014).

Sherif, M. (1965). *The psychology of social norms.* New York, NY: Octagon Books.

Sleeter, C. E. (2005). How White teachers construct race. In C. McCarthy, W. Crichlow, G. Dimitriadis, & N. Dolby (Eds.), *Race, identity, and representation In education (critical social thought)* (2nd ed., pp. 157–171). New York, NY: Routledge.

Smith, H. J., & Lander, V. (2012). Collusion or collision: Effects of teacher ethnicity in the teaching of critical Whiteness. *Race Ethnicity and Education, 15*(3), 331–351.

Snyder, T. D., & Dillow, S. A. (2015). *Digest of Education Statistics: 2013.* Washington, DC: U.S. Department of Education. Retrieved from National Center for Education Statistics.

Steedman, C. (1985). "The mother made conscious": The historical development of a primary school pedagogy. *History Workshop, 20*(1), 149–163.

Steinberg, G., & Hall, B. (2000). *Inside transracial adoption.* Indianapolis, IN: Prespectives Press.

Stevenson, H. C. (2014). *Promoting racial literacy in schools: Differences that make a difference.* New York, NY: Teachers College Press.

Stocking, G. W. (1965). On the limits of 'presentism' and 'historicism' in the historiography of the behavioral sciences. *Journal of the History of the Behavioral Sciences, 1*(3), 211–218.

Sullivan, S. (2014). *Good White people: The problem with middle-class White antiracism.* Albany, NY: State University of New York Press.

Torres, C. A. (Ed.). (1998). *Education, power, and personal biography.* New York, NY: Routledge.

Transracial and Transcultural Adoption. (1999). Retrieved 2014, from U.S. Department of Health and Human Service, Administration for Children and Families, Child Welfare Information Gateway: https://www.childwelfare.gov/pubs/f_trans.cfm

Trepagnier, B. (2010). *Silent racism: How well-meaning White people perpetuate the racial divide* (2nd ed.). Boulder, CO: Paradigm.

Tschannen-Moran, M. (2014). The interconnectivity of trust in schools. In D. Van Maele, P. B. Forsyth, & M. Van Houtte (Eds.), *Trust and school life: The role of trust for learning, teaching, leading, and bridging* (pp. 57–81). New York, NY: Springer. doi:10.1007/978-94-017-8014-8_3

Twine, F. W. (1999). Bearing Blackness in Britain: The meaning of racial difference for White birth mothers of African-descent children. *Social Identities, 5*(2), 185–210.

Twine, F. W., & Steinbugler, A. C. (2006). The gap between Whites and Whiteness: Interracial intimacy and racial literacy. *Du Bois Review, 3*(2), 341–363.

U.S. Depatment of Health and Human Services, Adminitration for Children and Families, Office for Civil Rights. (2009). *Ensuring the best interests of children: Through compliance with the Multiethnic Placement Act of 1994, as amended.* Retrieved from http://www.hhs.gov/ocr/civilrights/resources/specialtopics/adoption/mepatraingppt.pdf

Wang, Y. (2015, October 5). "Workers" or slaves? Textbook maker backtracks after mother's online complaint. *Washington Post.*

Weber, R. (2011). *Understanding parents' child care decision-making: A foundation for child care policy making.* Washington, DC: Office of Planning, Research and Evaluation, Administration for Children and Families, U.S. Department of Health and Human Services.

Woodward, K. (2003). Representations of Motherhood. In S. Earle & G. Letherby (Eds.), *Gender, identity and reproduction: Social perspectives* (pp. 18–32). Houndmills, Basingstoke, Hampshire, England: Palgrave Macmillan.

Yoon, I. H. (2012). The paradoxical nature of whiteness-at-work in the daily life of schools and teacher communities. *Race Ethnicity and Education, 15*(5), 587–613.

ABOUT THE AUTHOR

Jennifer L. S. Chandler, PhD, is in Leadership for the Advancement of Learning and Service from Cardinal Stritch University, Milwaukee, Wisconsin. She is a Lecturer in the Leadership and Interdisciplinary Studies Program at Arizona State University, in Tempe, Arizona. There, she also conducts leadership research and education within the Center for Bio-mediated and Bio-inspired Geotechnics (CBBG) which is a National Science Foundation (NSF) Engineering Research Center (ERC). Previously, Jennifer conducted organizational analyses with federal agencies such as the United States Treasury; United States Secret Service; Bureau of Alcohol Tobacco, Firearms, and Explosives; United States Navy; Unites States Army; and NASA; for not-for-profit organizations such as the Association of American Medical Colleges, and Voter News Service; and for multinational corporations such as Motorola.